PORCELAIN FOR THE EMPEROR

KAI JUN CHEN

Porcelain for

MANUFACTURE AND TECHNOCRACY IN QING CHINA

University of Washington Press / Seattle

the Emperor

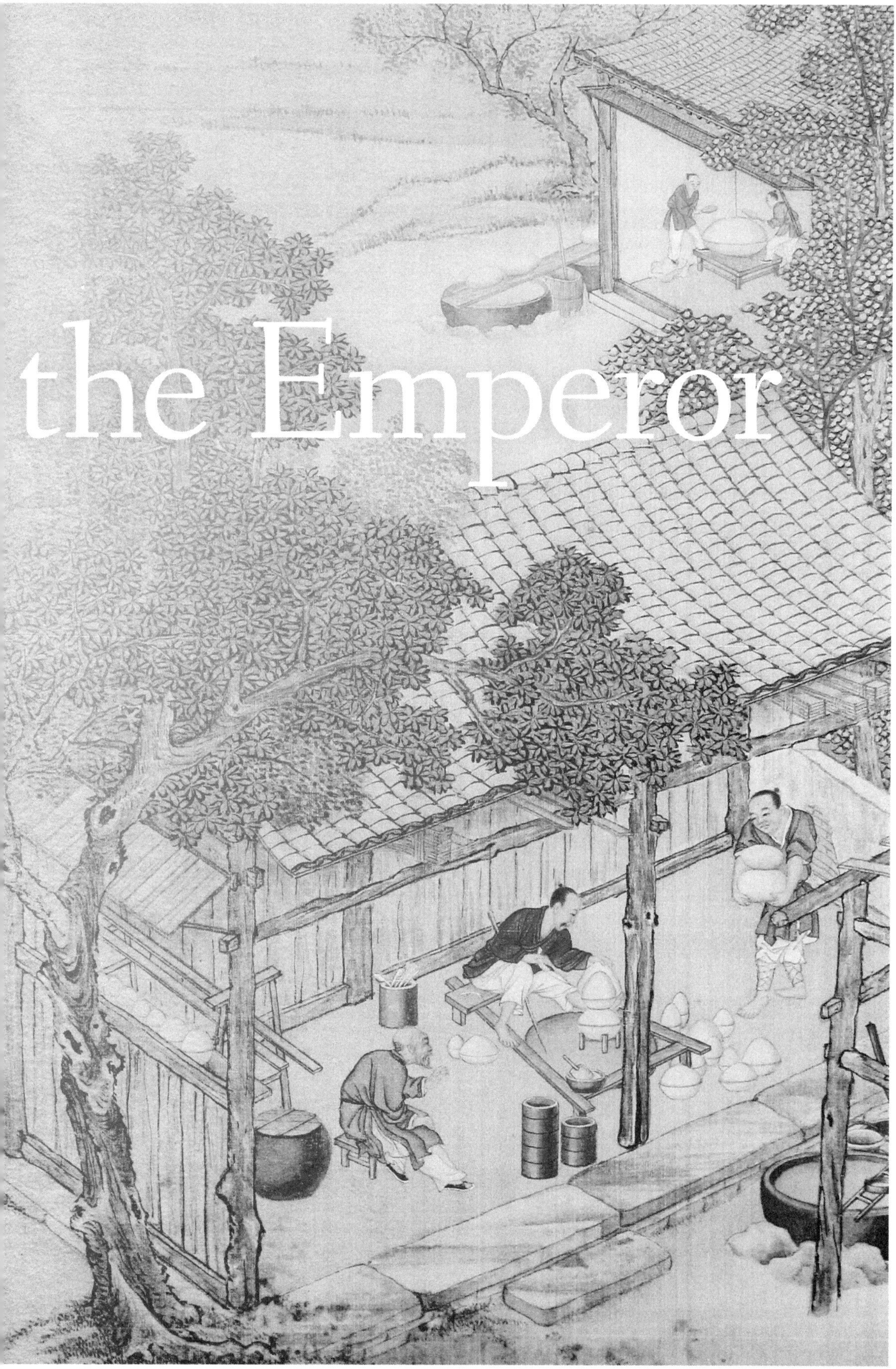

Porcelain for the Emperor was supported by a grant from the Traditional Chinese Culture and Society Book Fund, established through generous gifts from Patricia Buckley Ebrey and Thomas Ebrey.

GEISS HSU FOUNDATION

This publication was made possible in part by an award from the James P. Geiss and Margaret Y. Hsu Foundation.

Publication of this book has been aided by a grant from the Millard Meiss Publication Fund of CAA.

The Metropolitan Center for Far Eastern Art Studies provided additional support for this book.

Design by Mindy Basinger Hill
Composed in 11/15 pt Fanwood and Leifa Medium

27 26 25 24 23 5 4 3 2 1

Printed and bound in the United States

UNIVERSITY OF WASHINGTON PRESS uwapress.uw.edu
LIBRARY OF CONGRESS CATALOGING-IN-PUBLICATION DATA

Names: Chen, Kai Jun, author.
Title: Porcelain for the emperor: manufacture and technology in Qing China / Kai Jun Chen.
Description: Seattle: University of Washington Press, [2023] | Includes bibliographical references and index.
Identifiers: LCCN 2022015086 (print) | LCCN 2022015087 (ebook) | ISBN 9780295750828 (hardcover) | ISBN 9780295750835 (ebook)
Subjects: LCSH: Porcelain industry—China—Jingdezhen—History—18th century. | Art and state—China—History—18th century. | Art and technology—China—History—18th century. | Tang, Ying, 1682–1756. | China—History—Qing dynasty, 1644–1912.
Classification: LCC HD9610.8. C62 C49 2022 (print) | LCC HD9610.8. C62 (ebook) | DDC 338.4/773820951212—dc23/eng/20221125
LC record available at https: //lccn.loc.gov/2022015086
LC ebook record available at https: //lccn.loc.gov/2022015087

♾ This paper meets the requirements of ANSI/NISO Z39.48-1992 (Permanence of Paper).

CONTENTS

ACKNOWLEDGMENTS

I AM MOST GRATEFUL to my mentors who read the early versions of this book. Dorothy Ko helped me conceptualize the project and navigate through the ocean of scholarship, as well as the labyrinth of career paths. Shang Wei transmitted his deep knowledge of Chinese literature by tutoring me in close literary analysis while encouraging me to bring multidisciplinary methods to investigate literary phenomena as an integral part of the larger cultural pattern. Lydia Liu reminded me to make legible contributions to different fields and taught me the theories of technology and media in and outside her seminars. Jonathan Hay's empirical observation and theoretical suggestions pointed me to exciting directions in the world of art history. Pamela Smith's generous engagement at the early phase of the project provided me with a model to explore artisanal ways of making and knowing.

My colleagues at Brown University form the core of a supportive intellectual home where this project has taken its final shape. I benefited immensely from various workshops and informal discussions with Cynthia Brokaw, Tara Nummendal, Harold Cook, Kerry Smith, Tamara Chin, Janine Sawada, Lingzhen Wang, Sam Perry, Rebecca Nedostop, Harold Roth, Dore Levy, Evelyn Hu-Dehart, Beverly Bossler, and my cohort Jason Protass, Jeff Moser, Brian Lander, and colleagues affiliated with the Joukouwsky Institute. Librarians Wang Li and Kimberly Silva tirelessly secured research materials across the globe for me. Curator Wai-yee Chong kindly opened the ceramic collection at the Museum of the Rhode Island School of Design, allowing me to find interesting comparisons.

I appreciate several funding agencies' confidence in this project. First, I thank the dean of faculty and the provost at Brown for their continued research and travel funds. Additional overseas fieldwork was supported by the Salomon Center and Haffenreffer Museum at Brown. The Chiang Ching-Kuo Foundation, American Council of Learned Societies' Henry Luce Foundation, and Andrew Mellon Foundation generously funded yearlong or semesterlong research and write-up periods, which were critical to the completion of the manuscript.

The Max Planck Institute for the History of Science in Berlin hosted me as a postdoctoral fellow for two blissful years, during which I was able to develop the project in conversation with Dagmar Schäfer, Francesca Bray, Ursula Klein, and many other historians of science and technology. In answering questions posed by colleagues who focus on drastically different time periods and regions, I stepped outside sinology to address our common interest in the relation between political force and the implementation of knowledge in industry of the early modern world.

The feedback I received at numerous conferences and workshops where I presented parts of the manuscript nourished its growth. I thank Matthew Mosca, Andrea Goodman, and Denis Leidy for their careful reading of the complete version, and Susan Naquin for meticulous comments on two chapters. Guest talks on related topics per colleagues' kind invitations made me broaden the case study of porcelain supervisors' careers and ponder the deeper significance of politicized expertise in industrial art. I therefore express my gratitude for the opportunities offered by Judith Zeitlin and Jacob Eyferth (University of Chicago), Patricia Ebrey and Madeleine Dong (University of Washington), Jack Chen (University of Virginia), Tobie Meyer-Fong (Johns Hopkins University), Michele Matteini (New York University), Yeewan Koon (Hong Kong University), and Ao Wang (Wesleyan University), the Heidelberg University Colloquy funded by the Balzan Foundation, and invaluable dialogues with the audience in each venue. The literary and art historical analysis in the project was also improved through panel discussions at conferences as well as individual meetings. I appreciate suggestions and enlightening questions from Bruce Rusk, David Rolston, Patricia Sieber, Sophie Volpp, Liana Chen, Yulian Wu, Craig Clunas, Peng Ying-Chen, Wang Ching-Ling, Kristina Kleutghen, Stephen Whiteman, and many more co-panelists.

I received countless forms of support during my research on porcelain. Peter Lam at the Chinese University of Hong Kong generously shared with me his pioneering research on the subject and priceless leads. The Academia Sinica in Taipei, National Palace Museum, and National Taiwan University provided me with all sorts of conveniences during my visit. My project is richly informed by what I learned from Lai Yu-Chih, Wang Cheng-Hua, Chen Kuo-Tung, Wong

Yu-wen, Shih Shou-Chien, Chuang Chi-Fa, and Lin Shih-Hsuen. I want to extend special thanks to Fu Sheng, Hsieh Min-Liang, Shih Ching-Fei, and Yu Pei-Chin, who not only honed my skills in formal analysis but also opened doors to collections for me. In the Palace Museum in Beijing, Wang Guangyao, Sun Yue, and many scholar-curators kindly facilitated my examination of the collection and responded to my frequent requests for images and information. Lu Minghua, Li Zhongmou, and Chen Jie made my research at Shanghai Museum efficiently rewarding. My adventure in Jingdezhen, the porcelain town, benefited tremendously from scholars at the Institute of Archaeology and the Jingdezhen Ceramic Institute, especially Jiang Jianxing, Huang Wei, and Huang Qinghua, who guided me through archaeological sites and local ateliers. My fieldwork in England, hosted by the Needham Research Institute at the University of Cambridge, was cheerfully accommodated by John Moffret. Christopher Cullen, and Mei Jianjun; outside Cambridge, Stacey Pierson, Anne Gerritsen, Stephen McDowell, and Keeper Jessica Harrison-Hall all kindly supported my research. John Finlay is the American in Paris who shared discoveries and went out of his way to take photos at auctions for me. I hope our next dinner in the Latin Quarter will happen in the near future. Apart from the museums mentioned above, two collectors, the Victoria and Albert Museum and the Smithsonian's National Museum of Asian Art, graciously allowed me to reproduce images from their collections.

The Columbia University community has been a source of knowledge and inspiration. I especially thank Bob Hymes, Eugenia Lean, and Robert Harrist for teaching me histories of society, science, and art spanning from the medieval to the later imperial period. Li Feng generously tutored me on bronzes and archaeology from early China. And I cherish the cheer-ups from Kile, BuYun, Anatoly, Arunabh, Peng, Allison, Noga, Yuan Ye, Yurou, Lei, Gal, Shing-ting, Myra, Yijun, Kyoungjin, Greg Patterson, Stephen, Six, Ksenia, Joyce Tsai, Joseph Scheier-Dolberg, and many more who engaged in long chats in front of the C. V. Starr and Avery Libraries.

Teachers and colleagues from the wider Northeast have expanded my intellectual horizons. I learned a lot from fellow art historians at the Institute of Fine Arts, Institute for the Study of the Ancient World, and the Bard Graduate Center for Decorative Arts. Special thanks go to Lu Pengliang, who kindly shared with me his connections in the museum world, knowledge on ceramics and Shanghainess cuisine from our hometown. Moreover, I thank Benjamin Elman, Paize Keulemans, and Tom Mazanec, who engaged me in several workshops organized at Princeton University. Mellisa Moy and Yan Yang at Harvard Art Museum and Daisy Wang at the Peabody Essex Museum kindly opened their collections to me. Tom Kelly, Anne Feng, and Victor Seow have always been a source of good ideas. Probably without noticing it themselves, Haun Saussy and Kuriyama Shigehisa, in several of our conversations, fine-tuned the core of the project.

The project also bears an imprint of my early intellectual formation. I cherish the guidance of my college adviser, Chen Yinchi, in broad humanities studies back at Fudan University and his support for my study at each turning point. I am grateful for help from Claude Imbert (École Normale Supérieure, rue d'Ulm), Denis Kambouchner (Paris IV), Marianne Bastid-Bruguière (École des Hautes Études en Sciences Sociales), Ian McMorran (Paris VII), Marc Kalinowski (École Pratique des Hautes Études), Alain Arrault (École Pratique des Hautes Études), Romain Graziani (Paris VII), François Lecercle (Paris IV), and especially John Lagerwey (École Pratique des Hautes Études). They introduced me to French philosophy and sinology, which made my first period of study abroad exciting and fruitful. Mme. Cartron and Charles Wang made the life of an international student much easier than it could have been.

And I can never sufficiently thank my editor, Lorri Hagman, who patiently shepherded the project, as well as the anonymous peer reviewers, the copy editor, and the indexer, who save me from embarrassment and make the work presentable.

Without my parents' and my grandmother's moral support, this work would not have seen the light of day. It is an understatement to thank my wife, Sissi Liu, who is the happy reason for my life's current trajectory. Her talent in the arts and wisdom in life make me dare to pursue our dreams.

CONVENTIONS

ROMANIZATION: Chinese terms, mostly in Standard Chinese (Putonghua; Mandarin), are romanized with pinyin spelling unless original book titles and quotations use the Wade-Giles system. When available, Manchu names and terms are romanized with the Möllendorff system. Romanized terms are Chinese, unless identified as Manchu. When necessary, they are distinguished by "C" and "M."

DATES: All dates based on the Chinese lunar calendar are given in ordinal numbers—for example, the 25th day of the 6th month of the 3rd year of the Qianlong reign. In block quotations and notes, this date could be shortened to QL3/6/25. QL is abbreviation of the Qianlong reign; KX stands for the Kangxi reign; and YZ, the Yongzheng reign. In most cases, the corresponding year on the Gregorian calendar is also provided.

MEASUREMENTS: Chinese units are used only when they appear for the first time. Approximate English terms are used thereafter.

cun: inch
chi: foot
jin: catty
li: mile
liang: tael

CHRONOLOGY OF DYNASTIES AND QING REIGN PERIODS

Shang, 1600–c. 1045 BCE
Zhou, c. 1045–256 BCE
Qin, 221–206 BCE
Han, 206 BCE—220 CE
Three Kingdoms, 220–280
Western Jin, 265–317
Eastern Jin, 317–420
Southern and Northern dynasties, 420–589
Sui, 581–618
Tang, 618–907
Five Dynasties and Ten Kingdoms, 907–979
Song, 960–1279
Liao, 907–1125
Jin, 1115–1234
Yuan, 1271–1368
Ming, 1368–1644
Qing, 1644–1912
- Shunzhi, 1644–1661
- Kangxi, 1662–1722
- Yongzheng, 1723–1735
- Qianlong, 1736–1795
- Jiaqing, 1796–1820
- Daoguang, 1821–1874
- Guangxu, 1875–1908
- Xuantong, 1909–1912

PORCELAIN FOR THE EMPEROR

INTRODUCTION

A LEADING FIGURE IN THIS BOOK is a potter who put himself literally on a theatrical stage and metaphorically on the stage of the global early modern world. Here is bannerman Tang Ying (1682–1756), singing a self-introduction in his play *Dream about Yuxi* (Yuxi meng):

> I aspire to become a potter rather than an immortal so that I will not have to suffer condescending inspection nor pleas for pity. Half of my life has been spent on the business of poetry while tending to the five colors [ceramic manufacture] on Pearl Hill. The Buddhist Layman Who Made Pottery [Taocheng Jushi] is my name. By imperial orders, I was appointed the supervisor of ceramic production, and I work hard to repay this imperial favor. I reside in Jiangxi's ancient town [i.e., Jingdezhen]; the emperor resides in the palace far away in the north, so I am a solitary subject. Free from mundane burdens, I am an official who enjoys some leisure.[1]

Tang Ying presented himself as a craftsman, an imperial potter who enjoyed a certain level of autonomy. Though he held an imperially appointed position, his work as a "solitary subject" (*guchen*)—away from the prying eyes of the central government—allowed him to immerse himself in the social and cultural life of Jingdezhen, Jiangxi province, the site of the Imperial Porcelain Manufactory. His experiences as a ceramist and playwright reveal the workings of knowledge cultures that bannermen like him engendered during their long and prolific careers. Bannermen were from documented military households who were either Manchu or Manchu close allies in founding the Qing dynasty. Because of their special relation with the ruling house, generations of bannermen undertook particular responsibilities in the government.

Born in rustic northeast China, far removed from the cultural heartland of the empire in the south, Tang Ying knew close to nothing about ceramic production when he was appointed to the Imperial Porcelain Manufactory in 1728.[2] Yet a large proportion of the exquisite Chinese porcelains in major collections around the world date to the first half of the eighteenth century and were produced in kilns under Tang's official supervision. What kind of education or training made such a transformation from novice to expert possible? More importantly, what institutions sustained the transmission of necessary technical and artistic knowledge, and how extensive was the impact of this knowledge on statecraft and culture? These are the central questions this book aims to explore.

Porcelain wares are upscale ceramics with sophisticated decoration. They are fired under high temperature, resulting in a surface that is hard, spectacular, and easy to clean, and they are suitable for tableware, ritual use, and aesthetic display. While scholars disagree on when high-fired porcelain began to be produced and in which region of China proper, by the eighth century it had been widely manufactured and consumed by buyers across social strata and, more importantly, exported globally to regions as distant as East Africa. The second peak of global porcelain trade in the early fourteenth century gravitated toward the Islamic world, and blue-and-white porcelain was coveted merchandise. The porcelain town Jingdezhen, where blue-and-white and other new kinds of porcelain originated, became the prevailing supplier for the global porcelain market over the next four centuries.

Jingdezhen was an important node in the early modern world. Although far from the capital city of Beijing, it was located on a rich geological deposit of raw materials essential for porcelain manufacture. A French Jesuit priest, François d'Entrecolles (1664–1741), managed to visit Jingdezhen in the early 1700s. He observed that the town was populated by roughly eighteen thousand households in an area that extended about two thousand square miles on both shores of the Chang River.[3] On a plateau near the riverbank were the streamlined workshops of the Imperial Porcelain Manufactory, which since the early 1400s had shipped tens of thousands of pieces yearly to the imperial court in Beijing. Even before Jingdezhen became an imperial manufacturing center, private factories there produced celadons, *qingbai* (green-white), alternatively called *yingqing* (translucent green) porcelain, and the famous blue-and-white porcelain that was sought after in East Africa, the Islamic world, and Europe. Both the scale and organization of this specialized industrial town posed a sharp contrast to the incipient kilns elsewhere patronized by European princes. In Italy, France, Austria, and

England, alchemists and technicians such as Johann Böttger (1682–1719), who might be considered a European Tang Ying, were trying to crack the secret of porcelain making. Despite technological differences, early modern Chinese emperors and their counterparts in Europe shared tastes in art. Something else they shared was the desire to control their ever-expanding territories and populations.

While the history that unfolds in this book focuses on the Chinese empire, the issues discussed are of global relevance. In the second half of the seventeenth century, the Qing confronted challenges similar to those faced by other Eurasian early modern empires.[4] The first of these challenges involved resource management, logistics, and infrastructure building. The increasing scale and complexity of domestic and international economies meant that an effective form of organization and control was needed to strengthen the imperium.[5] In China, where the industrial manufacture of textiles, porcelain, and salt was scattered across the empire, the rulers' desire to monitor their production required long-distance communications. Bannermen such as Tang Ying played an important role in this process.

A second challenge was that of managing ethnic tensions in a multiethnic polity. As in comparable colonial empires that aimed to achieve grand cultural integration, ethnic tension was a thorny challenge for the Qing (1644–1912), the last imperial Chinese dynasty. The ruling house of the Qing originated in Manchuria, on the northeastern edge of the empire.[6] The ruling royal lineage and aristocrats constituted only a small fraction of the empire's population. The Manchu rulers had to find a way to govern the expanding territories inhabited by Mongolian, Tibetan, and—particularly—Chinese subjects. The latter, who had governed themselves through previous dynasties via a bureaucratic system based on civil examinations, posed the largest threat to Manchu monarchic power.[7] In military campaigns, it was necessary to mobilize the army and supplies across the vast territory, while during peacetime, flows of tax, labor, materials, and information had to be amassed and redistributed throughout the regions. Thus, specialists—and a trustworthy officialdom dominated by Manchus and allies who were equipped with practical skills concerning manufacture, finance, and intelligence—became indispensable to governance.[8] This officialdom consisted of technocrats who, in the term's classical sense, combined technological expertise and managerial power.[9]

The Qing deployed bannermen technocrats to exert control over the production of knowledge generally—and of court art in the Imperial Porcelain Manufactory, in the specific case examined in this book. During the early to mid-Qing, bannermen specialists effectuated an epistemic change toward hands-on knowledge and pluralism in the technological and cultural spheres by appropriating both literati and regional knowledge. In discourse and in practice, Tang Ying and his peers increasingly distinguished their position as technocratic subjects from the position of the Han literati. The difference in knowledge production between the Qing bannermen technocrats and the equally proficient Chinese scholars-cum-moral-philosophers of the late Ming (1368–1644) stems not from the different structures of governance but from the changed identities of Qing imperial agents, which resulted from the multiethnic nature of the Qing ruling class itself.

The bannermen technocrats contributed significantly to a "material culture of state control," to borrow Chandra Mukerji's words in her study of the imperial French gardens of Versailles as both symbolic and technological domination over the imperial territory.[10] My exploration is based on, but pushes further, previous investigation of the Qing institution, which has established a thorough understanding of the bureaucracy, military operation, and finance during this period. Yet we are left wondering how this early modern court extended political control over technology and natural resources—recently a matter of interest in the history of science, as well as the history of East Asia.[11] Historians of art and material culture have analyzed the spectacular visual materials created at the Qing court to show that multiethnic cultural integration was achieved through eclectic artistic forms, but we have yet to understand how imperially commissioned art forms spurred on technological experiments and ensured cultural integration on the material level.[12] This study of technocrats in the porcelain industry addresses these questions because the porcelain supervisors extended the court's political control over regional technology, directly carrying out technological experiments and dictating designs to achieve cultural integration in artistic forms.

Bannermen technocrats' work can be most fruitfully examined with insights drawn from the history of science and technology. Since the 1970s, historians who study the sociology of knowledge have been investigating how particular networks within social institutions affect the formation of knowledge and skill.[13] This perspective allows us to see how technocrats at the Qing court developed their specialist skills through apprenticeships with artisans and merchants, as well as their often interrupted literatus schooling.[14] Recent scholarship on embodied knowledge also is useful for examining technocrats' production and transmission of knowledge across geographical regions by means of tangible objects such as kiln tools, blueprints, and finished products, which complemented textual communication.[15] Another relevant area of scholarly attention is the cultural embeddedness of knowledge—in this case, the value-laden way of knowing nature and crafting artifacts in early modern China.[16] Bannermen technocrats appropriated skill sets from the available cultural repertoire of theater, design, and so on, in response to the propagandistic agenda of the mid-Qing court. Thus, this work draws on the sociology of knowledge, unpacks technocrats' embodied knowledge, and emphasizes the cultural embeddedness of knowledge, to make sense of the bannermen technocrats' work, position, and meaning.

What is the difference between technique and technology in terms of their level of abstraction and their social and cultural embeddedness?[17] Anthropologist Tim Ingold calls the less codified interactive process a "technique," "skill," or "craft," using "technology" to mean "a corpus of generalized, objective knowledge, insofar as it is capable of practical application."[18] However, anthropologist Francesca Bray draws on Chinese agriculture and other technical processes, such as family rituals, to emphasize the inseparability of technology from the social and cultural contexts.[19] As Ingold himself suggests, the articulation of a technical process and the detachment from sensory and interpersonal interaction are historical. The separation between physical experience and verbal articulation is a matter of degree rather than a dichotomy between premodern craft and modern technology. This book tries to delineate this historical process, in which imperial ideology conditioned bannermen's technical skills in both hands-on manufacture and articulation of knowledge. In the context of porcelain production, "technology" refers to a cluster of techniques that involved the systematic development of a porcelain industry, as well as to the technical knowledge analytically transcribed in treatises or pictures. In contrast, "technique" refers to specific procedures and devices deployed to achieve certain artistic styles desired for particular commissions.

Technocrats in the Imperial Household Department

The term "technocrat" is used in this book to indicate a combination of technological specialization and managerial responsibility, as well as acknowledging the difference between bannermen elites in this position and Chinese bureaucrats of Han ethnicity.[20] The bannermen elites were concentrated in certain ethnically marked institutes the Qing ruling house established to keep on top of the complex governing machinery and to curb multiethnic tensions in its empire. These institutes were based on the Manchu military-civil banner system.[21] Under this system, the ruling house registered extended military lineages of the Manchu, Mongolians, Han, and occasionally Koreans and Russians under eight banners, led by royal household members and elite clans.[22] Originally military legions, each banner consisted of a varying number of companies (M: *niru*), whose members were entitled to certain financial and legal privileges, depending on their rank and station.[23] Some bannermen who were in charge of logistics or working at the periphery of military operations were of slightly lower status, and later formed military companies of *booi*, sometimes translated as "bondservants."[24] The elite clans outside the *booi* companies tended to provide primarily military service, although offspring of such families sometimes also worked in logistical divisions at the court.

Elites from the upper three banners (Bordered Yellow, Plain Yellow, and Plain White) formed the Imperial Household Department (C: Neiwufu; M: Dorgi Baita Be Uheri Kadalara Yamun, lit., "bureau supervising all the internal affairs"), where bannermen elites received practical training and carried out strategic commissions.[25] The Imperial Household Department consisted of fifty-six major bureaus.[26] Princes or major military figures served as the chief supervisors of this department. The divisions were so elaborate that their responsibilities overlapped with those of the Six Boards of central government. Thus, this court department intervened in many financial and manufacturing affairs crucial to the state. The founding date of the Imperial Household Department is still open to debate, but it must have existed before 1636.[27] Its personnel grew from roughly 402 individuals in 1662 to 1,623 in 1796.[28]

The technocratic bannermen of concern here were primarily affiliated with the Imperial Workshops (Zaobanchu) within the framework of the Imperial Household Department. The Imperial Workshops were a cluster of handicraft workshops responsible for the large-scale production of artifacts. They had been making everyday necessities and weapons during the Kangxi emperor's reign (1662–1722) and must have been formally established before 1690.[29] The main working body of the Imperial Workshops consisted of three kinds of artisans: bannermen selected from the upper three banners to complete at least three years' apprenticeship; skilled artisans recruited from the south, especially the Lower Yangzi Delta region or Guangzhou; and visiting artisans from Tibet. In addition, European missionaries equipped with special skills formed a very important group of cultural envoys at court.[30]

Besides the Imperial Workshops inside the Forbidden City, three textile manufactories and one porcelain manufactory were supervised by bannermen elites in the southeast of the empire.[31] Historian Evelyn Rawski notes that the Imperial Household Department, especially the Imperial Workshops, "carried out a bewildering variety of activities," including "printing, the salt monopoly, the ginseng trade, the manufacture of textiles, porcelain, guns and cannons, and an entire panoply of artifacts, as well as diplomatic gifts."[32] The production of textiles, porcelain, and other luxury goods was financed by the levy from nearby custom houses, whose revenue went directly to the emperor's Grand Storage Bureau (Guangchusi), which was also a bureau in the Imperial Household Department, not part of the public Board of Revenue (Hubu). Textile commissioner Cao Yin reportedly carried out a variety of tasks, including reporting local weather, recommending skillful artisans to the court, finding rare books, and spying on local elites' political movements.[33] Thus, the factories' versatile and powerful supervisors were crucial for what historian Laura Hostetler terms the "Qing colonial enterprise," as these supervisors incorporated regional intelligence, techniques, and resources in the project of empire building.

Bannermen's training and service in the Imperial Workshops endowed them with a technocratic approach to statecraft in the multiethnic or even cosmopolitan Qing court.[34] This internalized approach in turn enabled them to contribute to empire building. The first component of the technocratic approach was an archivist disposition in collecting local intelligence from all over the empire for the court. Most bannermen technocrats began their apprenticeships by recording seemingly trifling details and running errands (C: *chai;* M: *baita*) in the palace rather than memorizing Confucian classics, as the Chinese examinees would have done. After gaining promotion to higher ranks and often appointment to regional strategic posts, they could communicate information regarding funding, raw materials, labor, and technical procedures directly to the emperor through a "secretive" system of memorials, circumventing the civil officialdom.[35] The information they collected was based on firsthand observation and local interviews rather than book knowledge. The Qing court institutionalized the multiethnic group of supervisors selected for their specialized skills, and carefully archived the process of developing and applying technical knowledge to control manufacture by means of standard measurements and fixed fiscal quotas. *Archive of the Imperial Workshops in the Imperial Household Department of the Qing Dynasty* (Qinggong Neiwufu Zaobanchu dang'an zonghui; hereafter, *Archive of the Imperial Workshops*) provides us with a vast paper trail about this production, from 1723 until the end of imperial China.[36] In the rhythm of working routine at court, the bannermen technocrats honed their archivist skills to put materials in order and obtain information according to a schedule of specific tasks.

The second component of the technocratic approach is the quasi-ethnographic methods that bannermen developed in their mediation between the court and regional bureaus on practical projects.[37] These methods consisted of direct observation and description of regional people and their material resources and productive processes.[38] Following cultural integration during the Kangxi reign, bannermen elites had supported the throne in exercising control over regional resources and technology in commercial centers, industrial towns, and borderlands. These bannermen not only transcribed regional technical knowledge into handwritten technical reports and printed treatises but also produced pictorial explanatory documentation for the audience at court, not for popular circulation. Moreover, they recruited virtuoso local artisans for the Imperial Workshops at court, which became a center of craftsmanship that enabled intensive exchange of technological knowledge.[39]

While extending their network in various regional societies, court-trained bannermen technocrats disseminated knowledge and artistic forms from the political center, where Western missionaries exposed the ruling elites to a wide range of wares, such as clocks, glassware, and European optical devices.[40] The worldwide techno-political connections in Chinese porcelain manufacture are more relevant to our subject than are the well-surveyed networks created through the global trade and consumption of Chinese porcelain.[41] The missionaries' epistolary exchange with the Republic of Letters in Europe reveals their extensive interaction with bannermen elites. In this sense, bannermen technocrats connected multiple communities of experts scattered across different regions, and even continents.

The impact on Chinese culture, especially knowledge culture, of these technically inclined and well-connected bannermen elites, especially their experimental ways of making and knowing, was significant. Since the turn of the twenty-first century, Qing historians have deepened our understanding of how bannermen negotiated, performed, and preserved their ethnic identity through the banner system and through language, the crucial tool for producing knowledge and aesthetic judgment.[42] The "technology of occupation" in manufacture, trade, and the intelligence service were also defining traits.[43]

Bannermen technocrats' experimental ways of knowing and making lie hidden in the relationship between their hands-on official tasks in empire building, such as porcelain production, and their private cultural production, such as literary writing and painting. Evidential scholarship (*kaozheng*), which flourished among Chinese philologists, occupied a surprisingly marginal place in bannermen technocrats' knowledge production, plausibly because of the often military and menial nature of their work.[44]

With the mentality of newcomers confronting an immensely diverse cultural heritage, bannermen elites, and emperors themselves, showed a particular predilection for trying new materials, techniques, and artistic forms in cultural production. Very little attention has been paid to analyzing bannermen elites' work in fine arts and literature as a technocratic mode of representation under strong central control.[45] The institutional structure of porcelain manufacture and the private production of paintings and literary writing—as disparate as they appear to be—are therefore integral aspects of bannermen's technical struggles to fulfill their imperial commissions. The synergy of archivist, ethnographic, and experimental approaches was essential for accomplishing imperial tasks.

Thus, this study's research questions and methodology both lie at the disciplinary intersection of the history of technology, material culture, and literary studies. The example of a bannerman in ceramic manufacture allows us not only to observe his lineage, training, and career path but also to view the Qing empire from the previously little-studied vantage point of technological knowledge.

Tang Ying, the Polymath Bannerman

Our central informant, Tang Ying, conveys a dualistic experience of the imperial center and the borderlands that is rarely seen from Chinese scholar-officials' points of view. Tang and his peers will guide us behind the high walls of the Forbidden City, where they learned technical skills from artisans and Jesuit missionaries. Once appointed to strategic posts in local society near Jingdezhen, Tang enveloped a large network of peer bannermen, magistrates, merchants, and private secretaries. In Jingdezhen, right beside the smoking chimney, as a hands-on potter instead of a lofty connoisseur, Tang Ying came to understand the whole process of porcelain production. In accordance with the Qianlong emperor's order, he contributed to a detailed, illustrated technical treatise on porcelain production. As Tang Ying was simultaneously a tax collector in local custom houses and the fiscal manager of porcelain production, he also wrote numerous memorials to advise on, and account for, the Qing court's expenditure of silver for porcelain production. Tang Ying's most overlooked role was as an innovative playwright, whose theatrical works drew on a specific regional repertoire, which he modified to fit the imperial ideology. His multifaceted work reveals much about his craft, which involved a technocrat's consistent artistic and technical choices.

The space for such choices was delimited by the ideological and rhetorical boundary of court culture, or "imperial decorum." The term "decorum" summarizes the visual and textual rhetoric designed to naturalize norms in the name of appropriateness.[46] The term tends to be used in medieval and early modern contexts where a monarch attempted to regulate close elites' words, comportment, and appearance. Depending on their willingness to comply, court elites chose to submit to these ideologized regulations in the name of appropriateness. The term "decorum" is a useful interpretation of the Chinese term *li*, usually translated as "rite" or "ritual," as it not only prescribed appropriate behavior at court but was also a legally binding force in statecraft.[47] A few important studies on court ritual and art imply that the ruling class of the Qing empire deliberately assumed multiple cultural identities through a sophisticated integration of literary and decorative forms from Chinese, Mongolian, Tibetan, and Manchurian repertoires.[48] Imperial decorum bore equally on the transcription of technological knowledge and on artistic form, both integral elements of porcelain production. Analytical concepts such as "craft" and "decorum" are relevant to the distinct cultural forms and values created by bannermen technocrats.

As impressive as the autodidact Tang Ying was, he was not a singular case. Following his trajectory will help us grasp the life and work of three generations of his family, as well as many peer technocrats who shared the same kind of careers combining technological work and managerial responsibility. As a perfect example of a bannerman technocrat contributing to empire building, Tang extended his archivist approach to regions far from the center. His poetry, drama, and technological treatises, which were written in the area around Jingdezhen, take a quasi-ethnographic approach in representing local society, as his representation "distinguish[ed] the knowledge about 'other' peoples that was based on direct observation from descriptions based on legend and hearsay."[49] The habit of systematically archiving information and experimenting directly with material permeated Tang's cultural production within and outside his official obligations.[50]

The Technocratic Knowledge Culture

Bannermen technocrats' ways of knowing and making were not simply individual habit. They formed a knowledge culture nourished at the multiethnic court yet exerting influence on regions at the empire's border. The technocratic knowledge culture consisted of shared archivist language conventions for discussing technical matters and a shared value system, including the purpose of such knowledge, methods of validation, and aesthetic ramifications. Bannermen technocrats' work exemplified the mutual formation of technological knowledge and socioeconomic institutions.[51] Similar to Egyptian experts in the British colonial regime, Qing bannermen elites developed a way of reproducing knowledge and honing skills in the process of tax collection and managing manufacturing.[52] In turn, the institutional valorization of hands-on experience, systematic planning, and normative regulation strengthened the state's centralized control over regional resources and labor forces.

Bannermen elites' apprenticeships at court and their in situ learning illustrate how skills are physically embodied and socially embedded.[53] Later on, in the regional factories, they had to open their senses to the feel of materials, to acoustic cues, the fire's temperature, and the air's humidity. The process of making and using knowledge in the Imperial Household Department leads to two questions central to the technocratic culture shaped by the Qing institution: What knowledge did bannermen technocrats produce in the manufacturing process? And how did bannermen transcribe their knowledge?

It seems as though the ruling house imposed a division of expertise by establishing the Imperial Household Department and its affiliated factories. Even though some Chinese scholar-officials were engaged in the promotion of agricultural production, hydraulics, and disaster relief, they scarcely played any role in the Imperial Workshops' manufacturing, according to what was archived after 1723.[54] In fact, Chinese scholar-officials were carefully kept away from the strategic posts in factories and custom houses, simply because these establishments were parts of the Imperial Household Department, where only bannermen were employed.[55] The Confucian examinees' method of learning was sustained by both the civil exam curriculum and the reforms resulting from their encounters with Western missionaries.[56] By and large, literati-bureaucrats' ways of knowing and making gravitated toward textual knowledge.

The technocrats' schooling and apprenticeship in the Imperial Household Department differentiated them, as cultural agents, from literati knowledge makers. As Tang Ying's career trajectory shows, bannermen elites' repertoires of skills often revealed their military origins, which distinguished them from Chinese bureaucrats. Although some bannermen also studied the Confucian canon and took civil examinations, more of them explicitly acknowledged their limited writing skills and distanced themselves from the scholar-officials. More importantly, bannermen technocrats like Tang Ying and his peers did not consider their familiarity with Confucian philosophy to be a moral high ground from which they could negotiate official ideology with the monarch in the way Chinese officials often did. Instead, the bannermen elites' knowledge and technocratic skills strongly correlated with their functionalist position in the Imperial Household Department. Historian Benjamin Elman has noted how active the Manchu bannermen and Hanjun bondservants were in the Imperial Workshops.[57] His term "expert" calls attention to technocratic bannermen's close affinity with artisans (*gong*) and merchants (*shang*) in large-scale practical projects.[58] As opposed to more visible Confucian scholars who produced voluminous texts, technocratic experts in this context were specialists who accumulated empirical and often nontextual experience by working on practical tasks for a long period of time.[59]

Similar to the alchemists hired by Central European princes, technocrats developed an eclectic way of transcribing knowledge, mediating among the ruling house, craftsmen, Western missionaries, and scholar-officials, who all acted according to different modes of knowledge making.[60] Bannermen technocrats augmented their manual skills with an expanded range of media, including diagrams, pictures, and models, for transcribing embodied knowledge. Broadly speaking, this notion of knowledge transcription means abstracting working experience and expressing it in a durable medium, indeed a process of manipulating symbols.[61] This method of transcribing knowledge loses some sensory information and trades accuracy for transmissibility.[62] In other words, the transcription is an equivalence forged within a sociotechnical regime of rhetoric.[63]

Although a written treatise was still an often-used medium for transcribing knowledge in the porcelain industry during the Qing, a more disparate assembly of media, such as preparatory sketches, drawings, and three-dimensional models, all record the technocratic supervisors' experience of designing and planning.[64] Tools, including kiln furniture, test pieces, and specimen shards, demonstrate their experimentation with materials. Moreover, the porcelain supervisors archived their tools and consulted them from time to time. These artifacts were highly effective in communicating technical details between the court and the local factories. In this sense, systematically archiving the artifacts loaded with information facilitated the management of labor, fiscal flows, and the transport of goods. As part of the myriad processes in empire building, bannermen technocrats' expertise served to manage the assemblage of material artifacts as well as interpersonal relationships in the factories and at court.[65] In summary, the physical and intellectual disposition of archivist, ethnographer, and experimenter undergirds the technocratic craft of these bannermen.

Craft and Decorum: Rhetoric in Articulation and Making

The term *gong* (craft) in this book points to a consistency in formal and referential choices that porcelain supervisors made in their artistic production and management.[66] The term draws on the rich semantic range covered by the use of *gong* in this period. In the imperial archive, *gong* is used as a noun, referring to craftsmen who specialized in a particular medium, such as wood, porcelain, or lacquer.[67] Compared with terms like "poetics" or "style," "craft" emphasizes physical labor and nontextual primary materials, in contrast to textual proficiency. The term "craft" highlights the physical labor that left traces on artifacts, and we can retrieve makers' and users' physical decisions and delimitations by examining such traces as clues.[68]

Gong is also a unit for measuring human labor via the language of archival documents. This measurement permeates the rigid system sustained by routinized reports, inspections, awards, and more often, punishments to calculate and standardize labor in the Imperial Household Department. Through standardization, the technocrats' senses and attention were trained to fashion artifacts according to the imperial judgment of appropriateness, or "decorum." As a porcelain supervisor, Tang Ying needed to consult information that he, as an archivist, arranged in the Imperial Workshops, as well as advice and tips that he, as a quasi-ethnographer, collected from regional societies to produce porcelain wares in compliance with this decorum.

As an evaluative term, "craft" also covers wordsmiths' and painters' toil. *Gong* can mean "regulated," and it was used in this sense to praise verses that were neatly composed according to rhyming rules and parallelism. This meaning originated in a much earlier period, but the literati still used it to appraise bannermen elites' poetry. Many bannermen's poems were not considered *gong* but glowed with the aura of virtuous and practical workmen who cared more about sincere self-expression than ornamentation. Bannermen technocrats only selectively appropriated the literati's skills on a basic level, namely literary writing and some knowledge of the Confucian classics. "Craft" is an even better term for capturing some bannermen's color-saturated painting style.[69] In contrast to the performative brushwork emphasized in some literati paintings, some bannermen's painterly approaches very likely related to their functionalist training.

Across a variety of material media—textual or nontextual—craft was inherent in technocrats' representational strategy, as seen in technical treatises and in their quasi-ethnographical references to the "other."[70] Close reading of Tang's pragmatic technical treatises and routine archival documents reveals his rhetorical strategy.

The *Yang* System

The politicized industrial *yang* system of design centered at court was central to all technocratic work. The imperial decorum took material shape through this design system, within which technocratic supervisors communicated with emperors about budget, measurement, shape, decorative pattern, and everything else related to manufactured goods. The cross-institutional *yang* system was installed not only for aesthetics but also for standardizing expenditure and technical procedures in general. Operation of the *yang* system demonstrates how political control was imposed and negotiated through decisions on technical and artistic matters, and therefore how the system made imperial decorum visible.

A *yang* was a prototype of whatever objects were to be produced, ranging from monumental architectural structures to small teacups. Though most often painted as a polychrome blueprint, a *yang* could well be a wooden model, a bundle of cardboard, or even an antique from a previous dynasty.[71] Supervisors and artisans could use these *yang* as templates to transmit the design from one object to another across media, as well as to regions far away. Beyond decorative art, *yang* were also widely adopted in the production of weapons and the construction of architecture, bridges, and hydraulic structures throughout the empire.

Yang were deployed following a procedure that organized the production process. A formulaic archival record first noted the preparation of an initial *yang*. In some cases, a follow-up memorial may have reported that successfully made products had been sent back to court. The emperor's judgment ultimately delimited imperial decorum that was visualized in *yang*.[72] Such was the imposing discursive and practical decorum in the institution of the mid-Qing regime. However, the apparently comprehensive planning and frequent inspections could not exhaustively control all the minute variables in the process of production. Individual bannermen's experimental decisions highlight their agency and explain the diversity of technocratic culture.

Technocratic Culture on the Early Modern Stage

A unifying craft cut across Tang Ying's porcelain manufacture, technological treatises, and literary productions.[73] Those aspects of cultural products not commissioned by the ruling house—his private writing, some paintings, and private porcelain wares—reveal how far he had "internalized" imperial decorum in his archivist, proto-ethnographic, and experimental approach to creative work.[74]

Tang Ying's literary writing is congruous with the ruling house's keen interest in representing the flowers, animals, minerals, and regional customs of the empire through texts and pictures.[75] Ideological propaganda and moral didactics prevailed in such representation. And textile and porcelain factories served as hubs, as well as censors, of information. Tang Ying's plays are famous for having appropriated repertoire from a type of regional theater, the clapper drama (*bangzi xi*), into a Kun style of opera that is imbued with moral didacticism. This dramatic style is similar to the one he used to produce porcelain. Moreover, many bannermen's poems recounted what they encountered in their jobs in regional society. Thus, Tang Ying and his fellow technocrats' private literary work and paintings reveal what they thought about their social and ethnic identities, their beliefs, and their relations with local society, alongside their repertoire of technical skills. Placing the bannermen technocrats' local instantiation of their skills within their institutional context enables us to navigate the world of craft (*gong*) in early modern China and to see how the imperial state's intervention in industry has left a lingering imprint on modern China through its modes of labor-intensive production, the division of domestic and foreign markets, and above all, a technocratic culture of centralization.

ONE

Bannermen Technocrats in the Mid-Qing

THE BANNERMEN TECHNOCRATS constituted the linchpin of imperial porcelain manufacture, for they possessed sufficient specialized knowledge to operate the manufactory, not to mention the financial experience to manage the flows of capital and labor. They differed from the Chinese literati in their education, skills, and knowledge cultures, not only because of their ethnicity as defined in household registers but because they enjoyed a special administrative status that enabled them to be close to the emperor and to serve in the Imperial Household Department.

The institutionalized banner privilege of the Imperial Household Department generated the similar career paths of bannermen elites and, by extension, a shared approach to knowledge and skill.[1] Elite bannermen came into being first through their alliance in the military conquest of China proper. After the Manchus secured rulership, administrative communication and cultural integration in the multilingual and multicultural population became the focus of statecraft. So before the 1680s, the most noticeable bannermen equipped with specialized skills were translators. After the 1680s, massive material production schemes had replaced translation projects and started to loom prominently in the Imperial Household Department's archival records. Thus, the court needed different kinds of specialized skills from the trusted officialdom as the empire evolved and the priorities of governance changed over time. The career of three generations of Tang Ying's family shows the degree to which a bannerman clan could secure its cultural and political capital by appropriating a mixture of technological and literary skills to meet the court's need.

Like many peer bannermen's retrospectively traced genealogies, Tang Ying's family allegedly originates from a military background. His ancestor Tang

Yingzu, who lived in the northeast of the Ming empire, had joined the Manchu troops prior to their conquests.[2] Later on, Tang Yingzu was "elevated" to the Plain Yellow Banner, part of the upper three banners, from which the emperor selected his personal household servants.[3] This family background afforded Tang Ying the opportunity, shortly after his sixteenth birthday, to attend the Kangxi emperor as a bodyguard,[4] a martial route reserved for bannermen elites.[5] The privileged civil route for bannermen was to become a scribe (M: *bithesi*), an entry-rank copyist or translator.[6]

The entry-level jobs of the male members of the Tang family show us bannermen technocrats' usual career starting points—from which the Chinese were excluded. Following in their father's footsteps, the first two of Tang Ying's three sons served in the Imperial Household Department. Tang Ying was highly conscious of the functionary social status of his family. His eldest son, Wenbao, already by 1740 held the rank of *zhishi* (M: *baitangga*), a clerk in the Imperial Household Department, which Tang Ying considered to be a huge step up.[7] Between 1739 and 1741 Wenbao was involved in producing several kinds of porcelain enamel in the Imperial Workshops, while his father worked in Jingdezhen at the other end of the production line that linked the Forbidden City to the industrial town. Wenbao took over his father's post at the Imperial Workshops at the age of thirty-seven.

Beyond the exclusive roles of scribe, bodyguard, and errand runner in palaces, bannermen could also attempt the civil service examinations, but they tended to fall back on the career paths reserved for bannermen.[8] Tang Ying was excited about the success of his second son, Tang Yinbao, in 1741.[9] Yinbao went on to attain the highest level at the metropolitan examination in 1748, after which Tang Ying introduced him to his network of famous scholar-officials.[10] However, even though Yinbao had passed his exams and seemed to be on his way to becoming a scholar-official, he was nevertheless selected for work in the textile manufacture in Hangzhou, in the Neiwufu circle of bannermen technocrats.[11] The third generation of the Tang family repeated this career pattern. Tang Ying's grandson supervised the salt monopoly in Yangzhou, a position typically reserved for bannermen.[12] This grandson successfully invited Yinghe (1771–1840)[13] from another powerful bannerman clan, the Socolos (C: Suo-chuo-le)—who was one of the chief directors in the Imperial Household Department—to write a preface for his grandfather Tang Ying's oeuvre.[14]

In brief, Tang Ying's family reveals how a bannerman household of moderate prominence could succeed across several generations in the specialized field of imperial manufacturing, a sector at the intersection of art, design, technology, and finance. This was made possible by the impressive practical skills they acquired in their early training at court.

From Apprentice to Supervisor

Bannermen elites in the Qing derived their power from their proximity to the emperor. Many adolescent bannermen served as emperors' bodyguards, accumulated considerable political capital, and developed an enduring focus on martial skills and military affairs.[15] Tang Ying's friend Gu Donggao (dates unknown) stated that "he [Tang Ying] guarded the Shengzu [Kangxi] emperor for more than thirty years."[16] Tang Ying accompanied the Kangxi emperor on his southern tour three times.[17] Tang Ying himself recalls accompanying the Kangxi emperor to the northern desert:

> Besides my humble attendance, I traveled in rain and wind, back and forth in mountains, east and west of the river and as far as the northern desert beyond the Great Wall. Through it all I stumbled along without one moment's break.[18]

This early experience as a mounted soldier prompted him to keep track of major military campaigns on the northwestern border later on. Though Tang Ying did not participate in them, he had lengthy reports about the battles copied from the capital gazette (*dibao*) and sent to him in Jingdezhen.[19]

Information gathering was part of the Imperial Household Department's organized archival approach. For the Grand Council, a similar bureau controlled by bannermen elites, albums of copied documents served as the basis for compiling the military campaign history (*fanglue*) of the Junghar War on the northwestern border.[20] The content of a document could be informative, while the action of recording it could be performative, especially in a nonparticipant's case. It is therefore no surprise that Tang Ying composed poems to celebrate Qianlong's victory in the Junghar campaign.

His military duty enabled Tang Ying the adolescent bodyguard not only to develop his martial skills but also to gain a lifelong network of bannermen elites. For instance, he maintained a firm friendship with Gao Bin (1683–1755), who came from a powerful bannerman clan, after their years as bodyguards together.[21] Gao Bin was appointed to manage the imperial salt monopoly and, later on, hydraulic projects.

> Mr. Tang Jungong and I [Gao Bin] served together as bodyguards at the inner court in our youth. He is one year older than me. . . . We guarded the palace together for decades. After I was appointed elsewhere, we no longer met very often. After twenty years, in the spring of *bingchen* year [1736] he was appointed to supervise the custom house of Huai River while overseeing the porcelain manufacture in Jiangxi. . . . We strolled along the riverbank of the Huai and passed the days with a pure heart. Three years slipped away there.[22]

Among Gao's lineage, Gao Bin's son and grandson, Gao Heng (?–1768) and Gao Pu (?–1778), both became notorious because of their high-profile corruption in the state's salt monopoly and jade trade, yet their descendants continued to serve in strategic positions. In short, hydraulics, the salt production monopoly, and the manufacture of luxury goods were typical kinds of imperial business entrusted to bannermen technocrats, in addition to military campaigns, translation, and publications during the dynasty's early years. Gao Bin was especially knowledgeable about hydraulics. In poems he composed during a river inspection, he carefully explained the materials, tools, and structures required for dike construction in handwritten notes between the printed verse lines.[23] Gao Bin and Tang Ying represented a kind of technocrat who had personal experience handling specialized tools and raw materials, in addition to the comprehensive financial expertise they acquired as inner-court officials.

Embodied Experience as an Apprentice (c. 1725)

After his time as a bodyguard, Tang Ying began his artisanal training as a pattern painter in the Imperial Workshops—the kind of craftsman development not usually included in formal schooling, which instead focused exclusively on the civil or military examinations. Tang Ying's early official positions are hard to find, as the *Collected Statutes* (Huidian) does not record the name of bannermen apprentices recruited from the upper three banners to work in the Imperial Workshops.[24] Before Tang Ying received his official title in the Imperial Workshops, he had probably held the rank of production supervisor (*jianzao*), a position involving extensive manual labor, particularly pattern drawing. In the first year of the Yongzheng reign, 1723, Tang Ying was often ordered to make design drafts (*yang*) for luxury items in various media. After he was granted the rank of vice director of a bureau (*yuanwailang*) in 1725, his official remit extended to carrying valuable artifacts in and out (*chijin, chichu*) of the imperial vaults and workshops, reporting on the production process, and supervising craftsmen's performance in the Imperial Workshops. From 1728 to 1756 he was appointed to run the Imperial Porcelain Manufactory in Jingdezhen, and two successive emperors continued ordering him to submit *yang*, as shown in their confidential correspondence.

Thus Tang Ying became one of the supervisor-designers trained by the Imperial Workshops to manage the implementation of technological and artistic skills.[25] The information that scholars have started to piece together about other individual bannermen supervisors' skills and responsibilities shows that selected bannermen elites went through hands-on apprenticeships and took charge of technological empire-building projects, constituting an officialdom that was distinct from the Chinese bureaucrats in terms of institutions, networks, and skills.

Tang Ying's practical training is demonstrated by the operation of the imperial system of design—or *yang*—in the manufacturing process. Though *yang* could consist of wooden models, a bundle of cardboard (*hepai yang*), or even an actual artifact serving as a sample, drawing remained the most convenient medium.[26] As a key part of his training as well as his job, Tang Ying was ordered to draw *yang* for many different workshops inside the palace. Several archival records dating from 1723 exemplify his work across diverse media:

> Prince Yi [Yinxiang, the thirteenth son of Kangxi emperor] has some small Ding bottles, a Ding censer,[27] a Jiajing [reign period] box, a Guan vase, and a teapot in the shape of bamboo brought out and orders Tang Ying to draw design drafts [*yang*] based on these model objects [also *yang*].[28]

This archival entry is classified under the Jade Workshop (Yuzuo) and shows how the objects to be drawn were of various shapes and glazes. The procedure was "to draw design drafts according the model" (*zhaoyang huayang*). The origin and the target, though realized in different media, were both considered *yang*. Tang Ying's work was to analytically extract design elements such as shape and painting motifs from an object and realize these design ideas in another medium.

The Qing court, especially emperors, imposed strict rules for technocrats' preparation of the *yang* through regular communication and evaluation, honing their painting techniques and thereby exerting control over the visual presence of the Qing empire. Extant exemplary *yang* show that such design drafts involved laborious work with repetitive patterns. Tang Ying was instructed to patiently draw such patterns following strict rules. Though we have very few *yang* decisively dated from before 1795, the practice of this design system must have already been in place before the 1680s and continued into the second half of the Qing dynasty.[29] An archive entry from 1723 records that the Yongzheng emperor praised the style (*kuanshi*) of a beautiful woman that Tang Ying drew on the wall of an imperial mansion known as the Celestial Immortals' Banquet over Nine Regions (Jiuzhou Qingyan Shangxianlou).[30] The emperor liked this drawing so much that he asked for the drapery of the robe on another beauty to be modeled after it. In the paintings of beautiful women of that time, such fabric was usually represented as a textile bearing complex patterns. These patterns were widely shared as motifs on artworks in other media as well, such as bronze, ceramic, and lacquer, and were made to comply with decorum—that is, a visualized courtly order that conformed to imperial ideology.[31]

Although Tang Ying's figure paintings have been lost, fellow bannermen painters' many highly detailed portraits exemplify the laborious approach taken to pictorial representation. Mang-gu-li (1672–1736), a powerful technocrat of Mongolian descent,[32] painted Prince Yi and a palace lady wearing elaborate ornamental court apparel. From Mang-gu-li's extant and recorded portraits, scholars note that he extensively integrated traditional Chinese figure painting with Western methods of applying shading to create visual depth and meticulously painted intricate patterns that cover the costumes and objets d'art in court paintings.[33] The brushwork in bannermen's landscape painting also exhibits skillful yet slightly mechanical control rather than an interest in performative brush strokes. The highly structured patterns depicted on the deep blue mineral-like square rocks by the bannerman court painter Tang Dai illustrate this kind of craftsmanship.[34]

The hands-on training and exposure to Western painting techniques in the Imperial Workshops nourished these technocrats' predilection for depicting sartorial embellishments accurately and inspired their pursuit of verisimilar representation. This court style owes much to the production of large-scale documentary paintings of military campaigns, imperial tours, and court rituals, where the highly regulated workmanship is evident, even at draft stages.[35] Alternatively, we could claim that this highly regulated method of revision and correction in the *yang* system, as a physical discipline, contributed to the technocrats' distinctive visual approach to documentary depiction. The administrative process of preparing pictorial blueprints for imperial inspection, approval, and feedback was similar to the process inner-court deputies followed in drafting policy recommendations for emperors—whereby each successive draft was archived after completion.[36]

COURT MANAGER-TECHNICIAN (1725–1728)

Bannermen technocrats' managerial agility in addition to technical skill distinguished them from master artisans recruited at court. Like other bannermen who rose from craft apprentices to become managers who could carry out imperial commissions beyond a specific field, Tang Ying is recorded as working with handicraft workshops near the Hall of Mental Cultivation (Yangxindian) specializing in jade, inlay works, miscellaneous works (like glasses and medicine), enamelware, picture mounting, paintings, cannons and muskets, ivory, flowers, wood, leather, lacquer, archery, container cases, helmets, carvings, and inkstones.[37] His wide experience with various materials could partly explain how he was able to pick up porcelain technology so quickly later on. For most of these projects at court, Tang Ying's task was to "commission" (*chuanzuo*), which refers not only to hands-on design but also to management. Some archival records indicate that he was also responsible for policing the flow of materials and keeping records of expenditures.[38] In reporting to his superior, Prince Yi, the proper term was to "inform" (*qi*).

> On the 11th day of the 3rd month in the 6th year of the Yongzheng reign, bureau vice director Shen Yu and Tang Ying respectfully report [*qi*], the number of tin panels for glass mirrors sent from Wuying Hall is 135. . . . Now the storage of our imperial workshops has not been completely built. We would like to temporarily store these panels in Wuying Hall.[39]

Apart from technocrats' involvement in fiscal and material management, this record also indicates the expansion of the Imperial Workshops in the early Qing, which likely demanded more managerial manpower. Tang Ying was promoted to positions with greater responsibility within a year. He had just been promoted at the beginning of the same year to manager with seal (*huaya banshi*), in charge of the movement of raw materials and products from imperial storages to workshops, and before long he became vice director of a bureau (*yuanwailang*).[40] Tang Ying's rapid promotion exemplifies the career opportunities reserved for bannermen.[41] Starting from pattern drawing, he rose to supervise every aspect of production. Apart from routine communication and supervision, when an imperial commission was complicated or its production involved particular technical experiments, supervisors were required to write confidential reports to the emperor. Expenditures on luxurious materials might be kept hidden, and more secretive information was kept confidential in relation to the military industry operated by the Imperial Household Department.[42]

MAKING WEAPONS

Technocrats' training in nontextual skills and logistical management was rooted in bannermen's military obligation. Even if many were appointed to oversee projects not directly related to military conquests, their familiarity with practical tools, intelligence gathering, and resource extraction—and above all a strong loyalty to the throne—served them over time and across a variety of cultural endeavors. During Tang Ying's years at court, his participation in the production of cannons, muskets, and bullets illustrates the military preoccupation inherent in the work of bannermen technocrats.[43] The records of Tang's involvement in producing model cannons and trial firing provide rare insight into how planning and experimentation went hand in hand. Archival records referring to Tang Ying's weapons-related projects mainly date from the beginning of 1727 and continue intermittently until the beginning of the next year. Early in 1727, Prince Yi ordered the craftsmen to replicate a cannon called "Mighty General" (Weiyuan) at his mansion. He also compared the model of Mighty General with abandoned cannons and ordered a *yang* of a recently found mother-and-son cannon to be drawn.[44] At the same time, the Board of War asked for one thousand muskets (*niaoqiang*). This was a large order. Prince Yi approved the order after he had ascertained that the Imperial Workshops would be able to build the cannons.[45] Then Tang Ying was ordered to participate in the weapons testing.

> On the 22nd day of the 1st month in the 6th year of the Yongzheng reign . . . the order was received. [Prince Yi ordered], pass the mother-and-son cannon and the Western firearm [*jiaoqiang*] sent as tribute by Yue Zhongqi to vice director Tang Ying and . . . bring one each of the large and small newly built mother-and-son cannons and new firearm to the imperial workshops in Yuanming Yuan. Tomorrow they should meet Centurion [*baizong*] Zhu Guojie and take the weapons for testing [*shifang*] near Lugou Bridge. . . . On the same day, director Haiwang and vice director Tang Ying turned in a report noting the quality and firing range to Prince Yi.[46]

The rest of the report in the archive specifies the numbers, kinds, and firing ranges of the weapons used in the military exercise. Tang Ying's experience in weapons supplemented his lifelong interest in military activities, begun when he was a bodyguard for the emperor.

The spectacles in Tang Ying's theatrical work drew directly from military exercises. Five years after he completed his longest play, *Turning the Mind of Heaven* (Zhuan tianxin), he added an entire aria to enhance the scene of a military maneuver of rebels in the mountains. The aria describes the rebel leader imagining his victory over an official army. The climax begins with the leader's order to attack.[47] At this point, Tang Ying added the aria "Ascending a Small Pavilion" (Shangxiaolou), precisely dated, to "assist the performance of the exercise" (*duizhen gunpai zhizhu*). The aria's relatively long lyrics, in an addition separate from the main text of the play, appear in his work logs.[48] Singing the aria provides time for soldiers armed with cane shields and cannons to perform. Moreover, Tang Ying wittily conflated the language of military maneuvers and theatrical performances. In an aria immediately preceding this one, the leader sings that they will "perform the magic military alignment called mysterious gate" (*banyan qimen ao*). Then he orders them to put on armor to "exercise" (*caoyan*). Eventually, in the added aria, the leader imagines himself being crowned as the new emperor and dressed in a yellow robe. He uses the theatrical term "change costumes" (*huan xingtou*) in its metaphorical as well as its literal sense. By employing this theatrical vocabulary seamlessly integrated into a military exercise, Tang Ying played a metatheatrical game with the boundary between military maneuvers and theatrical performances.

The staging of this military scene in the theater shows the same concern with decorum he showed when he participated in testing cannons and muskets in Beijing and Guangzhou in 1750. Tang Ying noted in his journal, "The general and the chief commander conducted the annual military maneuver with cannons in the camp south of White Cloud Mountain. The scene was solemn and organized."[49] His comment refers to the battle array, which had both practical merit and symbolic power, that is, imperial decorum, or appropriate presentation of the army in this case. This pursuit of decorum permeated weapons manufacture. For instance, serial numbers were engraved on the cannons with gold and silver and surrounded by gems, for both practical identification and self-glorifying decoration:

> On the 1st day of the 2nd month, director and vice director, Haiwang and Tang Ying, etc. . . . received Prince Yi's order: Carefully draw the *yang* of this chamber cannon [*yaotang pao*]. Decorate it with some inlaid gems. It is to be used to guard the storage area and to guard the emperor. As for the remaining ten large and small mother-and-son cannons, select the best ones to be gilt with a

> gold dragon and gold inscription, and attach a serial number. The inferior ones should be gilt with a silver dragon, silver inscription and have a serial number attached.[50]

In weapons production, the separation between design and execution thus necessitated increased communication and quality control. Meanwhile, this system of design made adjustment and improvisation possible, although the end products were still subject to the established decorum, over which emperors had the last word.

IMPERIAL AGENTS IN LOCAL SOCIETY (1728–1756)

Moving our focus outside the court to the Imperial Porcelain Manufactory in Jingdezhen, we find that two of Tang Ying's immediate predecessors at the imperial kilns came from important bannermen clans. Archival records document the gradual recovery of the Imperial Porcelain Manufactory from private commercial operators into the hands of bannermen technocrats.[51] The development of the manufactory in the first half of the eighteenth century reveals the court's attempt to control a regional industry with remarkable success in the middle period but much irregularity in the beginning and the end.

An Qi (c. 1683–1742), whose Plain Yellow Banner family made a fortune from the imperial certificate to conduct the salt business in Tianjin, single-handedly paid for porcelain manufacture and transport to the court between 1720 and 1726.[52] The family also dispatched servants to oversee porcelain production in Jingdezhen. As the court had not yet rigorously imposed regulations regarding the shape and color of porcelain, some features of products made in this period plausibly resulted from the An family's artistic choice. For instance, the family amassed a vast number of antique paintings.[53] And polychrome figure paintings prevailed on porcelain wares made during this period, likely related to the supervisor's individual interest.[54]

In 1725, Nian Xiyao (?–1738), from the Bordered Yellow Banner, became the first formally appointed supervisor of the manufactory, though he oversaw production from afar while managing tax collection in the Huai'an Custom House.[55] During Nian's tenure, the Yongzheng emperor clearly intended to control porcelain manufacture in Jingdezhen. During the year of overlap between the two porcelain supervisors, the emperor ordered Nian to audit the finances of An Qi's manufacture and to investigate the impact of the An family's porcelain manufacture on the local labor force. Shortly afterward, in 1727, the Yongzheng emperor wrote a trenchant articulation of imperial decorum regarding the artistic style of porcelain. On the 3rd day of the 3rd month in the 5th year of the Yongzheng reign (March 25, 1727), he resolutely declared the regulatory nature of the *yang* system:

> As for the products that I once [ordered to be] made, you should keep a model as a copy for reference [*shiyang*]. If not, I am afraid it would be impossible for later production to reproduce its original style. In my opinion, the Imperial Workshops used to make a smaller amount of good products but they were in the honorable style of the inner court [*neiting gongzao shiyang*]. Recently they have become artful but permeated with styles from outside workshops. Next time you produce something, do not lose the honorable style [of the model] from the inner court.[56]

Supervisor Nian's artistic preference is supplanted by imperial taste and is hardly discernible on vessels made in the Yongzheng reign. The Yongzheng emperor's frequent archived instructions regarding the form and quality of porcelain products match the meticulous potting, glazing, and painting of porcelains dated to this period. The emperor's preferences significantly shaped imperial decorum and, in turn, set the artistic style for the supervisor to achieve technically. Nian Xiyao was a mathematician who collaborated with the Jesuit missionary Giuseppe Castiglione (1688–1766) to translate, incorporate, and transform Andrea Pozzo's (1642–1709) *Perspectiva Pictorum et Architectorum* into *The Study of Vision* (Shi xue, 1729), a treatise on the application of perspective drawing.[57] The treatise includes perspective drawings of about ten kinds of vessels on whose forms porcelain was often modeled. This kind of development and transmission of technical knowledge was encouraged by the Yongzheng emperor, but technocrats' value judgments, if they did not closely follow imperial decorum, were rendered completely invisible, whether in aesthetics, religion, or moral discourses. The role of the technocrat was to carry out the emperor's moral authority, whereas many Han scholar-officials assumed Confucian moral authority themselves.

Nian's influence on the works of his follower Tang Ying could be understood as the shared bannerman-technocrat approach to manufacture. Later, when Tang Ying's name was absent from the Imperial Workshops' archive between 1728 and 1735, Nian Xiyao was the person who corresponded with the emperor and Prince Yi. Nian probably had taught Tang Ying some basic mathematical formulas for calculating the cost of porcelain production.[58] The master and the protégé even followed similar career paths. During Nian Xiyao's early service in Guangdong, he was in charge of purchasing European artifacts as well as reporting about the foreign ships anchored at Guangzhou customs, which was exactly what Tang Ying did at the same place in 1750.

Yongzheng's son, the Qianlong emperor, intensified imperial intervention in design via the *yang* system. When Tang Ying succeeded Nian Xiyao, taking full responsibility for the manufactory in 1728, the court frequently sent *yang* for Tang Ying to realize. Like the inscriptions on cannons, even the reign mark on porcelain vessels could be standardized by the application of a standardized *yang*. For example, in the very first year of the Qianlong reign, a design draft of seal script (*zhuanzi kuan ziyang*) was distributed, in which the emperor ordered, "From now on, all the [marks on the] porcelain pieces should be based upon this style [*kuanshi*] of seal script."[59] Thus, trained in this practice of *yang*, a technocrat like Tang Ying became accustomed to the two sequential phases of production: design and execution.

Nevertheless, the increasing scale of manufacture and Tang Ying's proactive experiments in the regional manufactory seemed to loosen rigid control from the court and negotiated a space for local agency. Tang's hands-on expertise in regional materials and procedures made his technical as well as artistic opinion indispensable for the court in making decisions concerning production. The following case illustrates how, as supervisor, he executed imperial control while engaging in formal innovation within the *yang* system. In mid-1736, the Qianlong emperor wanted a kind of porcelain coated in white glaze, called "sweet white" (*tianbai*).[60] The court dispatched nine different design drafts to Tang Ying for production, and at the end of the year, Tang Ying sent eight new porcelain prototypes back.[61] The emperor rejected the further production of one type of vase and specified that, for the next order, Tang Ying should command the people at the local kiln site (*yaoshang ren*) to "improvise some *yang*" (*suiyi huayang*).[62] This was a rare instance where the practice of *yang* might well have facilitated stylistic variation, and it was the supervisor who made it happen.

Although Tang Ying's bannermen peers, such as Nian Xiyao and Gao Bin, might not have been experts in the same trade or at the same technical level, they shared training in specific practical skills, which were universally required and developed further through their management of large-scale projects crucial for empire building.

Self-Cultivation in a Technocratic Network

The mastery of languages was less a matter of social status or aesthetic virtuosity for bannermen than an occupational skill for archiving and technical communication and a marker of ethnic identity.[63] Yet communication using a knowledge of correct official protocol and adequate cultural allusions required considerable time to master. There is evidence that not only was Tang Ying proficient in literary Chinese but he also knew enough Manchu for his documentary work. By the time he became active at court, many of his bannermen peers seemed to primarily use standard Chinese to communicate about manufacture. Although the mastery of Manchu language was an ideological ethnic marker that the court hoped to promote, the population's Manchu proficiency did not match the aspiration. Yet Tang Ying's working journal preserves a few textile terms and numbers in Manchu. The fragmentary note mixes Chinese counting units, Manchu numerals, and Suzhou numerals, a numerical system often used by merchants, who apparently were one source of Tang Ying's managerial knowledge (fig. 1.1).

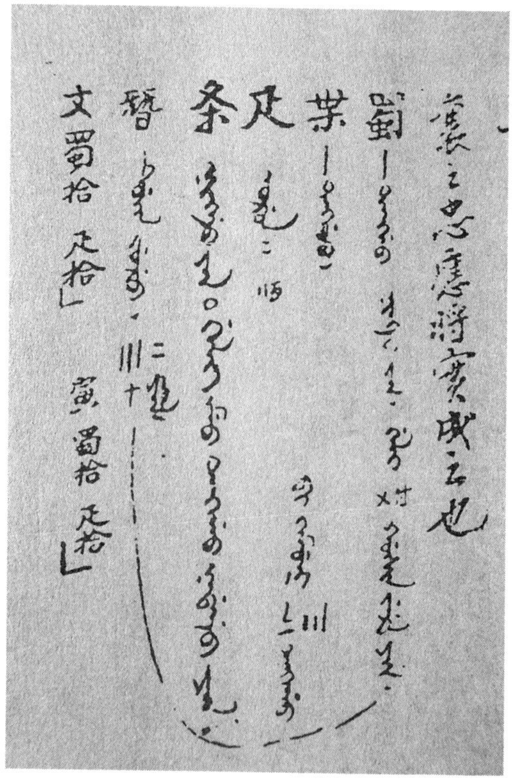

FIG. 1.1. Manchu terms and Suzhou numerals, from *Tang Ying quanji*, 398

The occasional mistakes in Manchu scripts suggest Tang's limited mastery of the language. Tang Ying was not responsible for any textile manufacture, but he may have been involved in counting the textiles collated in one of the six vaults annexed to the Grand Storage Office (Guangchusi) of the Imperial Household Department. Another possibility is that he copied these Manchu accounting entries for training purposes. After all, the textile manufactory was one of the regional bureaus to which bannermen elites from the Imperial Household Department were most frequently appointed. In fact, Tang Ying's grandson worked in the textile manufactory in Hangzhou. In any case, this partial evidence proves Tang Ying's skill at communicating in a language that circumvented Chinese officialdom.

We can find many other bannermen's voluminous Manchu correspondence in the Archive of Accounting (Zouxiao Dang), discussing military operations, funerary constructions, and the celebratory rituals of royal families, as well as detailed fiscal arrangements.[64] In the early Qing dynasty, language skills could earn a bannerman translator an illustrious career. Depending on historical circumstances, bannermen elites would choose which language and what level of proficiency to pursue. Tie Bao (1752–1824), later a key civil service examiner and the compiler of several authoritative imperial anthologies of bannerman poetry in Chinese, decided as a young man to take the civil service examination rather than the military examination, which might have been less challenging—and to take it in Chinese rather than in Manchu.[65] He was concerned about having to rely on translators when working outside Beijing if he chose to focus only on Manchu.[66] This particular bannerman's multilingual proficiency reveals the thinking behind his linguistic choice as well as the available educational resources. This kind of decision regarding language proficiency would eventually shape bannermen's careers because language skill was the basis for building their network and extracting information linked to a region or a social community, such as Chinese literati.

APPROPRIATING LITERATI SKILLS

Being proficient in literary Chinese might give a bannerman access to vast cultural resources—and sometimes a career trajectory. Tang Ying was born in Shenyang in the Manchurian homeland and was not tutored directly in the erudite literati community in the Lower Yangzi Delta, as Cao Yin had been in his early years. Official schools for bannermen, including Prospect Hill (Jingshan) and Xian'an Palace, were established within the framework of the Imperial Household Department as early as 1685, educating young men from only the upper three banners—not all bannermen and no bondservants.[67] As a bondservant, Tang Ying was not qualified to enroll in one of these schools, and he was probably not living in Beijing at the right age, so he had to begin at a local school in Shenyang at the age of seven, studying outside the capital until he was ten years old.[68] We do not have information regarding what kind of curriculum the local school offered. Yet according to his recollection in verse, we know that Tang Ying taught himself classical Chinese. He was fascinated with calligraphy from an early age and practiced on his own in his spare time while on duty as an imperial guard:

> After ten years old, though I achieved little in my studies, I was obsessed with the appreciation and practice of calligraphy. I did not completely understand the meaning but read regardless from dusk to dawn and lost myself in writing. At the age of sixteen, I entered the inner court to serve. . . . I traveled as far as the northern desert beyond the Great Wall. Through it all I stumbled along without one moment's break. However, even while toiling, at dawn and under lights at night, I still held up books to read and soaked my brush to write freely.[69]

Thus, Tang Ying's cultural literacy was neither at the same level nor of the same kind as that of a Chinese literatus or scholar-official who had mastered Confucian classics and their multiple annotations, and learned a vast body of literary anecdotes (*diangu*). To make up for this deficiency, Tang Ying employed two strategies.

First, he diligently practiced literati-scholars' skills, such as poetry composition, calligraphy, seal making, landscape painting, and drama. His journal contains many rhyme words, poetic couplets, literary and historical anecdotes, musical tunes, and lists of inscriptions on placards (*bian*) hanging in eminent historical spots. These fragments were preparatory templates for his practice. The journal demonstrates his inclination for technical archiving—even in literary composition. Tang Ying often humbly solicited critiques of his writing.[70] The Chinese literatus Jiang Shiquan (1725–1785), later regarded as one of the most eminent playwrights of the Qianlong reign, made Tang Ying's acquaintance early on. After the young Jiang succeeded in the provincial exam, he attended a performance by Tang's family troupe in Tang's bureau in Jingdezhen in the 10th month of 1747: "Custom Overseer Tang Woji invited me to drink in the bureau on Zhoushan Hill. I thank him for arranging for his family troupe to perform his own *zaju*, the so-called northern drama."[71] Then Jiang Shiquan failed his metropolitan examination in Beijing when Tang Ying happened to have just completed an official visit to the emperor, so they sailed back south together. During the long trip, which lasted more than sixty days, they exchanged many poems and discussed drama and music. Jiang must have read at least part of Tang Ying's next two plays, *Bedding Made of Reeds* (Luhua xu) and *Repayment of the Champion in Three Exams* (San yuan bao), when they journeyed along the river, as he eventually wrote prefaces for them.[72] Tang Ying's interaction with Jiang Shiquan is only one example of his frequent efforts to seek friendship and literary advice from Chinese literati. However, this polite and even convivial socialization did not mean that Tang Ying wanted to forsake his identity as a bannerman and loyal imperial supervisor.

Tang Ying's second strategy was to distinguish himself from literati by his stylistic and referential choices in painting and literary writing. He never identified himself as a Chinese literatus for he would incur no benefit, probably only peril, from identifying himself with ruled subjects. Many details in his manuscript indicate that he kept an intellectual and personal distance from literati such as Jiang Shiquan. Tang noted his reply to Jiang's poem in his working logs with a quibble about correct rhyming.[73] In one of his occasional poems responding to Jiang's, Tang pointed out the incorrect rhyme of Jiang's original poem.[74] This was either a gesture of emulation or a plea to stick to the dogmatic approach to rhymes. On a personal level, the fissure suggests a more fragile relationship. The bannerman would later censor his own correspondence with the Chinese literatus to avoid a politically sensitive implication.

> In the intercalary 7th month of year Wuchen [1748], I left my imperial audience to return to Jiangxi. After seven days, our boat anchored at the Circuit Jinmen. I bought a bunch of chrysanthemums. . . . This is truly a lonely but peaceful moment in my late years. *My companion, Jiang Shenyu, the Juren degree holder, aspired to eremitism. So we wrote short poems for our records. I spilled out thirty-one poems out of excitement and did not care too much about their refinement. Those who would laugh at or criticize me are all that know my capacity.*—dated the 26th day of the 7th month.[75]

Of the text in italics above, Tang Ying noted, "delete this passage" (*ciduan shan*), because he had become alerted to the political sensitivity of Jiang Shiquan's aspiration to eremitism, which potentially implied political dissidence. In 1748, Tang had become frustrated by the difficulty of selling inferior porcelains, as he had been ordered by the Qianlong emperor to sell the projects rejected by the court. After a stressful meeting with the emperor, Tang was in low spirits and so could sympathize with his traveling companion Jiang, who had just failed his examination. However, upon later reflection, Tang Ying expunged the whole section recording the company of Jiang Shiquan.

Just as Tang Ying was well aware of the differences in status and culture between himself and the literatus, no Chinese would have mistaken him (or his fellow bannermen from the inner court) for a member of the Chinese literati. Tang intentionally avoided certain "highbrow" themes favored by the literati, instead embracing plain language and appropriating repertoires from "lowbrow" regional drama. He said his verses were like "words from a potter's mind" (*taoren xinyu*) rather than poetry:[76]

> The reason I write "words," not poetry, is that I am a petty clerk in the inner court, so I dare not group myself with poets and civil service examinees. I merely express myself with "words" that convey my touched heart.[77]

In this preface, he openly states his preferred genres:

> Boudoir laments, poetry related to courtesans or immortals and the untitled, these are romantic poets' forms of expression. Humble and clumsy as I am, I am not merely unwilling to, but also unable to [compose on those themes]. I have never attempted them in sixty years. This is what I mean by "words from my mind."[78]

His poetry, often precisely dated, reads like an everyday working log. The majority of his poems record his observations and feelings on his business trips between Beijing, the Jiujiang custom house, and the Imperial Porcelain Manufactory in Jingdezhen.

Like many bannermen, he valorized literary austerity, a quality of literary language devoid of embellishment and allusion. Gao Bin, Tang Ying's close friend and belonging to the bannerman elite from the powerful Gao clan, composed his poetry using the same kind of simple language.[79] Tang and Gao prefaced each other's anthologies and praised one another's verses, criticizing extravagant vocabulary and erudite references. Gao comments that "his [Tang's] poems and prose all use honest, considerate, and sympathetic words." Tang puts forward his own principle of poetic composition in the preface, before commenting on Gao's poetry:

> For what were the poems handed down across generations? They were transmitted due to the upright nature [of the poet]. . . . Later poets indulge their own preferences and deliberately imitate others. They take pride in using flowery language and elaborate on the literary allusions in order to embellish and show off their ability to pile up and stick together [allusions]. This means losing the uprightness of their nature. . . . His [Gao Bin's] works do not imitate others, but are in line with the ancient poets, since his natural honor manifests itself.[80]

Both of them valued poetry as an expression of one's righteous and honest nature, and they derided precise wording and ostentatiousness as a derivative imitation of literati poets. The point of view of a Chinese official further testifies to the technocratic style:

> [Gao Bin] does not care about strict rhymes and parallelism in couplets. He contents himself with the pleasure of mildness and ease; he furthers the intent [of *The Book of Songs*] to be warm, mild, and gentle. . . . People say his poetry is well crafted. They do not know that he actually does not intend to craft his poetry.[81]

Technocratic elites actively gathered Chinese literati around them by means of collaborative projects or banquets. Tang Ying was able to compile a whole anthology of poems written in friendly collaboration at Pipa Pavilion, a scenic spot built for such gatherings. The governor of Fujian, Zhou Xuejian, who was apparently Tang Ying's friend, wrote a preface to the anthology that highlighted the technocratic identity and corresponding stylistic choices:

> The inner court is a seminal place from which everything sprouts. The outstanding men there are all appointed to be mandarins and commanders. As the master [here referring to Tang Ying] has been acquainted with the emperor for a long time, he is the right-hand man to rely on. . . . [His words are like] the resonance of ritual bronze bells, so he is not merely the leader on trivia about the wind and moon.[82]

The subtle relations between the bannerman and his literati friends reveal Tang's strategy of knowledge appropriation and distance keeping. Chinese literati's evaluations of Tang Ying's literary work should be regarded as etic perspectives on bannermen technocrats' cultural identification.

Tang Ying overtly explained his literary genre and stylistic preference as having a potter's inclination. For instance, he never wrote a boudoir lament or a poem on the pursuit of immortality. This stance implicitly challenged the traditional Mencian (Confucian) hierarchy between the literati and artisans, whereby "those who use their minds rule and those who use their muscles are ruled."[83] Tang's manifesto in *Words from a Potter's Mind* (Taoren xinyu) unfolds within an imaginary dialogue with an unnamed guest:

> The guest, bewildered, asked: "Making pottery involves toil for the muscles. A potter is one who works with his muscles. One can imagine what his affairs and character must entail. What from his mind is worth conveying in words?"
> I said, "True. Do you know that every individual has his mind and his own mind generates his words? . . . Potters have their own world, seasons, joys and

sorrows upon separation and reunion, their own vision and sentiment. When I am ready for a drink or a meal, dealing with clothing and repose, traveling or making friends, I conduct it with a potter's mind. There is nothing I express in words that did not spring from a potter's mind."[84]

To debunk the common misconception that a laborer's mind and voice are easily imagined and, therefore, not valuable, Tang Ying makes an egalitarian argument emphasizing the distinctness of potters' cosmology, epistemology, and life scenarios. Then he claims to take on the role of a potter, thinking with a potter's mind and expressing himself in a potter's voice, emphasizing the affinity between technocrats and craftsmen of the Qing dynasty.

Another feature of Tang Ying's approach to knowledge was the mixture of miscellaneous records he kept in his working journal, including not only classical studies but also medical prescriptions, records of an eclipse, gardening notes, new acquaintances' name cards, and reports of battles along the northwestern border. He developed this approach during his early career as the emperor's bodyguard, when, constantly on the move, he had only enough time to jot down entries as short aide-mémoires for later consultation. Tang had no formal teachers but plenty of access to firsthand practical knowledge during his engagement on practical projects. Certainly his appointments had already mapped out where he would focus his attention, but he did not attempt to rank the information he acquired according to any aesthetic or moral hierarchy, as a literatus would have done. This nonhierarchical presentation of knowledge is evident in his notes on the practice of merchants.

CROSSING PATHS WITH MERCHANTS

The imperial archive and memorials document bannermen supervisors' assiduous work in fiscal management. Tang Ying's case provides rare evidence of bannermen technocrats' affinity with merchants. Showing no hint of the Chinese literati's expressed contempt for merchants, Tang appropriated merchants' knowledge and acknowledged friendship with traders. He also learned the Suzhou numerals that merchants used for bookkeeping (fig. 1.1). Some of his travel logs document his use of mercantile knowledge. His notes about routes, gathered as an imperial factotum, are similar to the travel route books produced for merchants.[85]

Among Tang Ying's notes about journeys are aide-mémoires and plans. The former summarize trips he had completed, tracking his experiences for future reference. He documents towns, distances, and official tasks, primarily for the purpose of time management. He needed to complete travels in time to return to the kilns in Jingdezhen during the right season, when the temperature and humidity were optimal for kiln firing. Any resulting failure in production would elicit criticism—if not punishment—from the emperor.

A detailed note inscribed on the upper margin of his poems written along the way is worth quoting in its entirety, as it illustrates not only the route but also his official obligations. It documents his journey after a formal visit to the Qianlong emperor in 1748. Tang Ying had three individual meetings with the emperor, traveled together with officials including a major court dramatist, Jiang Shiquan, met with an official, handled a task in the Imperial Textile Manufactory, and accommodated one or more Mongols from the Plain Red Banner, probably for their regional mission.

> On QL 13/6/9. Departed for Beijing via the water route of Jiujiang to meet the emperor.
>
> On the 13th day of the same month, arrived at Pukou and rose early to depart from Pukou on the 15th.
>
> Arrived in Beijing on the 11th day of the 7th month. [The emperor] called me in for the first time on the 22nd of the same month and the second time on the 6th day of the next month [an intercalary month between months 7 and 8]. On the 14th day was the third call and I received his order.
>
> Left Beijing on the 22nd and was boarded together with elder friends like Zhang, Jiang, and Xu at the pier at Zhangjia Wan, heading south.
>
> On the 15th day of the 8th month, passed by Qinzhou prefecture; on the 21st we passed Jining prefecture and arrived at the Qingjiang riverbank. On the 24th day, [corrupted text] on the 26th day were hosted at Official Gao's for three days.
>
> On the 29th day passed by the custom bureau of Huai pass and stayed one night. On the 1st day of the 9th month stayed in Baoying county. On the 3rd day we passed Yangzhou, the 4th day Yizheng prefecture.
>
> On the 6th day visited Official Yin in Nanjing and dealt with something about textiles.

> On the 10th day, passed the Wuhu custom and I received some Mongolians from the Plain Red Banner in Wuchen of Anhui prefecture. On the 17th day of the 9th month I resumed my work at my office.[86]

This sort of terse yet informative report format is not ubiquitous in Chinese officials' travel logs, though they wrote profusely about welcoming and farewell banquets in their poems. In less than 250 words, Tang Ying provides substantial information about a technocrat's typical itinerary and tasks on the road. Archiving this information en route very often preserved his experience for future consultation.

The second kind of note regards plans for trips. These probably copy merchants' handbooks directly. Safe travel was a major concern in Tang Ying's travel notes as well as in merchants' route books. The most informative log in Tang's journal records a journey along the so-called Eighteen Rapids (Shiba Tan) on his way to Guangzhou in 1750.[87] One month after departure, when he passed the fourth rapid in the middle of his trip, Tang included an illustration in his notes titled "The Complete Water Route with Distances and Place Names from Wan'an Prefecture to Ganzhou Prefecture via the Eighteen Rapids."[88] This log is written in exactly the same format as merchants' travel guides, where each section begins with a number giving the distance calculated in miles (*li*), followed by the name of the location. Each section ends with a very short comment, such as "dangerous" or "extremely dangerous."[89] He was not archiving past experience here, because he had not yet passed the remaining fourteen rapids. In this instance, he very likely was copying from existing merchants' travel guides.

Such binary rational logic of review and planning is at the core of the technocrat's approach to archives. Tang Ying's journals are far from a polished record. Each entry is an immediate account of a journey or a template for travel or other action. For example, in a very different field of work, printing, he would write down *ad hoc* directions about the layout of his verses in woodblock publications.[90] Throughout his career, Tang Ying communicated directly with craftsmen and merchants, either to acquire knowledge or to intervene in the process of production. By contrast, the majority of Chinese officials hired private secretaries (*muyou*) to handle practical business and assigned support staff to work with merchants and artisans. Yet bannermen like Tang Ying *were* emperors' private secretaries. The technocratic experience of both artisanal work and merchant transactions was integrated in Tang Ying's management of Western goods in Guangzhou.

EXPOSURE TO WESTERN CULTURE

While European alchemists were struggling to decipher the clay ingredients used in Chinese hard-paste porcelain, Chinese emperors and educated elites were fascinated with European glass and the related technique of painted enamel.[91] Because of the very nature of cultural eclecticism in the Imperial Household Department and Imperial Workshops, technocrats like Tang Ying did not make a stark distinction between Chinese and foreign cultures. Non-Chinese artifacts are listed in his business writing in a dispassionate, matter-of-fact manner. For instance, when Tang Ying prepared a "list of tributes" (*gongdan*) submitted from domestic provinces as well as from Westerners, he did not separate the category of "exotic" Western glassware from the Han dynasty jade and celadon flower beakers on the same list. In the Imperial Workshops near the Hall of Mental Cultivation (Yangxindian) at the southwest corner of the Forbidden City, a bannerman would interact on a daily basis with artisans who had come from disparate regions such as Jiangnan, Tibet, and Europe.[92] In contrast to the Chinese literati's enthusiasm about glass, which was expressed in their literary fantasies, Tang Ying was not particularly impressed by these spectacular glass devices.[93]

Routinized enumeration and description take the place of imagination in his poetry anthologies, archival records, and confidential memorials to emperors. After assuming his position in Guangzhou, Tang Ying still listed the goods sent to the court dispassionately: "Four telescopes [*qianli jing*], to be sent to the clock-making workshop, two timepieces [*tuizhong*], eight hanging mirrors."[94] The memorials were all written in an indifferent yet meticulous tone, giving the impression that Tang was always eager to show his dedication to the job despite having no emotional attachment to any of the exotica. The records are just as fastidious in reporting cracks on a replacement crystal:

> On the 3rd day of the 1st month in the 16th of the Qianlong reign, [for Yue custom house] Zhun Tai once gave as tribute a clock with an accordion decorated on top with a pearl made of glass. The pearl was damaged in transportation. I ordered Liu Daishan to mend it as an indemnity. Up till now this [order] still has not been turned in![95]

On the 2nd day of the intercalary 5th month, Tang Ying answered, "Foreigners have brought the glass pearl that superintendent Zhun sent from the custom house to Guangzhou. . . . Please allow me to submit a slightly cracked glass ball to replace the glass pearl on the top of the accordion clock."[96]

Such pressing practical tasks left Tang Ying very little leisure time to peruse the wonders of Western artifacts. Some scholar-officials and bannermen amassed considerable numbers of antiques and exotica through embezzlement or forced transactions—items that would be confiscated only after the officials' demise; in contrast, Tang Ying was not interested in collecting at all. His entire oeuvre only contains one poem written in response to an antique dealer, and that expresses his lack of interest. Instead of gathering luxuries and using them to display his social status, he was much more excited about actually making things—whether ceramics, poems, calligraphic work, or bonsai.

Another characteristic distinguishing technocrats from traditional literati-officials may be the practitioner mindset revealed in Tang Ying's writing. During his brief but intense service at the Guangzhou custom house in 1751, Tang was extensively exposed to European glassware, but this experience is completely omitted from his drama, poetry, and literary prose; very likely, he deliberately avoided any disclosure of specific or technical information. The Qing emperors discouraged the circulation of information about finance and technology outside the technocratic community of correspondence.

Recent scholarship on Eurasian cultural encounters often overlooks the fact that intercultural exchanges could take the form of indirect mediation. A technocrat like Tang Ying was continuously learning, not from European missionaries themselves but from peer technocrats who had worked with Westerners. Yet his encounters with Western culture were strictly delimited by his official training and responsibilities. He could access Jesuits' designs when involved in particular commissions or could work with people who once were Jesuits' pupils or collaborators. For example, in 1751, the court sought some special rocks from Guangzhou and Macau, sending down thirteen models of rocks prepared by the Jesuit Giuseppe Castiglione (Lang Shining; 1688–1766) and a letter written in a Western language, and ordering Tang Ying to find boulders similar to those models and send them back.[97] Tang must have had a translator, and he definitely needed local interpreters to provide assistance when he collected tariffs and purchased "big clocks and watches" in Guangzhou from consignments from England, France, Holland, Germany, and Switzerland.[98] A table in his work logs registers the names of European cargos that Tang Ying very likely inspected and traded with in Guangzhou (fig. 1.2). He put a little square as a phonetic radical by each character to mark the transliteration of these foreign names.[99]

The court institution enabled and demarcated technocrats' exposure to Western culture. Technical knowledge was mediated and archived for prac-

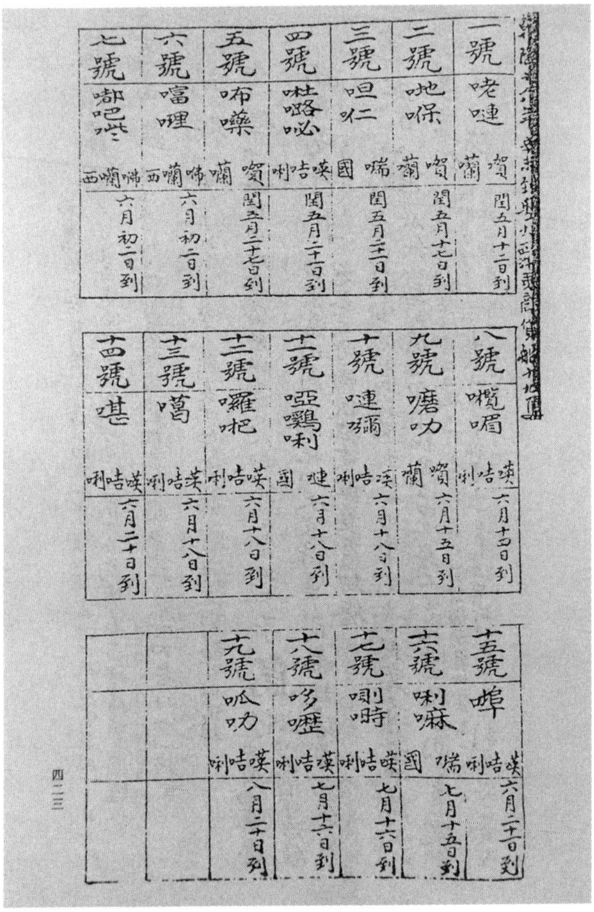

一號	咾嗹	〔口賀〕囒	閏五月十二日到
二號	吔㖙	〔口賀〕囒	閏五月十七日到
三號	呾〔口仁〕	喘國	閏五月二十日到
四號	〔口壯〕〔口路〕咇	〔口英〕咭咧	閏五月二十日到
五號	〔口布〕〔口樂〕	〔口賀〕囒	閏五月二十七日到
六號	〔口富〕哩	咈囒西	六月初二日到
七號	〔口都〕吧〔口些〕	咈囒西	六月初二日到
八號	〔口覽〕〔口眉〕	〔口英〕咭咧	六月十四日到
九號	〔口磨〕叻	〔口賀〕囒	六月十五日到
十號	嗹〔口彌〕	〔口英〕咭咧	六月十八日到
十一號	啞〔口鷄〕唎	喘國	六月十八日到
十二號	囉吧	〔口英〕咭咧	六月十八日到
十三號	〔口萬〕	〔口英〕咭咧	六月十八日到
十四號	〔口甚〕	〔口英〕咭咧	六月二十日到
十五號	啅	〔口英〕咭咧	六月二十一日到
十六號	唎〔口麻〕	喘國	七月十五日到
十七號	咧〔口時〕	〔口英〕咭咧	七月十六日到
十八號	哆嚦	〔口英〕咭咧	七月十六日到
十九號	呱叻	〔口英〕咭咧	八月二十日到

四二三

FIG. 1.2. List of Western cargos, from *Tang Ying quanji*, 423

tical purposes. Meticulous documentation in confidential memorials and the conspicuous absence of such experience in the Tang's literary writings attests to this controlled connection with Western culture.

TANG YING WAS ONE NEXUS in a constellation of bannermen who served in the Imperial Household Department. Biographical records reveal that his extended family was bonded to this department. The career trajectories of many parallel and interconnected bannermen clans unfolded along a similar pattern. They differed from Chinese scholar-officials in their recruitment system and their extensive engagement with projects related to military campaigns, the emperors' private revenue, empire-building construction projects, and manufacturing. Equipped with martial skills during the early years of their service, the technocrats continued to guard the ruling house's security by collecting intelligence all over the Qing empire.

Tang Ying maintained a martial identity, cultivated friendships with artisans and merchants, and was exposed to Western knowledge. As a typical agent of the system, he facilitated the development of technology within the framework of imperial decorum—meaning, according to what the emperor sanctioned as appropriate. His work was circumscribed by a politicized industrial art: the separation between design and execution, regular and documented communication among various participants in the manufacture of goods, and division of labor. This technocratic approach to cultural production cannot be sufficiently explained by the literati's self-cultivation or Confucian doctrine; the overarching Qing technocratic approach to technology, art, and literature is, in fact, not explained in current scholarship at all. The next chapter examines this cultural and technical integration within the framework of imperial regulation.

TWO

A New Knowledge Culture in the Imperial Workshops

THE QING PORCELAIN INDUSTRY, the center of which was concentrated in one town—Jingdezhen—produced high-quality porcelains for domestic consumption and global distribution; in turn, this fueled the consumer revolution that spread across Western Europe during the seventeenth and eighteenth centuries.[1] Examining the rise of bannermen technocrats against this global background reveals their impact across regions and their contributions to the long and uneven process of industrialization in the Eurasian world. In the Qing Imperial Workshops, separation between design and production was key to facilitating both the high quality and the endless variety of imperial manufacturing, through which the court achieved a cultural synthesis on the material level. Tang Ying internalized the cultural pluralist ideal and tactic, as evidenced by the technical assemblage in his theater, his painting, and most importantly, his porcelain design.

The ceramic industry in Jingdezhen consisted of a massive private sector deeply enmeshed in the global trade and a state-owned sector that was seemingly unresponsive to global demand. But this separation was more apparent than real. The Imperial Porcelain Manufactory by and large relied on and exercised control over private commercial kilns. By the time Tang Ying arrived in the bustling center of porcelain manufacture in 1728, the central government had been regulating the industry by operating the Imperial Porcelain Manufactory for more than three hundred years. The Imperial Household Department was also involved in other regional industries, such as salt production and pearl and fur trading, yet bannermen's technical expertise is not as easily visible in products from these industries as it is in porcelain.[2] The knowledge cultures revealed in both imperial porcelain commissions and Tang Ying's private projects further distinguish the technocrats from Chinese literati.

Rich geological deposits of porcelain ingredients and kaolin around Jingdezhen made possible the massive porcelain production here. Yet the state did not take close control over manufacture from the beginning. Governmental supervisors' technological engagement in porcelain manufacture also changed over time. They gradually transformed from tax collectors equipped with theoretical knowledge into hands-on ceramic specialists. At its beginning, Jingdezhen was named after a Song dynasty reign, Jingde (1004–7), during which the court sent a supervisor to collect taxes in kind. There is no evidence to suggest that the Song supervisors were systematically involved in design or technological oversight. In the Yuan dynasty's Porcelain Bureau (Ciju), supervisors from the Islamic world probably assumed a more hands-on role.[3] During the Ming dynasty, official supervisors—including many eunuchs—were known to be involved in communicating designs to the Imperial Vessel Manufactory (Yuqichang), and they had been producing porcelain for the court since 1369.[4] However, the scarce remaining evidence about eunuchs does not clearly show eunuch supervisors' technological expertise. Well-documented technocratic intervention in production reached its peak only during the mid-Qing period (1680s–1795).[5]

The technology of the porcelain industry in Jingdezhen underwent major advances during four periods: the late Yuan, two early reigns of the Ming dynasty (Yongle, 1403–24, and Xuande, 1425–35),[6] the Chenghua reign in the mid-Ming (1465–87), and the mid-Qing era. In the last three periods, the imperial manufactory spurred on technological and artistic development. Complex imperial commissions demanded elaborate experiments using raw materials of superior quality. During the mid-Qing period in particular, private kilns in Jingdezhen benefited from novel technology and designs transmitted from the imperial manufactory, because the transformation of the labor system from registered households to paid employment allowed craftsmen to work for both imperial and private kilns.[7] This also meant that artisans with extraordinary skills could be brought into imperial workshops inside the Forbidden City. The supervisor-designers then had the opportunity to collaborate with such master artisans, including some Europeans, as well as many craftsmen from workshops focusing on products other than porcelain.[8]

During the peak of aesthetic and technical innovation in the eighteenth century, mid-level technocrats, including Tang Ying, acquired embodied knowledge related to porcelain in the specific (*yang*) design administrative system and, in turn, controlled local industry on behalf of the court. Other mid-level technocrats in the porcelain industry included Liu Yuan (c. 1641–before 1691), Nian Xiyao (late 1600s–1738), and Haiwang (before 1723–1755), all of whom had firsthand experience both in handling materials and in management.[9] To produce wares in sanctioned artistic styles that promulgated imperial ideology, emperors had to collaborate with these experts in the design system. After all, the rulers, who lacked specialized knowledge, could not single-handedly decide on the shape, glaze, and decoration of porcelain products. And even emperors had to correctly position their stylistic preferences within the matrix of archived artistic forms to generate suitable political and moral messages.[10]

The Design System: A Planned Economy of Art

In the multiethnic regime headed by the Manchus, the *yang* system facilitated the production of a wide variety of items, ranging from an entire palace and powerful cannons to delicate snuff bottles. *Yang* denotes the models circulated among workshops during the production process. As well as sketches and drawings, this term can also refer to finished products that the craftsmen used as models. Or, it could mean a model made on a reduced scale, made with less precious materials. Such designs were usually modified after inspection by emperors or supervising princes. The design system was far more complex and strictly enforced than sumptuary regulation. Arguably, *yang* were first and most frequently deployed in imperial architectural projects, much earlier than the Qing dynasty.[11] Yet the extant evidence can be traced primarily to solitary designers who were obscure officials or to the single most important official architect, Li Jie (c. 1035–1110), who wrote the *Building Standard* (Yingzao fashi; 1103), a treatise on architecture that includes many structural blueprints as well as nonstructural design drafts.[12] There is scant evidence of the design and production process itself. In contrast, the *yang* system in the Qing imperial workshops is well documented not only by the survival of many of the actual models but also by the considerable number of supervisor-designers who made, transmitted, and used the models to produce items of all sizes. A Lei family recruited to Beijing provided the chief architects at the Qing court for generations. The archive of *yang* they left behind covers a wide range of items.[13] The Qing *yang* system proved to be a quasi-industrial institution that aimed to transcribe and archive embodied knowledge in order to integrate technological experiments, political control, and fiscal planning.

The use of *yang* in ceramic production evolved from the governmental attempt to control ceramics' quality and impose standardization.[14] This standardization dates back to the fifth century BCE, if not earlier.[15] The last chapter of *The*

Artificers' Record (Kaogong ji), titled "Works in Pottery," lists the standard measurement of seven kinds of pottery vessels. The text ends by expressing concerns about quality control.[16] During the Tang dynasty, *yang* was officially used as the standard way to evaluate products collected as tax in kind.[17] The crucial transformation of *yang* from a sample for tax evaluation to a regulatory design for production likely took place from the tenth to the twelfth centuries.[18] The famous quote "During the Xuanhe reign, the court made samples for commission" refers to the production of a kind of celadon (*mise ci*) as a local tribute to the court during the late Northern Song dynasty.[19] In 1278, during the Yuan dynasty, the government had already established a bureau to make models and blueprints for producing all kinds of goods.[20] In the early Ming dynasty, there were also specific bureaus in charge of design. Academy painters designed ceramics in the Xuande (1425–35) and Chenghua (1465–87) reigns, according to late Ming literatus Wang Shixing (1547–1598).[21] When the system of design in general reemerged in the 1680s after the turmoil of dynastic transition, the institutional infrastructure evolved, but some court painters continued to provide similar designs for architecture, ritual wares, clothing, and everyday utensils for the court.[22] The design of porcelain was no exception, in that some very famous court painters, such as Giuseppe Castiglione, were involved.[23]

Yang and Court Style

Unlike painter-designers, technocratic supervisor-designers not only drew design patterns but also oversaw other technological procedures and exerted financial control in response to emperors' assessments. In the early to mid-Qing period, supervisor-designers, based on their technical expertise, negotiated with emperors about feasible production while Qing emperors' judgment on artistic style permeated the official correspondence and thereby defined imperial decorum.[24] Although the judgment of decorum cannot be divorced from emperors' personal tastes, it refers here to public enforcement of the politically appropriate and auspicious character of art. The Yongzheng emperor explicitly formulated the appropriate *yang* as the "style made respectfully in the inner court" (*neiting gongzao shiyang*).[25] Two frequently used imperial evaluations functioned almost as a form of central regulation. The first was "vulgar" (*suqi*). This critique concerned an awkward choice of color, imperfectly wrought shape, or inappropriate thematic reference, and it meant failure to conform to imperial decorum. The second term was "exquisite" (*jingxi*), often seen in an imperative phrase: "Make it as exquisite as possible!" Precisely incised outlines, perfect symmetry, and proper color choice were seen as embodying technological prowess and meticulous managerial control.

The pursuit of meticulous control in porcelain manufacture was in line with the emphasis on fastidious depiction in other documentary and quasi-ethnographic enterprises of the Qing court. The ruling house seemed to assume that truth value was somehow inherent in elaborate description, either textual or pictorial. It had been a lasting practice, in the first half of the Qing dynasty, for emperors to demand that bannermen supervisors report strategic information collected from the regional societies "in detail" (*xiangxi*).[26] Court painters were also ordered to carefully lift and remix images of animals from European prints, as well as ancient catalogs of mystical creatures.[27] The expansive repertoire of high-quality design models in the Qing dynasty extended its fascination with verisimilar depiction, especially in the illustration of collectibles at court. Both the Yongzheng emperor and the Qianlong emperor commissioned paintings recording their lavish collections of luxuries.[28] Projects that involved Western painters and their Chinese pupils revealed the prevailing interest in empirical observation and pictorial documentation.[29] Such illustrations were probably used as portable catalogs when emperors traveled.[30] The utility of this pictorial documentation overlapped with that of design drafts, themselves a kind of pictorial documentary, whose mobility enabled supervisors to overcome geographical distance, differences in media, and even time to some extent.

Numbered Design

The application of *yang* in actual manufacture at the Qing court was anything but straightforward and was systematically managed by inventory numbers. To successfully produce designed porcelain wares, supervisors and craftsmen went through innumerable rounds of trial and error. The pots might deform or collapse during the firing process, or the pigment might dissipate due to overfiring. Thus, the production of porcelain as an industrial art involved the collaboration of a large community and an elaborate array of tools, including models in a variety of media. Experiments were conducted on raw materials under the imperial control of the *yang* system, not in a commercial context.

Recent archaeological excavations in Jingdezhen have recovered many shards from firing tests during the Ming dynasty.[31] The misfired glaze and blurry decoration on some of these fragments testify to extensive experiments. There is even a broken dish excavated from a stratum dated to the Xuande reign. It is decorated with floral patterns and inscriptions in different shades of cobalt (plate 1). The inscriptions label the colored flowers as "*le* number one; *le* number two; *le* number three," presumably denoting three new kinds of cobalt blue, imported from Leping county and used in the firing test. Yet none of these test pieces shows an archiving effort as systematic as that illustrated by the following examples from the Qing dynasty.

These test pieces, which functioned both as design models and technical trials, register the stylistic regulation as well as the development of technical knowledge situated in the collective memory of a whole community of craftsmen and supervisor-designers. Collective memory stores the knowledge of technical procedures and artistic forms in a historical network of tools, work sites, and even organizational structures, rather than in any individual artisan's mind.

Numbers inscribed on these semifinished pieces, which are dated to Tang Ying's period of supervision, suggest the systematic organization of design models in production. This is consistent with the general archival approach internalized by technocrats working for the court. Official memorials and reports preserving information from specific commissions were dated and deposited in specific departments, and model products were also ordered to move between the porcelain storehouse at court and the imperial manufactory in Jingdezhen.[32] The combination of decimal numbers and characters from *The Thousand Character Classic* (Qianzi wen) on the following examples very likely indicates their posi-

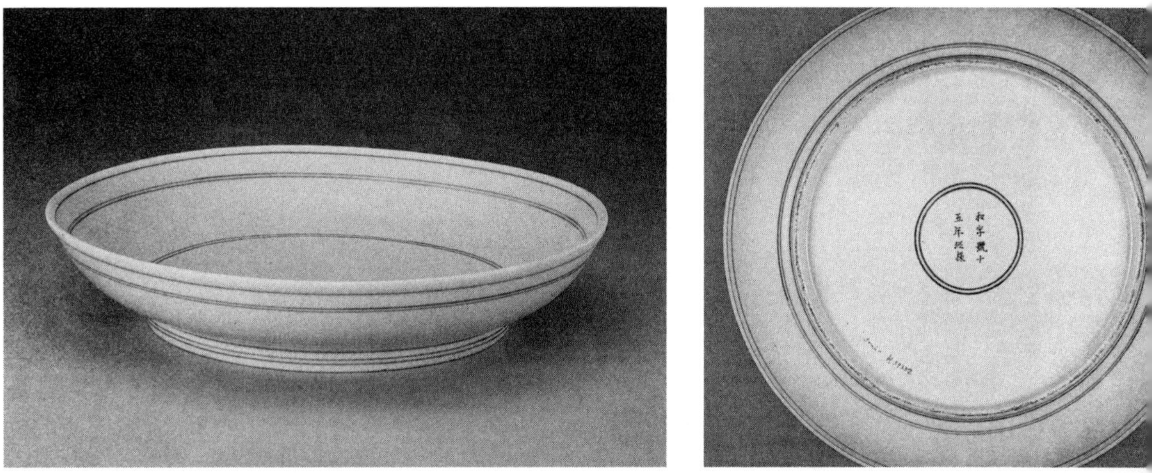

FIG. 2.1. Porcelain dish (*left*), decorated with four rings painted with cobalt blue, dated to 1750, and bottom mark (*right*), 34.4 cm in diameter, in Palace Museum, Beijing

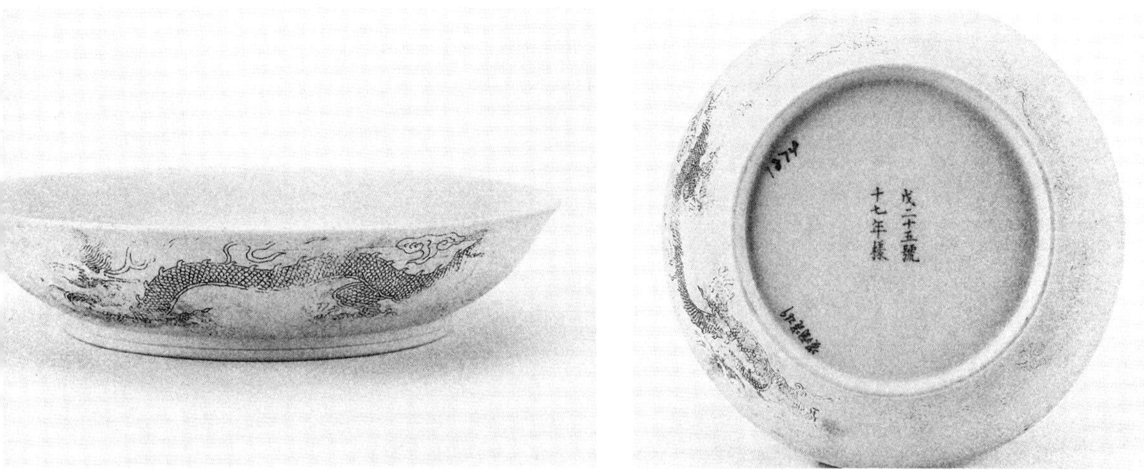

FIG. 2.2. Porcelain bowl (*left*), decorated with a dragon in mist, dated to 1752, and bottom mark (*right*), 18.5 cm in diameter, in Palace Museum, Beijing

tions in series of experiments or spatial positions in storage.[33] As the book consists of one thousand unrepeated characters, they had been used as an alternative to numbers. Premodern Chinese carpenters used characters from *The Thousand Character Classic* to mark matching woodwork tenons and mortises. On the following ceramic examples, numbers and dates functioned like coordinates to pinpoint the preparatory design models in specific projects.

The following three semifinished pieces all show obvious preparatory traits. The piece dated to 1750 is numbered 10 under the He group (Hezihao shi; fig. 2.1).[34] It is decorated only with four cobalt-blue rings. A design like this seems merely to provide a framework for further painting. The inscription indicates that it is a preliminary base (*pi*).

The piece dated to 1752 (*shiqinian yang*, the 17th year of the Qianlong reign), numbered 25 under the Wu group, is decorated with a dragon in mist, which provides a perfect comparison to other pieces bearing dragon motifs attributed to Tang Ying (fig. 2.2). This model seems to have been neither glazed nor fired at a high temperature. Moreover, its inscription groups it under the character *wu*, which is from a system of numbering that uses the celestial branches (*tiangan*) instead of *The Thousand Character Classic*, so it might belong to a different order of classification.

The third example, a dish with a cobalt-blue phoenix, held in the Shanghai Museum, is dated to 1741 (fig. 2.3). The inscription, "*Gu* group, pattern made in the 6th year," implies that it may already be a sample of combined designs, which means that the shape, glaze, and decorative motifs from different pieces were brought together in one new piece. The clay body was grouped under the character *gu*, while the phoenix and floral pattern was designed in 1741 (the 6th year of the Qianlong reign). This could be rare evidence of commissions combining the shape of one vessel and the decorative motifs of another.

These numbered and dated preparatory samples reveal a systematic effort to document numerous trials, which were necessary because of the high ratio of failure incurred from either technical difficulty or imperial dissatisfaction. In contrast to the test pieces signed by Tang Ying, these anonymous numbered models, though almost certainly overseen by the supervisor, point to the impersonal regulatory function of the imperial design system. Design models expressed supervisor-designers' technological and artistic skill, but the ultimate authority belonged to the monarchs, who could efface all subordinates' authorship. In short, the technocrats' archivist training was indispensable for operating the *yang* system, which deployed both paper trails and experimental models to control the material empire made in the Imperial Workshops.

The archive not only recorded the communication mechanism between the court and regional factories; it was also the information hub of ongoing projects. The archived information and products were consulted and reused in subsequent projects. By 1722 the Yongzheng emperor had established the Imperial Workshops archive to document entire production processes, and its scale multiplied many times during the Qianlong reign. The archive kept track of the dispatched design models according to the court's instructions. For instance, in early spring 1738, the archive record itemizes a large group of model pieces to be sent to Jingdezhen. Next to some entries, the sender wrote brief directions about the modifications required, like "drop the handles" or "heighten the four feet." At the end of the document, there is a note: "After you finish production, return the original porcelain pieces to the Porcelain Storehouse. Paint drafts of large vessels and take them with you. And you can take the small vessels [as models] directly," which unmistakably dictates the location and circulation of the design models.[35] In this case, the small vessels could leave Beijing to serve as models in Jingdezhen, but large pieces could not leave the palace and were depicted in design drafts. Most importantly, original pieces should all return to the Porcelain Storehouse. Transportation could be arranged differently during other commissions, but the point of the archive was to have routes clearly recorded.

This brief review of the design system across time periods indicates that neither the design drafts nor their governmental institutionalization was unique

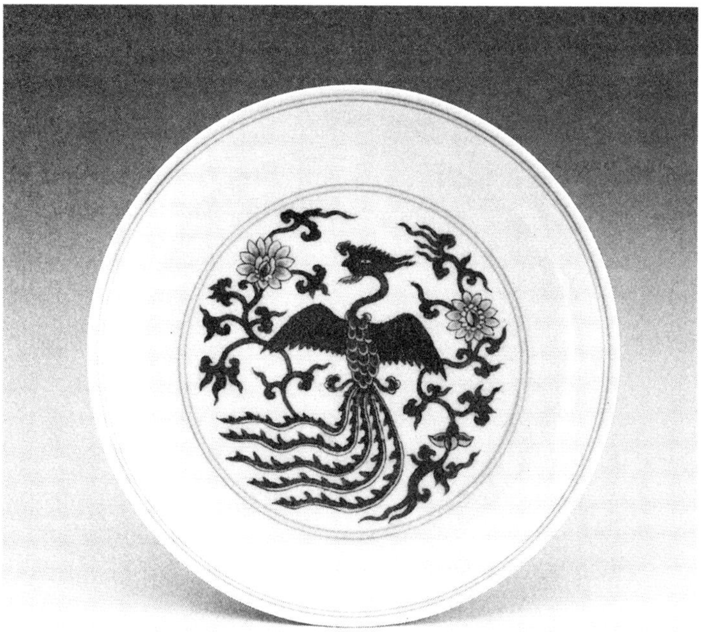

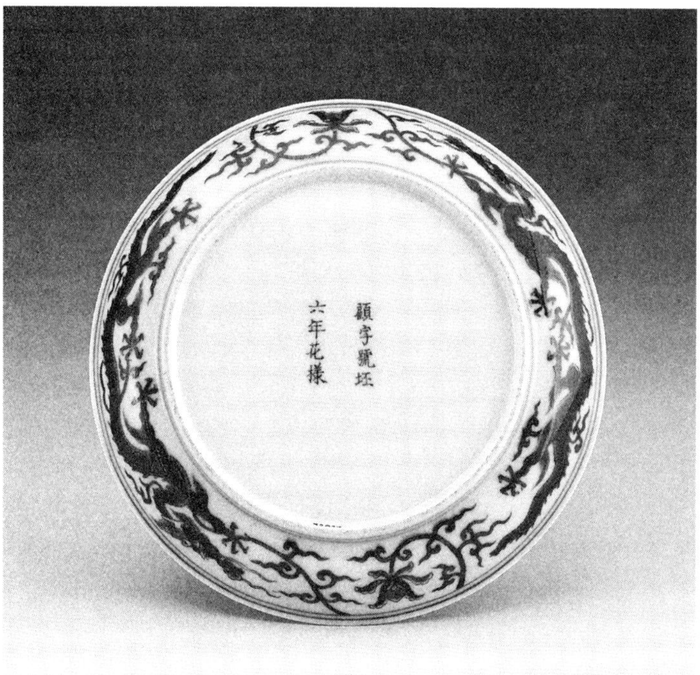

FIG. 2.3. Porcelain dish (*top*), decorated with a phoenix among floral motifs painted with cobalt blue, dated to 1741, and bottom mark (*bottom*), 15.5 cm in diameter, in Shanghai Museum

to the Qing court, but the systematic training and employment of a network of technocrats had never been recorded in previous dynasties. The series of bannermen porcelain supervisors also differed from both Chinese designers and craftsmen in that technocrats communicated visual qualities effectively using symbols, including letters and numbers, for the purpose of serving the emperors. The synergy of hands-on experience and an analytical approach enabled some of them to think critically and to create new decorative forms. The technocratic style even characterizes some private artwork beyond imperial commissions.

Bannermen's Design

The Qing dynasty supervisor-designers had two main functions in the design system. First, they were managers who transmitted orders, materials, and funding for production, and inspected products to control quality. Second, they made use of artistic forms from the established cultural repertoire to design products for the court. They had to perform simultaneously as inventive artists and pragmatic accountants. The overlapping roles resulted in an internalized courtly approach to artistic forms, which spilled over into their private art making, providing a particularly helpful trace of their internalized decorum. Visual evidence from two stylistic repertoires—ritual archaism and literati orthodoxy—shows how the institution induced supervisor-designers both to comply with decorum and to reveal what space was left for their own agency in the controlling system.

MODELS FOR RITUAL VESSELS

Following the ritual practice of previous dynasties, the Qing court commissioned many vessels made of porcelain instead of bronze, to rhetorically embrace an austere ideal. The *Illustrated Regulations for Ceremonial Paraphernalia of the Qing dynasty* (Huangchao liqi tushi) often prescribed porcelain, wood, and bamboo—that is, less valuable materials—to substitute for metal in making ritual vessels.[36] This regulation of material as well as form in ritual vessels was similar to the performance of frugal rituals since the Southern Song dynasty. In actuality, Song scholar-officials avidly participated in collecting and cataloging bronze ritual vessels.[37] Elaborate reports in *Ritual Affairs for Grand Revival* (Zhongxing lishu; 1184) indicate that extant bronze vessels in these high-ranking officials' collections, or vessels depicted in catalogs such as *Illustration of Three Classics of Ritual* (Sanli tu; 1109–25) and *Catalog of the Antiques of Xuanhe's*

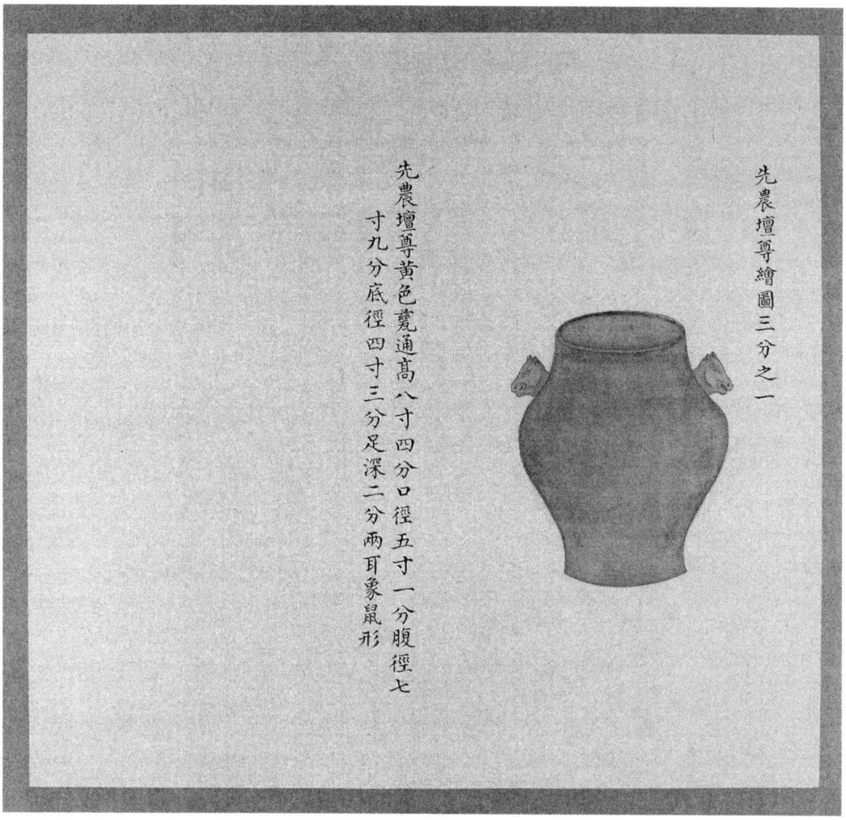

FIG. 2.4. Album leaf showing a *zun* vase in the main position on the altar of Earth and Grain (Ditan/Shejitan), in the *Album of Sacrificial Vessels* (Beiwu zhaocheng), ink and color on silk, dated to the Qing dynasty, 37.2 × 34.8 cm, in Palace Museum, Beijing

Reign (Xuanhe bogu tu) were employed as graphic designs in the reproduction of ritual vessels.[38]

Some colored versions of the *Illustrated Regulations* or their copies made at the Qing court were possibly used as design blueprints.[39] One example of such a copy is the *Album of Sacrificial Vessels* (Beiwu zhaocheng; fig. 2.4), originally kept in the Palace for Fasting (Zhai Gong). The small format of this album would have facilitated its circulation among workshops.[40]

This album, or one very much like it, served as the model for a well-documented set of blueprints from 1748. On the 26th day of the 3rd month, Fuheng (1720–1770), then director of the Board of Rites, and Wang Youdun (1692–1758), then director of the Board of Punishments, brought in a twelve-leaf album of sacrificial vessels. Based on this, two court painters were ordered to draw preliminary drafts and then make bundled paperboard models of wares to be produced in the Imperial Workshops. On the 2nd day of the 5th month in the same year, paper blueprints as well as wooden models of vessels for various altars were ready. Depending on which materials would be used to make the vessels, these *yang* were distributed to various workshops. Drafts for metal vessels went to Prince Zhuang, models of bamboo and lacquer vessels departed for the supervisor of the Textile Manufacture in Suzhou, while models of vessels to be made with gourds went to the head of the Guangzhou custom house (Yue haiguan). Not surprisingly, Supervisor Tang Ying received models of vessels to be made with porcelain in Jiangxi province—that is, at the Imperial Porcelain Manufactory.[41]

In this case, although workshops across the empire made vessels out of various materials, all the *yang* designs came from the Hall of Self-Fulfillment (Ruyiguan). This office had already been established during the Kangxi reign to imitate painting academies of previous dynasties, yet the office quickly extended its function to producing decorative art:[42]

> The Shengzu emperor had heavenly gifted intelligence and was capable of various arts. . . . He further set up the Hall of Self-Fulfillment. The system imitates the Academies of Painting of previous dynasties, and it extends [its service] to handicrafts.[43]

The work of painting, writing, jade carving, and mounting are all here. At first it hired the artisans. Later the literati were gradually employed.[44]

The Hall of Self-Fulfillment provided a marketplace for regional artisans, literati artists, and Western experts to learn from each other.[45] Master artisans hired from the South and Jesuit experts from the West were not lofty recluses but rather workmen. From them, bannermen apprentices like Tang Ying learned embodied skills with decorative arts and some Western knowledge. However, everyone came to the system of design to learn about decorum, the appropriate way of making goods for the emperor.

Being skilled at painting—or, more precisely, being skilled at pictorially recording forms either from nature or from artifacts—could allow a worker to serve in more than one workshop because pictorial depiction was a resourceful way to communicate practical information among technocrats. Bannermen who were equipped with design skills could rise above working with specific material media and reach the managerial level. In addition to high-ranking ministers like Mang-gu-li (1672–1736), who was an accomplished painter, Tang Ying's contemporaneous bannerman peer Shen Yu (1649–?) painted practical works such as *The Picture of Transporting Grain to the Capital on the Tonghui Canal* (Tonghui he caoyun tu), and Haiwang painted topographical landscape pictures for land surveys.[46] Like Tang Ying, they were promoted to managerial positions.

Tang Ying was drawing design drafts in the Workshop of Falang Enamel (Falangchu) at the beginning of the Yongzheng reign.[47] Before long, he was promoted to vice director in the Imperial Workshops, making designs and handling commissions. Shortly after that, in the fall of 1728, he was appointed to the Imperial Porcelain Manufactory in Jingdezhen. The Yongzheng emperor had been satisfied with Tang Ying's work, but the succeeding Qianlong emperor apparently did not appreciate Tang's unique expertise in porcelain production. In 1736 Tang was dispatched to take charge of the custom house in Huai'an (Huai'an guan) for at least three years, until it became clear that Mo'ersen (dates unknown), a substitute bannerman supervisor in Jingdezhen, simply could not produce porcelain wares of the same quality.

While he was stationed in Huai'an, Tang Ying remained involved in the large-scale production of ritual wares.[48] The production was not very successful, in that many blue vessels were not properly glazed and were therefore unusable, but some yellow and white pieces were suitable for ritual use. Supervisor Nian Xiyao wrote to the emperor, "After we sent the design [*shiyang*] to the vice director of the bureau, Tang Ying, for production, the porcelains were completed and submitted. Your servant [probably Nian Xiyao] and the appointed staff selected as usable a porcelain *zun* [goblet], *jue* [beaker], bowls and plates in yellow and white colors."[49] Tang Ying was fined for the substandard pieces. We will see his recurrent fiscal liability for products deemed to be of unacceptable quality.[50] One extant piece is very likely the qualified kind of *zun* made of yellow porcelain (*huangci zun*; plate 2).[51] This piece roughly matches a piece depicted in *Album of Sacrificial Vessels* as well as a model from the Ming dynasty.

Standardization mattered for both quality and quantity. The imperial reign mark on thousands of porcelain pieces nearly effaced the designers' and local artisans' authorship. Although the Qing emperors commissioned fewer wares than the Ming emperors did, the annual output of the Imperial Porcelain Manufactory during the Yongzheng reign (1722–35) was required to be at least 25,000 pieces and no more than 50,000 pieces. The annual yield during the Qianlong reign (1735–95) ranged from 16,969 to 47,120 pieces.[52] The craft seen in these designs is evident in exemplar pieces inscribed with supervisor-designers' individual signatures, such as ritual wares made outside the realm of direct imperial commissions. Tang Ying very likely made such signed pieces with superior raw materials reserved for the court, so the pieces analyzed in the next section showcase the complex coauthorship of a supervisor-designer and the court in terms of appropriate design, or decorum.

IMPERIAL PRESENCE ON PRIVATE VESSELS

Just as court painters also sometimes worked for private patrons, Tang Ying and other porcelain supervisor-designers occasionally made porcelain for their own purposes. Tang Ying made at least eight blue-and-white altar vases that blurred the boundary between the private and imperial realms. They are inscribed with the titles of all the official posts that Tang Ying held up to 1740, though they were made for religious offerings within the household. The overlapping public and private character of these pieces suggests the indoctrination of imperial decorum. These vases come from several sets of five-offering wares (*wugong*).[53] One pair of tall candlesticks belonging to the Victoria and Albert Museum (fig. 2.5) may originally have formed a set, together with four similarly inscribed altarpieces, dated to the beginning of 1741.[54]

Inscriptions on the lowest lobes of this pair are dedicated to the deity Immortal Mother (Shengmu), worshipped in the shrine at Dongba—the suburb of Beijing where the graveyard of Tang's lineage was located.[55] One similar pair of beaker-vases dated to 1740 is housed in the Shanghai Museum.

These rather private porcelain offerings showcase a bannerman supervisor's religious practice in response to bureaucratic and familial stress. Tang Ying's life events suggest his motive behind making these offering altarpieces. Tang Ying turned sixty in 1741. He had been expecting the birth of his third son,

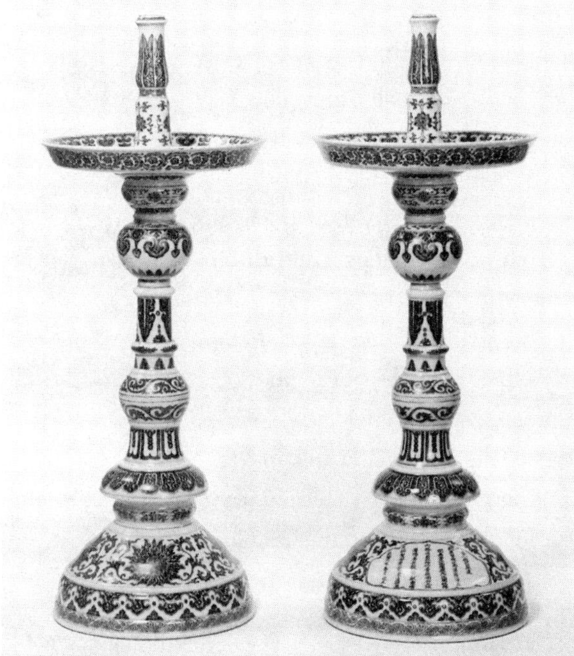

FIG. 2.5. Pair of porcelain candlesticks painted in blue with an inscription of Tang Ying's full official title in a cartouche on the foot, height: 67 cm, diameter: 23 cm, in Victoria and Albert Museum

Wanbao, which occurred on the 18th day of the 8th month. His second son was preparing for the civil examination and eventually succeeded on the 10th day of the 11th month.[56] And around that time, Tang received a harsh reprimand from the Qianlong emperor concerning the unsatisfactory quality of his porcelain products and unclear accounting:

> The so-called first-rate porcelains that Tang Ying produced are too shoddy. The glaze is not good. There are also broken pieces. . . . This problem concerns not only last year. The pieces produced in the past few years are much worse than those produced during the Yongzheng reign. Moreover, you have never submitted an accounting report. Investigate and submit for my reference reports about the cost and quantity of products during the eleventh and the twelfth years of the Yongzheng reign, and during the first to the fifth years of the Qianlong reign.[57]

Tang Ying was under considerable pressure during the first five years of the Qianlong reign. As mentioned previously, in 1739 he was again appointed to collect custom taxes at Jiujiang custom house, so he was able to oversee porcelain production only from a distance. The Qianlong emperor declined Tang Ying's repeated requests to be relieved from tax collection. The altarpieces were possibly made in response to anxiety compounded by an eventful family life and his demanding official obligations. The elaborate official titles written in cobalt blue on these pieces signal the formal presence of the government.

Tang Ying's altarpieces show how technocratic craft carried over to the private sector. Beyond these ritual wares, products with dual signatures embody the copresence of the supervisor-designer's craft and imperial decorum. Tang Ying's predecessor in the Imperial Porcelain Manufactory, Lang Tingji (1663–1715), also made porcelain pieces bearing both the imperial reign mark, "Made in the Kangxi Reign of the Great Qing" (Da Qing Kangxi Nian Zhi), and his individual studio title, "Hall of Purity, Imperially Bestowed" (Yuci Chunyitang Zhencang).[58] Scholars have discovered what they consider inferior pieces inscribed with only the studio title.[59] The sporadic memorials concerning handicrafts during the Kangxi reign have made it hard to specify the level of court interference in design. How exactly did supervisor-designers like Tang Ying affect the production of signed pieces after all? Did they outline the shapes and draw the decorative patterns? Did they paint and write by themselves or did professional artisans copy their painting and calligraphy onto the porcelain? Some questions can never be fully answered, but artifactual evidence indicates that these technocrats supervised production in a hands-on, cross-media way.

FROM LITERATI DESIGN TO TECHNOCRATIC DESIGN

The training and career paths of generations of bannermen supervisor-designers reveal the progression of the court's appropriation of regional cultural resources. Quite a few famous bannermen supervisors in the Kangxi reign learned painting and literary composition from eminent Chinese artists and literati from Jiangnan, the regional hub of artistic talent. In this early stage of cultural integration, the court directly hired regional painters who were once immersed in the culture of Jiangnan to work on imperial projects that involved visual representation, ranging from meticulous court portraits to diagrammatic maps or abstract design blueprints of monumental palaces and small stationery items.[60] Painting skill—or, more precisely, the capacity for pictorial extraction of information—was a distinct part of technocratic craft. Supervisor-designers were expected to be able to lift an image from one medium and rework it in another to fit the imperial order and budget.

Liu Yuan (c. 1641–1691), the first substantially recorded bannerman designer of porcelain during the Qing period, shared a career trajectory and a hands-on approach with his successors, including Lang Tingji, Nian Xiyao, and Tang Ying.[61] Liu Yuan had served as tax collector at the Wuhu custom house in Jiangnan and made designs for imperial ink stones and porcelains.[62] He nurtured his artistic skills during his early years in Suzhou by learning from eminent literati artists such as Wu Weiye (1609–1671) and Li Yu (1610–1680). He worked with four media: most famously, ink cake and ink stones, but also painting, woodblock printing, and eventually porcelain. For a woodblock album called *Chancellors in Lingyange* (Lingyange gongchen), Liu Yuan designed all the decorative frames for the illustrations and the last six leaves.[63] He also provided hundreds of designs for the Imperial Porcelain Manufactory in Jingdezhen.[64] Scholars have started to identify Liu Yuan's design by comparing the decorative motifs across the woodblock album, his imperial ink cakes and ink stones, and those on the porcelains.[65] The formal comparison of extant wares confirms contemporary comments on his "eclectic style"—an ambiguous craft that forged a literati style with an essentially artisanal predilection.

The eclectic style of court art visualized the cultural integration in which the Qing court indoctrinated bannermen. Designs resulted from the selection and combination of a variety of sources. Tang Ying's case is even more illustrative of this process of selection and combination, given the plethora of textual evidence discussing the details of the design process. Emperors or princes sometimes provided model pieces and instructed a designer to extract the shape, the color of the glaze, and the decoration from these various items and then combine the selected qualities into a new piece:

> Copy the design [*huayang*] of a landscape in four medallions on a flower brocade pattern of this *yangcai* [foreign enameled] bowl to make cups and plates. The cups should have handles. The saucers could be round or of mallow-petal shape. Make wooden models of cups and plates for inspection first. Start to produce only after approval.[66]

This instruction emphasizes that the decorative painting should draw from that on the enameled bowls, while the shape of the cup and saucer should draw from undecorated wooden models.[67] Thus, models of different kinds contributed diverse aspects of the design, and supervisor-designers were skilled in painting such formulaic motifs. For instance, Liu Yuan specialized in painting themes such as bamboo, dragons, and water patterns, as well as some types of flora. Tang Ying excelled in drawing beautiful patterns on draperies. Paintings or colored drawings were the most convenient tools used for design at the Qing court, partly due to the pervasive documentary use of painting and diagram-like images for transmitting information.

Technocrats' deployment of literati painting style in porcelain design extended the Qing court's appropriation of Chinese painting techniques in monumental imperial projects to everyday utilities. Since the Kangxi reign, the Qing court had involved eminent Chinese painters to make royal portraits that completed enormous documentary scrolls on rituals, military campaigns, and imperial tours to South China.[68] Aside from commissioned work, painters at court continued to use and disseminate established styles in the literati tradition, especially for landscape paintings. Some bannermen had integrated these styles with more technical, utilitarian ways of making images. For instance, Haiwang, a Plain Yellow bannerman, started as a commandant (*hujun xiao*) in the Palace Guards Brigade and a fiscal manager in the Neiwufu, then used his drawing skills to survey land for imperial tomb sites and hydraulic construction, as well as creating architectural designs for palaces and mausoleums.[69] Later in life, he was frequently summoned to inspect designs for vessels and provide advice on the production of tools related to Western learning in mathematics and astronomy. Such a disposition trespassed into private production work and imperial commissions because institutional training and production shaped the ways technocratic designers appropriated available artistic styles.

This cultural pluralism can be understood in the context of the cultural projects of "grand synthesis" at court that Tang Ying was involved with.[70] This eclecticism is evident in his porcelain design and his work as a literary writer, in which his most notable strategy was assembling. For example, Tang Ying tried a technique called "assembly of lines with altering tunes" (*zhuangdiao jiju*) in his play *The Imperial Singing Girl's String Ballad* (Nü tanci), which consists of only one scene.[71] This segment of the play derived from a small section in Hong Sheng's (1645–1704) *Palace of Lasting Life* (Changshengdian), a masterpiece in the literati repertoire. The entire programmed suite is called "Peddler in Alternating Tunes" (Zhuandiao huolang'er). Tang Ying's rewriting integrates songs from other music modes (*gongdiao*) into a single coherent suite of tunes by manipulating the structure of each aria in the suite. Modern scholar Wu Mei explains the technique of this musical assembly in "A Brief Survey of the Rules and Form of Southern and Northern Arias" (Nanbeici jianpu):

> In the fourth scene of an anonymous *Peddler's Carrying Pole* [Huolangdan], there are nine arias in the "peddler's song in nine turns." Each aria changes a rhyme. It opens a new horizon in the arias of the Yuan dynasty. The length of lines varies for each aria. And there are only three extant examples of this suite of tunes. One is in *Peddler's Carrying Pole*, one is in *Righteous Refusal of a Gift of Gold* [Yiyong cijin].[72] The third is in *Palace of Lasting Life*. The set in the scene of "String Ballad" in *Palace of Lasting Life* derived from that [in the anonymous *Peddler's Carrying Pole*].[73]

Tang Ying must have been extremely interested in this technique of selection and combination, as he recorded the same kind of southern tradition practice in his work logs.

This kind of assembly technique was used with tunes from northern and southern musical traditions, as well as different genres. Tang Ying extracted many couplets from a large pool of poetic works and reassembled them in his work. He wrote remarks next to the couplets to record his use of them. Some summarize the theme of the couplet, while others even designate the structural position of the couplets he collected.[74] This form of composition—using an assembly model for a technical exercise in poetry composition—was called "assembling lines from Tang dynasty poetry" (*ji Tang*), popular among Chinese literati.[75] Bannermen, who were fascinated by the literary technique, used it to hone their literary skill. Unsurprisingly, a former porcelain supervisor, Lang Tingji, compiled a handbook explaining how to carry out this kind of poetic exercise: *Principal Methods for Writing a Poem by Assembling Selections of Tang Poetry* (Ji Tang yaofa). In it, he introduces a method for writing compositions couplet by couplet:

> To assemble a composition from Tang poetry, you begin by deciding on the first two lines. Then you choose the fourth line and the sixth line. According to the categories, you should have little trouble finding the parallel line and completing all six lines. Then you can decide on the seventh line and search for the eighth in the rhyme [with the seventh line]. Or, you can decide the eighth line first and seek the seventh from the chosen category, as you like.[76]

The principle called "searching for the couplet according to categories" (*yilei midui*) is exactly what Tang Ying did in his collection of couplets. Following a similar logic of design in other genres and media, Tang Ying accumulated alternative templates for the same structural position in plays, such as more than two dozen tunes suitable for opening speeches, obviously for actual use.[77] His technical approach to composition suggests a technocratic model of cultural appropriation, which could be summarized as invention from inventory. In other words, archived templates provided the basis for new experimental assemblages. In this technocrat's theatrical practice, we see how the archivist approach extended from his court training to his private literary writing.

Tang Ying's eclectic playwriting craft was equally visible in his paintings and designs, as all of these cultural products reflect the process of cultural integration that he internalized at the court. Some of Tang Ying's paintings and calligraphic work are the best examples of an ambiguous style that implies artisanal training and yet literati influence. This ambiguous style testifies to the internalization of imperial decorum. Tang Ying's painterly craft shows a clear trace of artisanal training, even as he employed motifs often seen in so-called literati paintings.[78] In fact, recycling images was a common pictorial strategy in technocratic craft. Probably his only definite extant hanging scroll landscape, in the Palace Museum in Beijing, is composed in the style of the so-called orthodox school (plate 3).[79] The surface is broken into five slightly redundant horizontal land zones instead of the conventional three parts (foreground, middle ground, background). The lower half of the painting is crowded with mansions surrounded by many kinds of trees. Tang Ying seems eager to pack in numerous stock motifs from literati paintings: the dotted mountaintop, fishermen, a pavilion by the riverbank in the style of Ni Zan (1301–1374), and so on. The enumerative composition suggests a pictorial repertoire from which he drew motifs and generated the landscape by varying the image combinations. The question at hand is whether Tang Ying's painting was truly "orthodox," as he claimed. He had probably once been a follower of Wang Yuanqi (1642–1715), one of the foremost "orthodox" painters at court:[80]

> When I was young, I used to view the scrolls of the Fuchun Mountains. . . . I was studying with master Wang Lutai [Wang Yuanqi] from River Lou. I heard that he formulated, "You should know that the flavor and essential expression of Masters Ni and Huang could be summarized with no more than six words, namely *guang* [brightness or luminosity], *li* [a sense of withinness, in opposition to graphic flatness), *mao* [rough incompleteness, encouraging participatory viewing], *ku* [economy (of brushstrokes and washes)], *zhong* [alignment, overall balance], and *run* [lustrous effect]. I am ungifted and slow. I improved but did not master it. Nevertheless, I did understand it.[81]

Tang Ying recalled Wang Yuanqi's verbal instruction, but by stating, "I am ungifted and slow. I improved but did not master it," he held himself at a subtle distance from the school he eulogized, much like he respectfully distanced his dramaturgy from literati playwright Jiang Shiquan's approach. The painting in the Palace Museum in Beijing is meticulously executed. Parallel lines evenly streak across the riverbanks. All the shores are carefully outlined. Every terrestrial crease and border of the riverbank is covered with parallel grass. There is little tonal change in the brushwork. The architecture is painted very possibly with a ruler in some places. Tang emphasized the accomplished referentiality of an image rather than the virtuosity of his brushwork. In this, his painting craft is more consistent with porcelain paintings than with the literati's orthodox doctrine.[82]

Tang Ying must have directly painted on some ceramic brush pots. There is an artisanal repetitiveness in his depiction of tree leaves, grass, and architectural outlines, even in sections that most forcefully imitate the literati style. Similar to peer technocrats, Tang Ying's painterly craft was predominately shaped by his involvement in the decorative arts. The long hand scroll in the Palace Museum in Beijing, dated to 1727, further reveals the preparatory and documentary nature of Tang Ying's craft as an image maker (plate 4). The four sections of the scroll are not logically related but resemble a repertoire of exercises or drafts. A horse rolling in the dust is one stock motif from the received pictorial repertoire. This motif appears on porcelain produced during Tang Ying's appointment in Jingdezhen. The rooster in the second section could easily be a blown-up version of those on joined-color (*doucai*) cups. The inscriptions next to the rooster mainly preach moralism and loyalism. Yet the inscription on the first section refers to actual experience in the borderland:

> Long ago when I accompanied the emperor to hunt in regions beyond the Great Wall, I captured one or two squirrels in the forest. Fed for a long time, they became docile and close to human . . . so I painted them to record my feelings.

This nostalgic reference to a borderland experience shows that Tang Ying took the relationship between a particular image and the accompanying inscription very literally.

Tang Ying's interest in regional flora, animals, and technological tools went beyond official utilitarian concerns, and was rooted in his early service as an artisan and bodyguard who traveled widely in the empire. Born in northeast China and having grown up in Beijing, he was observant of southern weather, plant and animal species, and customs, as well as languages, in places where he supervised porcelain production. For example, in a poem to be inscribed on the wall of Zhenhai Tower, a semimilitary watchtower armed with cannons in Guangzhou, he carefully notes a minute observation about the differences between kite flying in the north and in the south.[83] Tang Ying's awareness of these differences emerged against a background of nostalgia for his hometown in the north but never led to any hierarchical judgment regarding regional differences. It was simply a fact learned during his journey of assimilation.

Tang Ying liked to document in painting what he observed in various regions and to explain the reasons for his interest, which are often different from those associated with literati's self-expression. He was an avid naturalist experienced in horticulture. Beyond appreciating beautiful flowers, he pursued specific knowledge of regional variations and asked assistants to bring seeds back so he could cultivate them. An example is an essay enumerating various kinds of *lian* (lotus or other species from a separate genus conventionally called by the same name in premodern China), which were often used as painting motifs to decorate porcelain wares. Tang wrote the essay to record an occasion when a friend showed him the depiction of a rare species brought from Sichuan. He evokes the famous Confucian philosopher Zhou Dunyi's (1017–1073) moral metaphor about lotuses, then identifies the particular species the philosopher alluded to. Next, as a good archivist, he lays out the kinds of lotus he has seen:

> Apart from the common ones, the red, white, and thousand-layered ones that are like brocade, and which are familiar to most people, I have seen the golden lotus in the border area. These grow in damp marshes. Being brilliantly golden, they have petals as large as walnut leaves. Their pistils are delicate. Their grass blades face the leaves. Growing in clusters, they cover the brooks in the valley. I could not see the end of them. Border crossers have sometimes transplanted them in China proper; but, since the soil is acidic, the shape and color [of the transplants] changes immediately.

This description is based on observation rather than book knowledge. Moreover, he pays particular attention to the difficulty of transplantation, and goes on to introduce lotus from another three regions, proceeding geographically counterclockwise.

> The Ao-han tribe grows three kinds including green lotus, yellow lotus, and lotus in the shape of a Buddhist cushion. They have the same shape as those in the Middle Kingdom but are of a different color. The petals of the lotus in the shape of a Buddhist cushion have no sharp tips. They roll back and retreat inside and also are pink. The tribal language calls it Ba-du-ma. These are the lotuses of Buddhist cushions found in temples.

"Ao-han" most likely refers to the Mongolian region.[84] Tang Ying likes to provide the term in transliteration from the native language, just as he did with ceramic terms when explicating porcelain technology in Jingdezhen. Furthermore, trained to work across several media in handicraft, he again promptly links the form of the Mongolian lotus to the cushion shape of lotuses in Buddhist temples. When he wrote this essay, his primary preoccupation was porcelain. The following description is reminiscent of the Indian lotus (*xifanlian,* literally "lotus of western aborigines") motif on porcelain wares.[85]

> In the northwestern region, there is *xifanlian*. They have jade-green leaves and slender stems, and purple flowers. Their shape is graceful and elegant. There is a thick palpus between the pistils and sepals. A bunch of these is about three or four *fen* tall. It sways and rotates because there is an axis growing under the cap like the axis in a grinder. It is indeed a marvelous flower from the remote region [*chongyi*].

Highly attuned to mechanical devices in his engagement with porcelain mass production, Tang Ying compares the stem between pistil and sepal with the pestle in a mortar. It is worth noting that he uses the metonymic term *chongyi*, meaning "repeated translations," to name the remote region where the extraordinary flowers grow, Chongyi, implying that multistage translation from one language to another via one or more additional mediating languages, had long been a standard term by the eighteenth century. The term suggests an aggressively expanding empire, where borders were constantly redefined, and relationships between self and other were ceaselessly reconstructed. The next kind of lotus in the essay is popular in the Yellow Mountains, not far from where Tang Ying worked. Geographical proximity does not reduce its uniqueness. It is as regionally specific as those in the borderlands. "There is *mulian hua* [wooden lotus, probably] in the Yellow Mountains. . . . It is not found growing elsewhere." Tang Ying eventually comes to the *daochui lian* (possibly tiger lily, *Lilium tigrinum*) in Sichuan:

> As for the *daochui lian* [lit., "lotus hanging upside down"], I really have not ever seen it. It grows in Shu [Sichuan]. Even local people cannot name it. Mr. Zhu from Xiuning visited the place on official duty and gave it this name. He transported it for replanting in Xin'an. His son painted the flower to record his father's hand-planted treasure. One day, he showed the original copy to me to identify it.[86]

Since the local people did not know the name of this plant, and Tang Ying and his informant were trying to identify the species based on a painting, that painting had to reject the amateurish brushwork of the literati and instead aim for verisimilitude.

The documentary quality of preparatory paintings reveals Tang Ying's artisanal disposition in his fashioning of images, which contrast with his stated aspiration toward the literati's orthodox style. The literal reference between texts and images, as well as the use of stock motifs, reveals how his craft had been shaped by his training at court and disciplined by his imperial commissions. Tang Ying's deployment of musical tunes from the regional repertoire and his eclectic painting style express the cultural pluralism of the Qing court. Bannermen's artwork reveals both individual artistic inclination and an imperial imprint.

COMPLEX AUTHORSHIP

Porcelain ware was made by many hands and betrayed many distinct intentions. Its complex authorship invites us to decode the intersubjective relationship materialized in the artistic design. The most obvious formal phenomenon is the juxtaposition of a supervisor's inscriptions and the imperial reign marks on some porcelain pieces. This dual scriptural presence displays how the supervisor-designers negotiated with imperial decorum in design.

Scholars have discovered fewer than two dozen extant pieces with Tang Ying's signature and seals.[87] Like some of the aforementioned designs by Liu Yuan and bannermen court painters' private work, Tang Ying's signed pieces were caught between imperial commission and private innovation, so they showcase a technocratic craft stepping across the public and the private realms. The writing on ceramic pieces took on a meaning beyond its function as marks of quality control or commercial branding.[88] The semantic function of writing dissolved and expanded to assume an aesthetic quality concerned with the choice of scripts and placement on the surface of wares. Writing—especially the signature and seals—became an unalienable part of the design while remaining linked to the authorship function.[89]

Sometimes, the placement of seals suggests the dual presence of imperial control and technocratic agency. On some such signed pieces, Tang Ying put his own seal at the bottom and registered the imperial presence elsewhere on the surface. This unconventional placement of marks suggests an alternative author claim, because the bottom of a porcelain vessel commissioned by the Qing court was usually reserved for a reign mark. One piece displays Tang Ying's skill in five calligraphy scripts—clerical, seal, standard, semicursive, and cursive styles (fig. 2.6a).

On each side of the square brush pot, he inscribed a poem in one script and signed in another so as to include five scripts on the four faces of the square pot. He chose to date and sign the piece with the cursive script on the side covered with his favorite clerical script. "It is in the 12th month of the 13th year in the Qianlong reign [1748]. I respectfully write from the west wing of the Bureau of Ceramics. Tang Ying" (fig. 2.6a). The bottom of the piece bears a red seal reading, "Ceramic connoisseur's elegant plaything" (*zhentao yawan*), which is regarded as Tang Ying's trademark (fig. 2.6b).[90]

Yet one side of this piece is inscribed with an imperial poem ending with "Made by Qianlong's imperial commission" (*Qianlong yuzhi*; fig. 2.6c). It conspicuously states the imperial presence and therefore complicates the overall authorship of the piece. This brush pot was unlikely to have been commissioned by the emperor, as Tang Ying would not sign a piece made for the emperor. It must be Tang Ying's test piece and yet it bears an imperial poem.

A similar inscription, "imperial" (*yu*), appears on an interlocked square brush

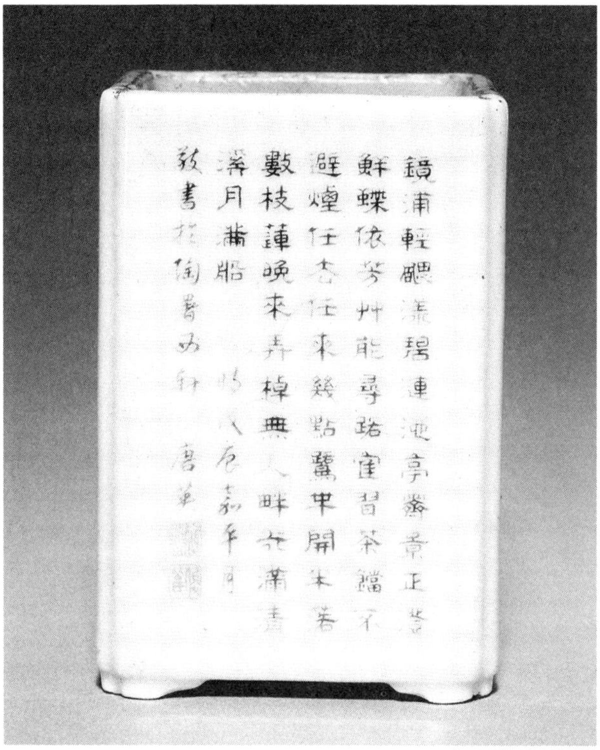

FIG. 2.6A. Square porcelain writing-brush holder, four sides inscribed with imperial poems written in four calligraphic styles, with one side inscribed with a poem written in clerical script, with date and signature "It is in the 12th month of the 13th year in the Qianlong reign [1748]. I respectfully write from the west wing of the Bureau of Ceramics. Tang Ying." Underglaze black pigment on porcelain, dated to 1748, height: 10 cm, diameter of foot: 9.5 cm, in Palace Museum, Beijing

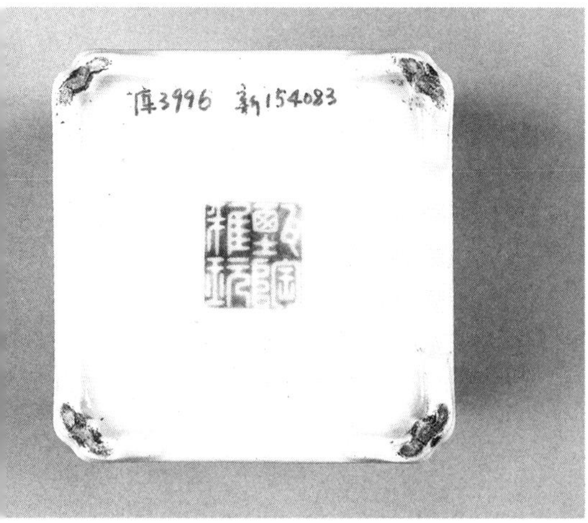

FIG. 2.6B. Bottom mark "Ceramic connoisseur's elegant plaything" (*zhentao yawan*) on 2.6a

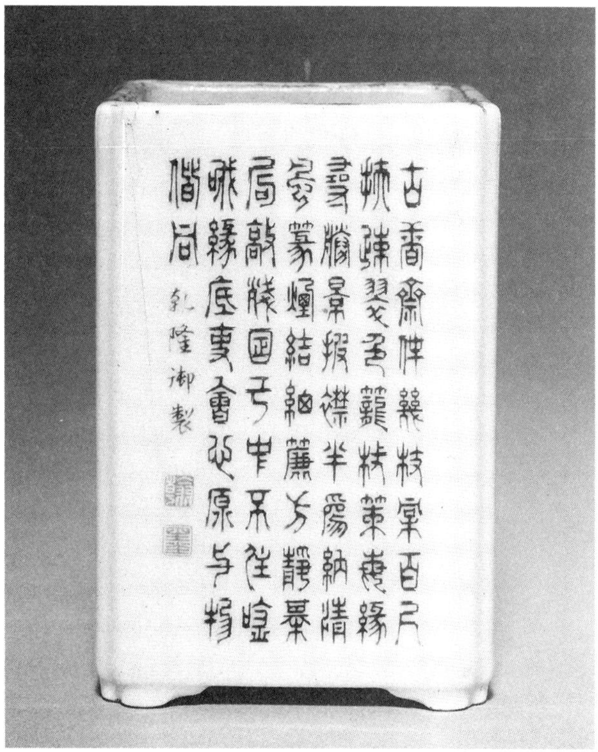

FIG. 2.6C. Side of 2.6a inscribed with imperial poems written in seal script, "Made by Qianlong's imperial commission"

pot decorated with monochrome ink painting, dated to 1755 (plate 5).[91] The pot seal refers to Tang Ying's studio: "Made by [the owner of] the Mu Studio" (Muzhai zhi). These pieces with Tang Ying's own trademarks might have been produced as early prototypes associated with the imperial commission of square holders for writing brushes inscribed with poetry and prose. One example of such brush holders has a reign mark at the bottom, completely erasing the supervisor's presence.[92] Yet the pieces with Tang Ying's signature help us understand the complex authorship of porcelain designs and the subtle negotiation between the emperor and the supervisor-designer visible on artwork. Similarly, court painters signed their paintings with "subject" (*chen*) before their names to suggest a close yet subordinate relation to the emperor.[93] The absence of *chen* in Tang Ying's porcelain work might result from conventional practice in this medium, or it might imply that these pieces with supervisors' signatures were not to be presented to the emperor but would be used locally either as gifts or as models.

DESIGNS ACROSS MEDIA

Bannermen supervisors' designs were restrained by imperial decorum in terms of their partial authorship, but the luxurious and multicultural resources at court also exposed them to unprecedented possibilities in materials and craftsmanship and therefore had an enabling effect on supervisors' design across diverse media. They were encouraged to combine design patterns, palettes, and shapes drawn from newly integrated cultures. The supervisor-designers were capable of, and passionate about, overcoming material constraints and exploring the potential of several media, displaying a fascination with technical possibilities; thus, we can find one design pattern transplanted onto a variety of surfaces. Tang Ying was particularly interested in making porcelain calligraphy panels. On a blue-and-white placard, he publicly displayed his patronage to a local trade deity of ceramic production, coloring the characters, which were carved in relief, for the Shrine to Protect Ceramic Production (Youtao Lingci) in cobalt blue.[94] The placard for the ceramic deity is an early instance of porcelain calligraphy in Tang Ying's practice. Some exemplars with his seals dated to 1748 have recently been discovered in public and private collections.[95] In fact, Tang Ying had designed a series of placards for local deities during his journey in 1748, though they were not all necessarily produced in porcelain. In his working journal, he provided a carefully designed layout for the placards, which all follow the same design scheme. They begin with the precise date, followed by calligraphy of a couplet or an essay, and end with his signature. In the design drafts collected in his working journal, he indicated the placement of the seals by putting a square frame at the beginning of two placards (fig. 2.7).

A piece Tang Ying made in Guangzhou illustrates how he put these private placard designs to use. This couplet was dedicated to the Temple for the Queen of Heaven (Tianhou Gong) in the town, for the protection of travelers' safety. Tang Ying noted next to the couplet, "On the festival of the Winter Solstice, on the 11th day of the 5th month in the 16th year of the Qianlong reign [1751], the calligraphy should be sent to the placard shop for production. After it is made, I will hang it up piously."[96] The well-archived application of design again seemed to govern production in both private and public spheres.

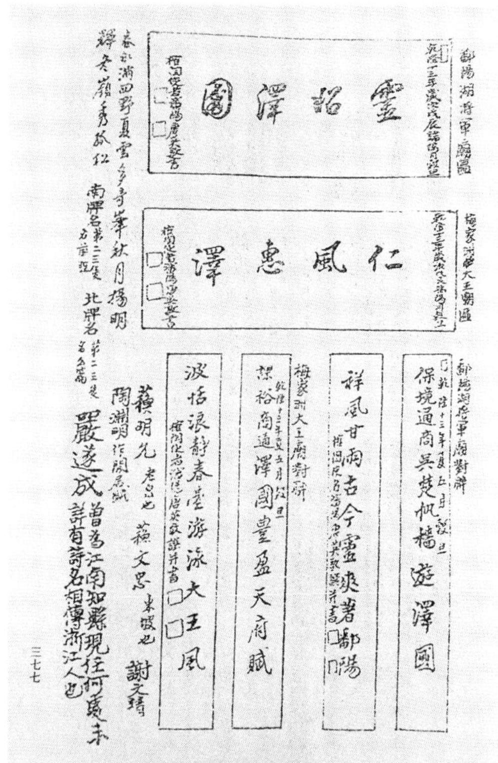

FIG. 2.7. Designs of placards, drawing on print, reproduced in *Tang Ying quanji*, 377

Tang Ying's cross-media explorations went far beyond mere ceramic realization of calligraphy. A realistic brush rest that is a ceramic imitation of a scholar's rock showcases Tang Ying's deft manipulation of both shape and glaze (plate 6). Ceramics had long been made to imitate vessels in other materials to reduce cost. Mutual appropriation between ceramics and bronze vessels had started as early as the Shang dynasty,[97] and as mentioned earlier, ceramic imitation of ritual bronze wares became intensively practiced in the Southern Song and the Ming dynasties in order to save money and symbolize virtuous frugality. Silver wares served as models for ceramic imitation throughout early and medieval China.[98] However, by the mid-Qianlong reign, ceramic imitation of lacquer, jade, rocks with special patterns, bronze, and many more media became a playful display of the technical prowess of the era. In the brush rest, Tang Ying has successfully conjured up the rock's porous structure and the mineral surface quality in this ceramic piece, which shows that his work took place in the context of imperial fascination with multimedia masquerades, where designs of both shape and surface were transferred across the design system. For instance, the architect family Lei not only drafted blueprints for palaces and gardens; they also designed wooden furniture, metal candlesticks, and textile patterns, to name just a few.[99] Thus, many surfaces made of distinct media were adorned with similar decorative patterns using dramatically divergent techniques. Both the frequent collaboration between nearby handicraft workshops near the Cining Palace and the institutionalized monarchic interest in cross-media performance gave supervisor-designers acuity in cross-media practice.

THE PRIMARILY TAX-ORIENTED *yang* system in previous dynasties evolved into a more communicative institution that allowed for direct technological and artistic intervention in the mid-Qing period. Within the elaborate *yang* system, bannermen supervisors assisted in schematizing creation and institutionalizing innovation. The *yang* they deployed turned a plan into symbols, both conceptually and with graphic assistance. The technocratic supervisors were able to articulate and transfer their newly acquired embodied knowledge from regional society. And they were able to realize the abstracted forms in diverse media. Their preoccupation with, and predisposition toward, producing preparatory works for the industrial art of porcelain production affected their craft in painting and calligraphy. The crossover between private and public work, illustrated by the complex authorship of their artworks, reveals the negotiations between imperial commissioners, supervisors, and coworkers during the production process. These negotiations were encoded in eventually specific choices of shape, palette, motifs, and decorative inscriptions for the porcelain pieces. The archived *yang* registered the technocratic experience that bannermen supervisors like Tang Ying gained in their technological experiments. Yet the expression of technocratic knowledge was inevitably sporadic in project-centered documents. Systematic articulation of this is preserved in a technological treatise compiled by Tang, which is the focus of the next chapter.

THREE

Tang Ying's *Illustrated Manual of Ceramic Production*

LOCAL CRAFTSMEN HELD the most intimate knowledge about porcelain production, but it was technocrats who used words and pictures to communicate this knowledge to the political center and other parts of the empire. Illustrated treatises were a way to archive and shape knowledge about porcelain production in Jingdezhen. A comparison of Tang Ying's treatises on regional ceramic processes with his rewrites of regional theater works reveals the hidden political agenda behind the choice of words, images, characters, and actions in both. Tang's technical treatise, like his refashioned plays, was part of the culture of technocratic knowledge that the Qing court fostered in the empire. The treatise documents how bannermen appropriated local knowledge as part of the intelligence service provided to their rulers. In this sense, "technology," "politics," and "arts" were one and the same in Tang's early modern world. His selection and combination of regional techniques and resources served to visually glorify the current rulership and its legitimacy.

Literary writings document bannermen technocrats' firsthand empirical observation and their interaction with regional populations. Tang, like bannermen supervisors before and after him, faced a vast handicraft industry full of complicated techniques and rich artistic conventions, just like the immense theatrical traditions he appropriated and transformed. Poetry and drama might not preserve much technological knowledge in the strict modern sense of the term, but literary writing was "empirical" in that it was the primary vehicle used by bannermen experts to make sense of the empire. Their literary creations, an important component of their knowledge cultures, reveal the fundamental political ideology and motivation with which they managed regional cultural resources and created artistic forms.[1]

The technocracy sustained by the Imperial Household Department brought together the production of technological knowledge, literary writing, and art, as they all grew out of the practical demands of large-scale projects related to statecraft. Tang Ying's *Illustrated Manual of Ceramic Production* (Taoye tushuo; 1743) depicted and described raw materials, tools, factory space, and technical procedures, translating an otherwise impenetrable process into a linear sequence.[2] Some have argued that these treatises merely explain the technical details of ceramic production.[3] Close inspection, however, reveals an unspoken political agenda. Technocrats were required to collect and articulate information about local resources and technology for the court. The Qianlong emperor's ultimate ownership of such information in the form of the treatises enhanced his authority in both technological and regional governance. My analysis is based on close intertextual reading of an extant copy of the illustrated treatise with treatises on the same subject authored by Chinese literati.

Understanding of the Qing technocrat's unique knowledge culture, however, begins elsewhere, in a selection of Tang Ying's plays, which reflect the broad knowledge culture at the Qing court, which affected his description of regional society. Tang's way of articulating regional society to the emperor is reflected in his choice of words and in plots absorbed from the local repertoire. In theater as in ceramic production, Tang's transcription of local experience is characterized by three approaches: ethnographic, archivist, and experimentalist. The necessity of addressing the emperor and his political prerogatives meant that Tang's appropriation of porcelain technology and local theater was by nature different from that described in instructional books and plays intended for literati, merchants, and artisans.[4]

From Apprentice to Master in Jingdezhen

Although the Qing technocratic method of cultural appropriation implied hands-on experience in activities such as regional manufacture and theater, some experts in porcelain production were not directly involved in production. To display authority, the writer of a treatise could focus on the bureaucracy governing production, as a section in *The Artificers' Record* does.[5] To facilitate local magistrates' quality control when they collected ceramic products as tax payments, Jiang Qi's (c. 1214–1234) *Notes on Ceramics* (Tao ji) systemized technological information.[6] The chapters on ceramics in the literatus Song Yingxing's (1587–1666?) encyclopedia, *The Works of Heaven and the Inception of Things*

(Tiangong kaiwu), were an integral part of his moral self-cultivation in terms of categorizing things (*gewu*). The authors of these three treatises display limited hands-on experience in ceramic production.

Tang Ying's physical experience of porcelain production in Jingdezhen distinguishes him from the tax collectors and literati observers. Although he had designed at court, the mass production of porcelain must have been a daunting industry that he had little grasp of when he was appointed to the Imperial Porcelain Manufactory in 1728. He volunteered to complete three additional years of apprenticeship to learn the skill of making porcelain from local craftsmen:

> In the 6th year of the Yongzheng reign [1728], I was sent to Jiangyou [Jiangxi] as a supervisor. Though ceramic production is a trivial business, there are things I had never been taught. Raw materials and the temperature of fire require the same effort as dealing with the five elements and alchemy. Furthermore, I was totally at a loss about how to imitate ancient [styles] and devise new contemporary [styles], nor did I know about spray cover or high and low forms. Every day I followed the craftsmen's instruction with great caution, being afraid of failing at my task and delaying the public mission. I closeted myself indoors, avoided socializing for fun, concentrated, and put all my efforts into living and working together with craftsmen for three years. By the 9th year of the Yongzheng reign [1731], though I could not claim to know all of the transformative principles of generating and subduing raw materials and fire, I was pretty well informed about the means of reduction, addition, and flexible modification. Before, I could only follow craftsmen's instructions, but now I am able to instruct craftsmen.[7]

Tang's account documented how authority was relocated from local craftsmen to the bannerman technocrat as he gained mastery of their knowledge and skill. When Tang was adept enough to modify the procedures and the ceramic recipes, the craftsmen would follow his instructions. The reversal of the master-disciple relationship suggests the tactful technocratic dominance assumed in the process of appropriating local culture. This progression from learning to masterful modification is even more clear in another area of Tang's life: his appropriation of regional theater.

PRELUDE: MASTERING THE REGIONAL SCENE

Tang Ying must have been exposed to both elite and regional theater starting with his years as Kangxi's bodyguard. He likely viewed a performance of clapper drama, a regional kind characterized by percussive music, when he accompanied

Kangxi during his southern tour, possibly in Hangzhou. His experience with acting, playwriting, music performance, and composition is, not surprisingly, absent from records of his early cultural pursuits, as technocrats tend to treat cultural productions in separate records. However, once he started writing plays in the 1740s, his poems from the period reveal an extensive interaction with local literati elites in playwriting and regional theater. Although outside his official duties, Tang Ying's dedication to the art of the theater, seen in a broader perspective, is political in nature, a form of preparation for capturing local manufacturing scenes in an illustrated manual.

Qing theater, because of its multimedia components and regional variations, opened up a wide arena for cross-cultural integration. The eclectic repertoire of court drama had developed since the 1680s, integrating Chinese elite drama and acrobatic pageantry into grandiose imperial rituals such as celebrations of military victories and performances for foreign envoys.[8] Such performances were also logistical exercises, similar to imperial handicraft workshops, which required working with an abundance of material objects and archiving information.[9]

The political significance of appropriating regional theater as a way to achieve control over a territory was further emphasized in the Qing discourse "Obtain Its Music and Turn Its Music In" (Huoqi yue, xian qiyue), as submitting regional music required local performers to entertain the ruler and hence enact a symbolic submission.[10] For instance, bannerman Cao Yin (1658–1712), the famous imperial textile commissioner, composed a celebratory play, *Festivity in Peaceful Era* (Taiping leshi), which included a scene featuring Japanese songs composed by transliterating Japanese vocabulary drawn from a military strategy manual.[11] The play suggests Japan's subordinate status by staging an alleged Japanese couple who perform folksongs in front of the imperial audience.[12] This play, very likely commissioned during Kangxi's southern tour, contains many short plays within a play performed by imagined subordinate subjects from regions such as Yunnan, Tibet, and even European countries. The generic scenes from a carnivalesque village festival were crafted to symbolize harmonious society under enlightened rule. A few decades later, Tang Ying appropriated regional theater within the same ideological framework.

Tang Ying lived near Jingdezhen for almost twenty-six years after 1728 and absorbed the regional dramaturgical culture. He very likely wrote the majority of his plays during this time, for none of his seventeen plays can be firmly dated to before 1740.[13] During Tang Ying's time, China witnessed a new flourishing of regional theater, which challenged the national dominance of Kun-style theater favored by Chinese literati, especially in the realm of urban commercial theaters and court entertainment.[14] Kun-style drama itself originated as a form of theater from Jiangnan but gradually shed its regional character as it evolved into a highly refined genre dominated by elite literati authors.[15] The rivalry between the Kun style and later regional theater styles was formulated as a competition between the elegant sector (*yabu*) and the miscellaneous sector—literally, the flowery sector (*huabu*)—two types of plays that the salt monopoly bureau in Yangzhou, managed by bannermen, collected for the imperial court.[16]

Many bannermen technocrats appointed to Jiangnan had been involved in recruiting actors or in theatrical censorship since the 1680s, so Tang Ying's peers played important roles in the politics of theater, specifically in the cultivation and appropriation of regional styles. Cao Yin's brother-in-law, Li Xu (1655–1729), once textile commissioner of the Suzhou Manufactory, recruited actresses for the court and received a theatrical master dispatched by Kangxi to train them.[17] Yiling'a (?–1795), who supervised porcelain production between 1768 and 1772, set up a Bureau of Songs (Ciqu Ju) in Yangzhou in 1780 to censor plays collected from the Jiangnan region.[18] Yiling'a showed his extensive knowledge of regional theater in a series of memorials to the Qianlong emperor.[19] These bannermen were the cultural agents who attended regional performances and communicated theatrical knowledge to the court.

Tang Ying was appointed directly by the court to Jingdezhen, where he was extensively exposed to regional theater. His deployment in plays of clapper drama tunes, a kind of music from the "miscellaneous sector," demonstrates the infiltration of regional theatrical techniques into Kun-style dramas. "Clapper" here refers to the percussive instrument used to accompany the performance. The arias of clapper drama often consisted of couplets of seven- or ten-syllable lines.[20] Kun-style arias from the "elegant sector" were based on long-established fixed tunes. Moreover, Kun-style lyrics require tonal harmony; that is, not all words can be used on any syllable.[21] Regional clapper drama imposes fewer rules on composition. The tunes of clapper drama acquired different regional inflections when performing troupes spread them across the empire. Consequently, the tunes of clapper drama had become almost interchangeable with both the tunes of the Qin region (*Qinqiang*) and the tunes of miscellaneous plays (*luantan*) by Tang Ying's time.

As a cultural mediator, Tang Ying's drama provides a missing link between court drama and literati drama. His noncommissioned plays are analogous to the porcelain brush bottles that bear both his personal signature and imperial poems (see figs. 2.6a, c). Like Tang's plays, these porcelain wares were not made to fulfill any imperial command, but he included the imperial presence in his design. Twelve of Tang Ying's seventeen plays range from one to four scenes and so are closer to performance chapbooks than full-length plays. Although he claimed that his plays were Kun-style dramas, he sometimes included a play within a play to highlight regional tunes. For example, in the celebratory wedding at the end of *Eyes on the Beam* (Liangshang yan), the clowns sing "tunes of the lass" (*guniang qiang*) and "tunes of clapper drama" (*bangzi qiang*).[22] As well as including regional musical styles, the fragmentary character of the plays deviates from lengthy Kun-style theater. Both the musical and the dramaturgical composition are highly eclectic.

The musical tunes and plots, which Tang Ying pulled from the regional repertoire, archived in his working journal, and eventually experimented with in his own plays, were supposed to be instruments for an eclectic style with which he could reiterate imperial values such as filial piety, righteousness, and loyalty, and criticize lasciviousness and disobedience. Tang Ying's archivist accumulation of regional musical tunes and arias, as well as his experimental initiative using them in compositions, exhibits a technocratic approach similar to the one he used for gathering and organizing regional ceramic knowledge, as revealed in his illustrated treatise. The *Illustrated Manual of Ceramic Production* presents labor scenes in an appropriate order, as commanded by the Qianlong emperor. The illustrated treatise (*tushuo*, narration by pictures) is like a work of theater in its staging of the scenes of porcelain production through painting and text.

COMMISSIONING THE TREATISE

In a global context, the *Illustrated Manual of Ceramic Production* (hereafter *Illustrated Manual*) may be the best-known premodern Chinese treatise on the ceramic industry. Its text and paintings have been transmitted along two trajectories. The text has been widely reproduced and circulated all over the world.[23] The illustrations, however, were believed to have been lost until a twenty-leaf album titled *Illustrated Manual of Ceramic Production* (Taoye tu) turned up at Christie's auction house in Hong Kong on April 28, 1996, and was acquired by a private collector (fig. 3.1).[24] I refer to this as the Qingwan album, after the society that published it.

Putting the textual and pictorial elements together, the treatise consists of twenty leaves of paintings and twenty sections of calligraphy. Each painted leaf

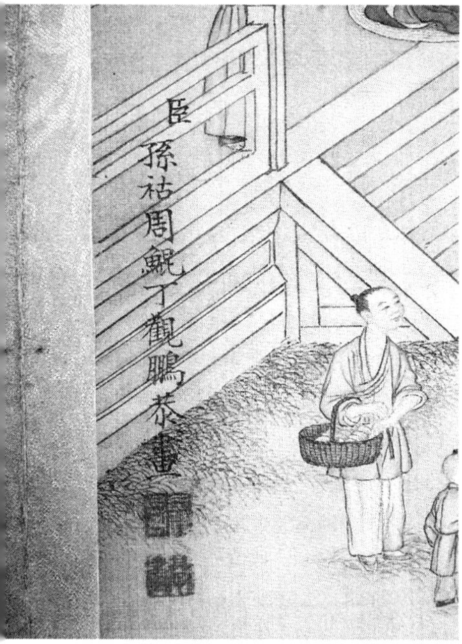

FIG. 3.1. Detail from the painting illustrating entry 20, "Worshipping the Deity and Rewarding the Fulfilled Wish" (Sishen chouyuan), signatures of Tang Dai, Sun Hu, and Ding Guanpeng, from the Qingwan album, *Illustrated Manual of Ceramic Production*, 1740–43, color on silk, 29 × 25 cm, private collection

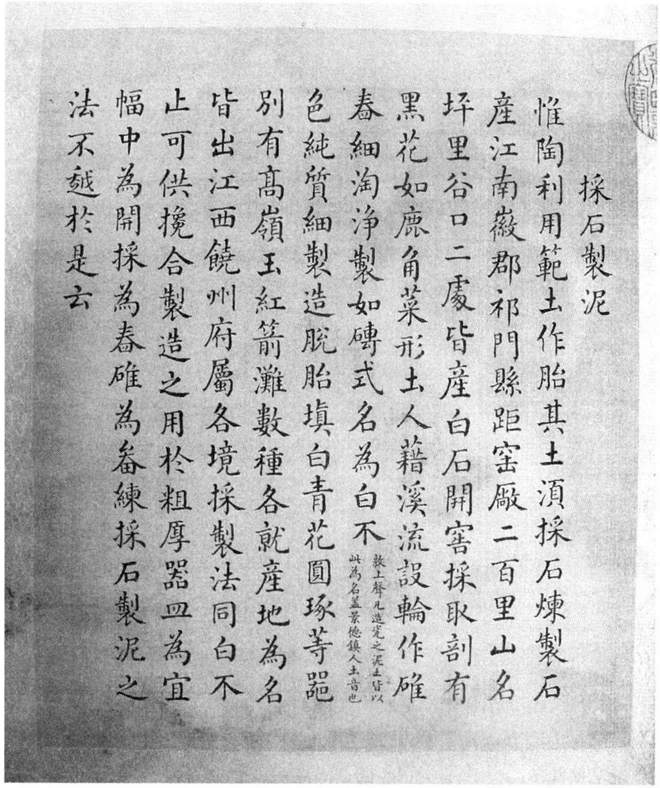
採石製泥

惟陶利用範土作胎其土須採石煉製石產江南徽郡祁門縣距窰廠二百里山名坪里谷口二處皆產白石開窨採取剖有黑花如鹿角菜形土人藉溪流設輪作碓舂細淘淨製如磚式名為白不（敦上聲凡造瓷之泥土皆以此為名蓋景德鎮人土音也）色純質細製造脫胎填白青花圓琢等器別有高嶺玉紅箭灘數種各就產地為名皆出江西饒州府屬各境採製法同白不止可供攙合製造之用於粗厚器皿為宜幅中為開採為舂碓為淘練採石製泥之法不越於是云

FIG. 3.2. Calligraphy, entry 1, "Collection of the Stones and Fabrication of the Paste," from the Qingwan album, *Illustrated Manual of Ceramic Production*, ink on silk, 29 × 25 cm, private collection

depicts a scene of porcelain production, which the text—given as a section of calligraphy—describes (fig. 3.2, plate 7).

As very few people besides the emperors would have seen the pictures (with related unique text) in the treatise, these images would have had little impact on later production. Given its limited viewership, what was the function of such a technological treatise? The cultural discrepancy between China's eighteenth-century technocrats and modern readers of a technical treatise alerts us to the alternative function of encoded knowledge. Modern readers of technical treatises usually expect the treatises to facilitate technical work, but the viewers of Tang Ying's treatise did not necessarily intend to use it this way. First, the technical information carried in this illustrated treatise might be relevant to quality control and to the calculation of cost. Second, the imperial ownership of the treatise indicates the emperor's authority and his control over the technology.

Imperial orders conditioned the process of making a treatise. The Imperial Workshops' archival record details the procedure for this imperial commission. First, the Qianlong emperor commanded three first-rate court painters to make a twenty-leaf album depicting porcelain production in 1740.[25] Once the album was finished three years later, Qianlong dispatched the paintings to Tang Ying and ordered him to describe in detail what was painted on each leaf.[26] The emperor commanded that the descriptive language be formal and that every entry consist of a similar number of characters. Tang Ying was also told to specify the mountains and lakes where the raw materials came from. Finally, he was required to put the album leaves in the correct order and send them back. Tang Ying returned the complete illustrated treatise in 1743.[27]

The description of porcelain production in earlier treatises, local gazetteers, and connoisseurship manuals had never included as many empirical details as Tang Ying's *Illustrated Manual*.[28] Unlike illustrated treatises on carpentry or tilling and weaving,[29] there were no illustrated treatises prior to Song Yingxing's *Works of Heaven and the Inception of Things,* which depicted human figures laboring according to procedures in ceramic production.[30] The elaborate color depictions in Tang Ying's treatise provided much more information on the minerals, tools, kinds of vessels, and structure of kilns than did monochrome woodblock illustrations. Tang Ying focused on the porcelain made in the Imperial Porcelain Manufactory instead of on other ceramic tiles and everyday vessels, as discussed in the *Works of Heaven and the Inception of Things*. The pictotextual relation in the *Illustrated Manual* makes for a productive comparison with the discrepancy between the textual descriptions and illustrations in *Works of Heaven and the Inception of Things*.[31]

Putting Knowledge in Order

The preface to the *Illustrated Manual* does not suggest any attempt to distribute the publication across geographic regions. Unlike *Pictures of Tilling and Weaving* (Gen zhi tu), an illustrated treatise on farming, sericulture, and textile production that reached a much larger audience through its reproduction in multiple media, the pictorial part of the *Illustrated Manual* was only available in the court.[32] Supervisors of ceramic production in other regions could not have used the manual, because production was dependent on local minerals and skilled labor available in Jingdezhen.

The *Illustrated Manual* highlights specific tools and production steps. The titles of seventeen of the twenty entries are active phrases combining a verb and an object. Tang Ying's preface quickly dives into a summary of procedures.[33] In contrast, an early section in the *Works of Heaven* provides numerical details about transportation as well as the cost of labor, raw materials, fuel, and so on. The gazetteer's compiler gathered information under the following rubrics: institutions (*jianzhi*), clay (*shatu*), labor (*renfu*), offices (*sheguan*), cobalt-blue pigment (*huiqing*),[34] kiln regulation (*yaozhi*), clerks (*gongyi*), artisans (*jiangyi*), fuel (*chailiao*), pigment (*yanse*), transport (*jieyun*), tribute (*yugong*), and price (*liaojia*).[35] The documents in the Ming gazetteer go to great lengths to record institutions and the industrial standards they used for measurement, including just a few scattered explanations about technical procedures.[36] In this respect, texts on porcelain production in gazetteers resemble Tang Ying's fiscal plans sent to the court. The *Illustrated Manual* does not provide data concerning budget, price, and transport. Tang Ying detailed these matters in an actual budget sheet, "Regulations and Precedents for the Manufacture of Round and Molded Porcelain Wares" (Yuanzhuo ciqi shaozao zhijia zeli).[37] And he reports on expenditure in regular memorials as well.[38]

Tang Ying's *Illustrated Manual* evenly covers every aspect of production, while the *Works of Heaven and the Inception of Things* is succinct about certain procedures, such as glazing. Thus, Tang fulfilled the imperial requirement to provide all the relevant information in order and to depict each procedure in an image, using texts of similar length. His titles of the twenty entries are active descriptions of procedures:

1. Collection of the Stones and Fabrication of the Paste.[39]
2. Washing and Purification of the Paste.
3. Burning the Ashes and Preparing the Glaze.
4. Manufacture of the Saggers.[40]
5. Preparing the Molds for Round Ware.
6. Throwing the Round Ware on the Wheel.
7. Fabrication of the Molded Ware (*zhuoqi*).
8. Collecting Cobalt Blue.
9. Selecting Cobalt Blue.

10. Molding the Body and Grinding the Colors.[41]
11. Painting the Round Ware in Blue and White.
12. Fabrication and Decoration of Molded Ware (*zhuoqi*).
13. Dipping into the Glaze and Blowing on the Glaze.
14. Turning the Unbaked Ware and Hollowing out the Foot.
15. Putting the Finished Wares into the Kiln.
16. Opening the Kiln When the Ware Is Baked.
17. Decorating Round Wares and Molded Wares in Foreign Coloring/Enameling.
18. The Open Stove and the Closed Stove.
19. Wrapping in Straw and Packing in Casks.
20. Worshipping the Deity and Rewarding the Fulfilled Wish.

The album leaves can be grouped thematically:

Preparing the raw materials of clay and glaze: leaves 1, 2, and 3
Preparing a sagger: leaf 4
Throwing and polishing a form: leaves 5, 6, and 7
Preparing color and decorating: leaves 8, 9, 10, 11, and 12
Glazing and marking: leaves 13 and 14
Firing: leaves 15 and 16
Special decoration and kilns: leaves 17 and 18
Packing and ceremony: leaves 19 and 20.

I compare these sections with three contemporary albums on porcelain production, to discern what information technocrats prioritized and described in detail, and what the painters left out of the *Illustrated Manual*.[42] My purpose is to reveal the technical, political, and aesthetic reasons behind the choices. Most of the dozens of albums on porcelain production in public and private collections around the world can be dated to the nineteenth century, or the second half of the eighteenth century at the earliest.[43] Based on their painting style and provenance, only three other sets of albums could possibly date from before 1750 and are therefore comparable to the Qingwan album. I call these roughly contemporaneous albums the Beijing album, the Sotheby's album, and the Lund album.

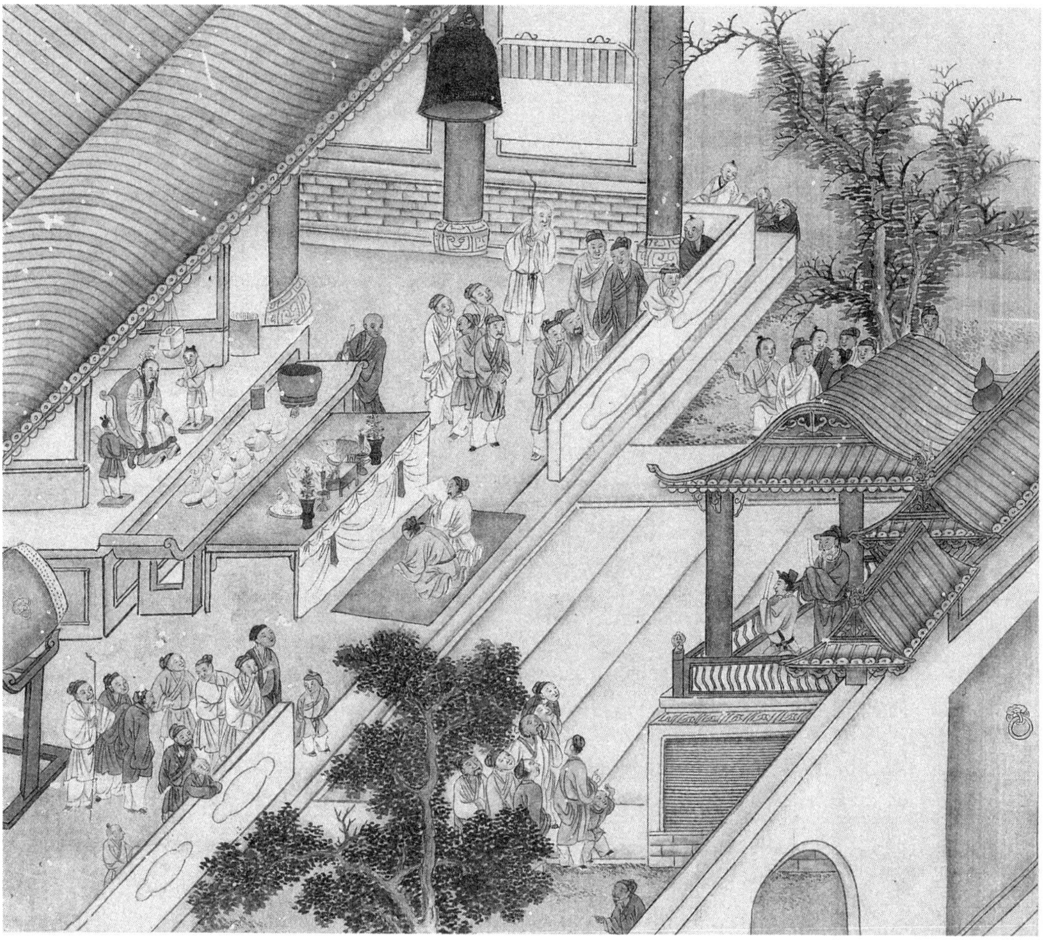

FIG. 3.3. Album leaf (not paginated), "Worship the Ceramic Deity," from the Sotheby's album, *Porcelain Production Illustrated.* Detail: flat bowls, ink and color on paper, Lot 476, 30.5 × 35.5 cm, Louis Blancard / Art Digital Studio © Sotheby's

CONTEMPORARY COMPARISONS

This pool of albums on porcelain manufacture provides a wealth of images depicting the industry, as well as comparable representations made with a different agenda. The Beijing album is incomplete, consisting of eight leaves of paintings but no calligraphy.[44] The Sotheby's album was sold at Sotheby's Paris auction house in June 2013 and comprises twenty-four pages of paintings without any accompanying calligraphy.[45] The signature on one leaf in the Sotheby's album reads, "Respectfully painted by Jiao Bingzhen [active c. 1680–1720]."[46] The vessel images, which lack three-dimensional volume or shading, distinguish the Sotheby's album from typical court paintings of the time (fig. 3.3).

Finally, the Lund album, probably made for a European audience, is a fifty-leaf album housed at Lund University in Sweden.[47] Twenty of its pages depict the sale and transportation of porcelain, which is not a theme of the other three albums. The stylistic differences among these four albums do not merely suggest their different representational approaches. The illustrations to Tang Ying's *Illustrated Manual* were produced before the textual descriptions, so the visual composition in each album leaf organizes Tang Ying's retrieval of his embodied knowledge. His agency shows itself in the order he gave to the album according to his understanding of technical procedures.

The eight groups of technical procedures that Tang Ying parses in the preface reveal the technocrat's logic in breaking down the process of porcelain production into five stages: the preparation of raw materials, forming, decorating, firing, and packing. He constructs a technical narrative with his ordering of the illustrated entries. On the one hand, this narrative puts specific aspects of porcelain production in a sequence that does not exactly mirror the temporal sequence of production. For instance, the preparation of clay and pigment usually takes place simultaneously, but Tang Ying chose to delay explaining pigment until the eighth entry. On the other hand, the technical narrative spatially situates the actions in their regional environment by describing the location of minerals, hand tools, and kiln sites. Three technocratic strategies are employed in extracting local technical knowledge: deployment of an indexical relation (or finger-pointing), differentiated articulation, and quantification. These represent bannermen technocrats' empirical and hierarchical approach in archiving regional intelligence.

PICTOTEXTUAL INDEX: PREPARING THE CLAY, GLAZE, AND PIGMENT

Tang Ying splits the technical narrative concerning the preparation of clay and glaze from the preparation of color pigment, which does not begin until the eighth entry, because of his logical separation of two categories of materials: clay and pigment minerals. This separate treatment facilitates an unbroken narrative of the sequential procedures for each material. Such attentiveness to material specificity in the manual shows technocratic hands-on experimentation in the field.

The indexical nature of the treatise means that the text directly refers to technical details depicted in the paintings. Tang Ying was acutely aware of the different media affordances of texts and paintings for communicating information. He complements the vividness of visual depiction with the strength of textual description to direct readers' attention to specific tools and actions. Without his textual reminder, the viewer might miss the water-powered wheel, half hidden behind two lush trees, that is connected to several crushers in the first leaf of the Qingwan album (plate 7).[48] Compared to the pages that depict the preparation of porcelain clay in the other three albums, the first leaf of the Qingwan album includes many more actions, and the textual entry highlights these labor tasks: "In the painting, there is quarrying, grinding, and sieving with a dustpan. The procedure to collect stones and to make clay uses no more than these."[49] This description not only directs the reader's attention to specific pictorial details but amplifies minute visual cues that cannot be magnified in a painting. One example is the visual character of first-rate white porcelain stones, "which when broken exhibit internally black markings branching out like deer's-horn seaweed."[50] In this way, the textual description adds information difficult to transmit through images alone.

In line with the emperor's request, Tang took an almost ethnographic approach toward documenting the pronunciation of technical terms in the local dialect, as well as the geographical location of special minerals. This attention to the local language was also visible in Tang Ying's theater. Thus, in the first leaf of the Qingwan album, the lower part of the painting shows workers in the pavilion tamping clay into bricks, and Tang Ying tells us that these were called white clay bricks (*baidun*) in the local Jingdezhen dialect (plate 7). "Petuntse," the transliteration of *bai dunzi* in the French Father d'Entrecolles's letter written in 1702, refers to the equivalent feldspathic rocks used in porcelain production in Europe. A more strategically important point is that Tang Ying indicates the distance between the ceramic manufactory and four kinds of mines producing clay for making the vessel bodies, ash to mix with clay to produce a glaze, coarse clay used to make the firing containers (saggers), and blue mineral pigment. Paintings without scale or labels cannot provide such information. However, they can depict complex groups of tools that are hard to describe in words. Such depiction could also function as aide-mémoire of physical gestures used in the production process.

Pictorial representations of the production procedures helped Tang organize his description of the embodied technical experience. A good example is the procedure for purifying paste given in the second leaf of the Qingwan album (plate 8). Tang Ying divides the whole process into a series of actions according to the spatial layout of tools, including an earthenware jar (*shuigang*), a wooden prong (*mupa*), a fine horsehair sieve (*mawei xiluo*), a bag made of double layers of silk (*shuangceng juandai*, not labeled), earthenware vessels for sedimentation (*guoni xiabo*), a wooden box with no bottom (*wudi muxia*), a large cloth of fine cotton (*xibu dadan*), a large stone slab (*da shipian*), and iron spades (*tieqiu*). His description enables readers to make sense of the procedure by scrutinizing the painting from right to left, top to bottom. The final sentence of this entry directly observes how comprehensively the painting depicts the tools and actions: "The tools recorded and human labor delineated in the painting cover both washing and purification."[51] Tang Ying's treatise includes multiple pictotextual comments of this kind, which note how accurately the paintings capture the technical details.

Tang Ying's comments on the technical accuracy of the pictures display his unbiased technocratic use of the painting album as documentary image, a predilection that literati observers lacked. Such pictotextual comments conclude six of the twenty entries. They were missing from Bushell's early translation because he was working from the texts that the literati Zhu Yan had collated in his book *On Ceramics* (Taoshuo). Zhu Yan probably never saw the accompanying album, and therefore chose not to include any pictotextual comments. This omission also betrays some literati's lack of confidence in, or familiarity with, the eclectic use of media to transcribe knowledge. Tang Ying's illustrated comments also reveal the limitations of using pictorial representations alone to transcribe knowledge, highlighting the discrepancy between hands-on experience and the images. In the eighth entry, Tang Ying comments, "The depiction in the painting is meticulous about collecting [the blue color]. As for smelting, it does not touch upon that." He had noticed the absence of the procedure called *zhilian*, which involved "burning the color pigment under the furnace floor for three days, then taking it out and washing it carefully again" prior to sale.[52] This comment reminds us how details may fall through the cracks between textual and pictorial representations.

The procedure for collecting the mineral materials of cobalt blue was similar to the preparation of clay. Endowed with a playwright's sensitivity to narrative coherence, Tang Ying avoids cutting back and forth between similar actions, positioning this as the eighth entry rather than the fourth. If the treatise's narrative structure implies the supervisor's authority over knowledge transmission, the paintings testify to the supervisor-designer's control over knowledge application. An old man in a blue robe is depicted overseeing production in the fifth, seventh, and eighth leaves of the Qingwan album, possibly Tang Ying himself. In terms of pictorial composition, the figure is the "eye" of a leaf, as he always directs the viewer's attention to a central technical scene.[53] In political terms, the figure indicates that the depictions form a documentary; it also personifies imperial control, right down to the level of technical inspection. The supervisor's watchful eye absorbs information about materials, products, and laborers in the local manufactory for archiving in a more analytical way—namely, to categorize and rank them.

DIFFERENTIATED ARTICULATION

Preparing the Color and Decoration The hierarchical logic of control dictated that raw materials and products were to be ranked according to their quality. The technocrat demonstrates his authority in categorizing pigments and products, citing only the top-quality cobalt pigments in the eighth entry: "The large round dark yellow pieces are the best. They are called *ding yuanzi*."[54] He glosses over the inferior kinds, only mentioning their origin from Jiangxi and Guangdong. After explaining the smelting treatment, Tang Ying further classifies cobalt minerals into three levels of quality in his ninth entry.[55] He asserts that color and luster are the two main indicators of quality. This classification is briefer and less specific than the cobalt mineral section in the Jiangxi gazetteer dated two hundred years earlier. Yet this categorization in broad strokes shows precise overall control. In contrast to the local gazetteer, which incorporated everything about cobalt blue, including quarrying, purification, grinding, and application, Tang Ying's treatise classifies the minerals into categories the emperor would understand. However, Tang Ying does single out one kind of cobalt mineral, the "chive sprout" (*jiucai bian*), to explain a crucial technical issue during firing:

> Should the firing be too prolonged, the blue dissolves and runs widely over the ground. It is only the type called "chive sprout" that makes very clearly defined strokes and does not "run" in the fire, so this must be used for the most delicate pieces.[56]

Some extant porcelain pieces bear the fine outlines of this decoration, often an imitation of the fine outline in cobalt blue on Chenghua porcelain wares that were intended to convey Qing court decorum (plate 9).

The Hierarchy of Quality Quality was, above all, a matter of political control at the Imperial Porcelain Manufactory rather than a matter of profit. The minerals' quality testified to the technocrats' ability to draw on local sources, while the products' quality symbolized the regime's technical prowess. Both contributed

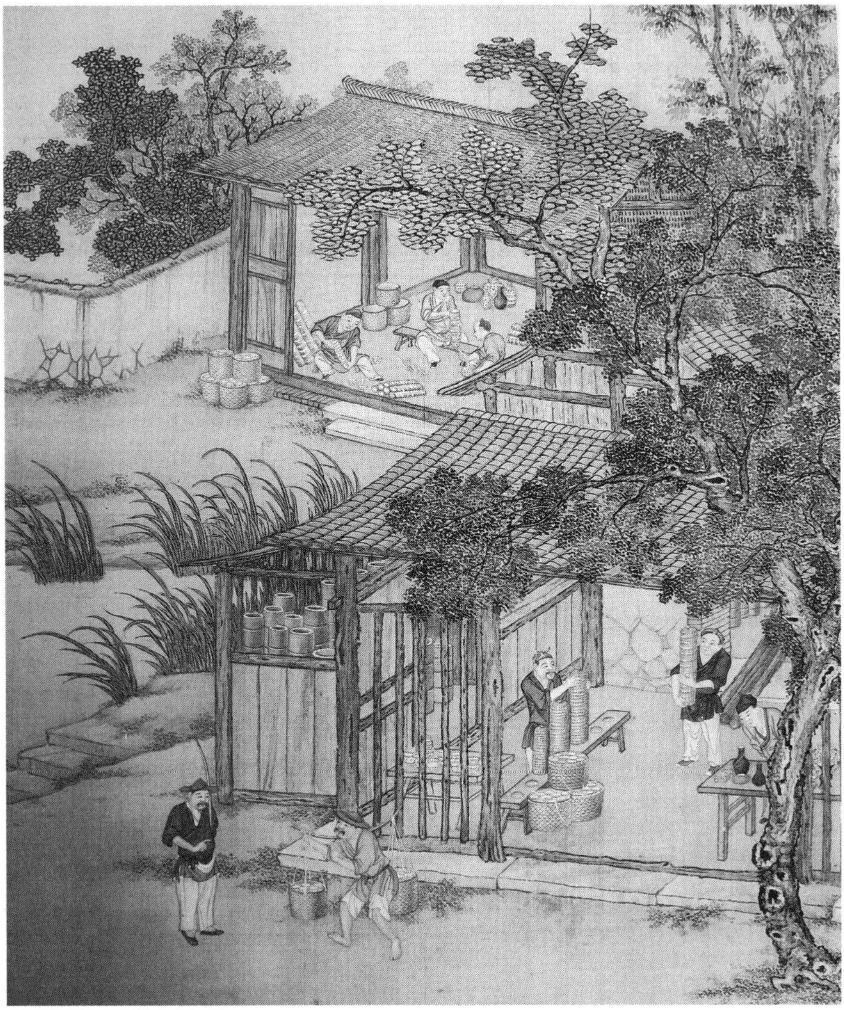

FIG. 3.4. Painting illustrating entry 19, "Wrapping in Straw and Packing in Casks" (Sucao zhuangtong), from the Qingwan album, *Illustrated Manual of Ceramic Production*, color on silk, 29 × 25 cm, private collection

to the performance of legitimacy. The display of classified products in the album reflects this fascination with order. The most prominent example is in the process of packing "molded wares" (*zhuoqi*) separately from round ware, shown in the nineteenth leaf of the Qingwan album (fig. 3.4).

Six molded wares are grouped together in the corner of a room in the upper part of this painting. In this room, two workers are stacking a dozen small blue-and-white round wares into a pile, tying them up with grass. In the room in the lower part of this picture, workers are piling second-rate round wares into baskets. Meanwhile, several large monochrome molded wares are laid out on a table for inspection. Accordingly, the textual description lists four types of packing, based on the quality of products.[57] Specialized packers (*zhuangtong jiang*) worked on first-class round wares and on first- and second-class molded wares. "The second-class round ware pieces are tied together in bundles of ten, called 'cylinders' [*tong*]."[58] The inferior wares are bundled in groups of forty, fifty, and even more. The difference in quality demands a micromanaged division of labor based on the skill of the packers.

This classification of skilled labor is represented in the painting and its textual description. Tang Ying stands at the top of the labor division and oversees production, keeping a close eye on expenses. To recoup part of the expense, he was responsible for selling defective products. The supervisors sent all products to the court until 1742, when the Qianlong emperor ordered Tang Ying to sell pieces of inferior quality at a discount in the local market.[59] The policy was finally established in early 1743, despite Tang Ying's repeated objections, about four months before he wrote this treatise. With one concise sentence, he includes this latest imperial regulation policy about defective wares: "All the third-rate pieces and inferior products are for local sale." There is no way to know where these pieces, some probably bearing imperial reign marks, eventually went, but they may have ended up in both domestic and overseas households.

The textual accounts and the albums of pictures are not straightforward instructions but carefully wrought discourses imbuing technological description with ideological rhetoric. The author ordered the topics to utilize visual art for communicating embodied experience. The text analytically expounds the body movements captured in the paintings. The text also narrows down the possible technical meanings of the gestures depicted and connects them with a linear rationale of the production process.

Throwing and Polishing the Shapes Forming the vessels was the most demanding procedure, requiring intensive labor along with many tacit skills. The potters had to take into account the shrinkage undergone during firing. Tang Ying highlights this thorny issue at the beginning of his fifth entry, while literati observer Song Yingxing skips this detail in his lengthy description of the throwing process of different round wares. There were no measuring tools or established formulas to accurately predict such contractions, yet an imperial commission required standardization. This calculation relied on the body of particularly experienced artisans:

> Artisans of this specialty must be familiar with the nature of kiln fire and clay so that they can calculate by adding and subtracting to build the mold. There are only two or three masters in the entire town of Jingdezhen.[60]

Then Tang Ying explains how several scenes in the Qingwan album capture the artisans' measurement and adjustment of the molds. Such explanations allow the viewer to differentiate between otherwise similar postures and tools, according to their functions.

The fifth leaf in the Qingwan album separates scenes of making molds and fixing molds (*xiumo*) into the upper and lower parts of the painting. A worker carries the preliminary mold from the workshop depicted in the upper part of the painting to another workshop for fixing (fig. 3.5).

In the upper right corner of this leaf, at a reduced scale according to perspective, two small figures are fashioning a round mold. A senior artisan in the lower workshop, as Tang Ying mentions, is giving advice about the appropriate measurement for fixing molds.

Differentiation—that is, careful classification of production, specialization, and tools—was an important centralizing strategy for articulating the otherwise tacit experience of local production, especially for the purpose of displaying control to both the emperor and the technocrats themselves. Tang Ying clarifies the two major categories of porcelain forms in the sixth and seventh entries, namely round wares (*yuanqi*) and molded wares. Round wares were distinguished from molded wares by the way they were formed rather by than their appearance.[61] The seventh entry indicates that molded wares also included some kinds of round-shaped vessels. Round wares and molded wares signify a difference in sophistication of the form, often related to height or size. A tall vessel, even one with a round shape, could not be formed on a wheel but had be molded in separated sections. Though all four albums represent the procedure of throwing round wares, the Qingwan album is the most accurate in delineating the specialization of craftsmen and tools:

> A wheel like a wooden table is fixed to a perpendicular axle so as to turn and revolve continuously. Then the thrown body is not too thick, too thin, or tilted. A carpenter repairs [the wheel] from time to time. Another workman puts the clay on the wheeled table. The craftsman who throws the body sits at the edge of the wheel compound and turns the wheel with a bamboo staff.[62]

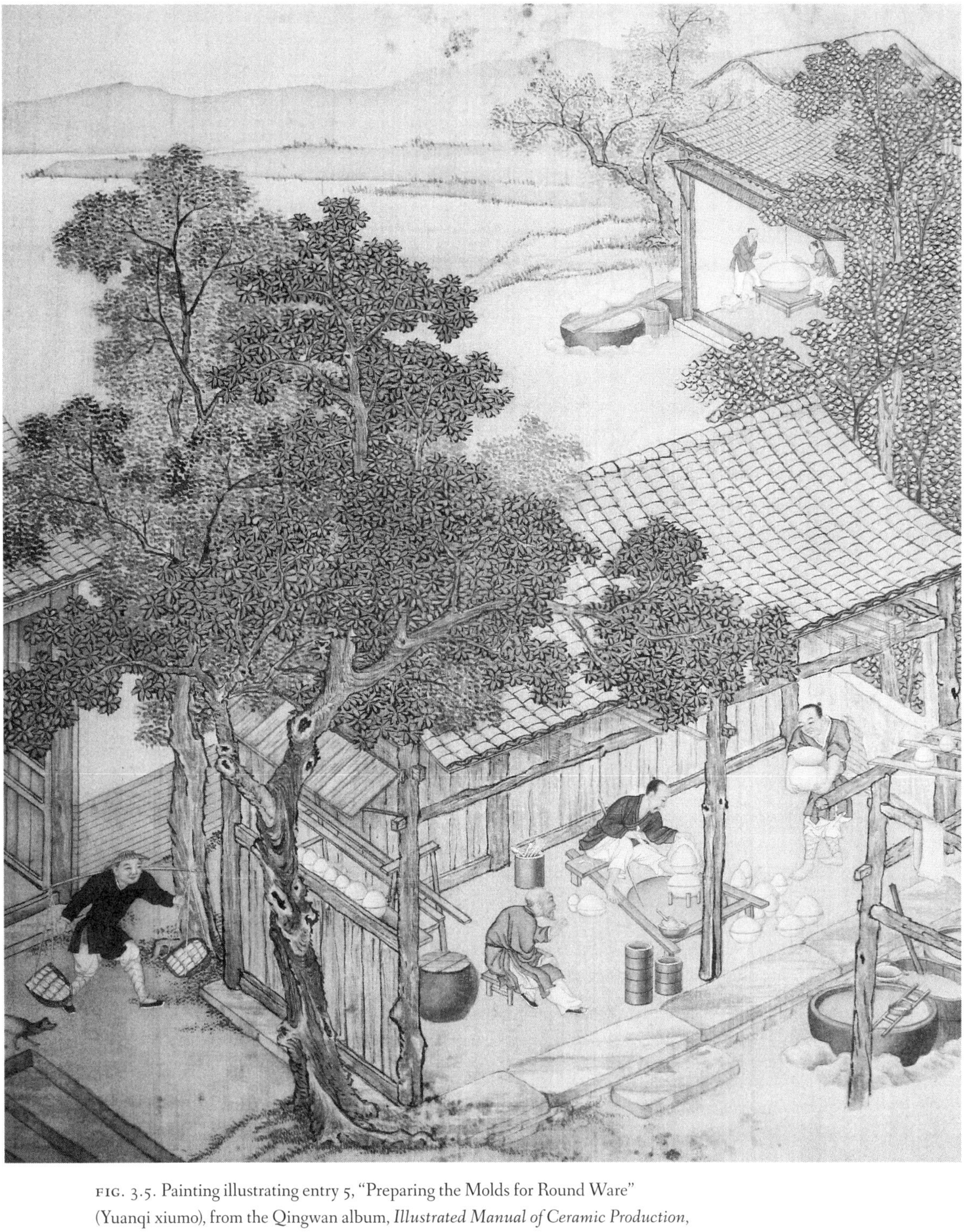

FIG. 3.5. Painting illustrating entry 5, "Preparing the Molds for Round Ware" (Yuanqi xiumo), from the Qingwan album, *Illustrated Manual of Ceramic Production*, color on silk, 29 × 25 cm, private collection

This description differentiates between the worker handling clay (*nijiang*), the worker throwing the body and turning the wheel with a bamboo staff, and the carpenter fixing the side of the wheel.[63]

The two main types of vessels that Tang Ying distinguished had their antecedents in previous supervisors' categorizations of porcelains in Jingdezhen. In the first extant technical treatise on porcelain production, Jiang Qi lists some kinds of porcelain in particular forms (bowl, plate, burner) according to their commercial potential in various regions.[64] Jiang Qi calls this the "kinds of vessels" (*qi zhi pinshu*). Song Yingxing classifies porcelains into two types, "molded ware" (*yinqi*) and "round ware" (*yuanqi*), which are very similar to Tang Ying's categorizations, although Tang Ying was much more specific about the types included in each category. The depiction of varieties of molded ware in the seventh leaf of the Qingwan album is so specific that we can recognize particular styles of glazes, including cracked and flambé (plate 10). *The Illustrated Manual* emphasizes that categorization of products and differentiation among tasks of cooperative labor were important for managing the division of labor.

Division of Labor in Decoration The painting album and written treatise indicate the division of labor and, more specifically, the leading role of specialized expertise. For instance, the eleventh leaf of the Qingwan album portrays compartmentalized workshops. Many craftsmen of different specialties in this painting are assembled around their table to work in a streamlined fashion (fig. 3.6).

The depiction stresses the crowded and busy workplace and the large quantity of almost identical small wares. There is no idle figure in the entire Qingwan album. Everyone is either diligently working or vigilantly overseeing. Tang Ying further describes the minute specialties into which labor could be divided and the demanding level of skills, which required years of training. The eleventh entry, "Painting the Round Ware in Blue and White," is most explicit about the rigorous division of skills:

> For this reason the craftsmen who draw the outlines only learn how to draw, not how to paint in colors. Those who fill in the colors do not learn to draw outlines. In this way, their hands become skilled at one task and their mind is not distracted. The outline drawers and painters are grouped separately. In a room, they ensure uniformity in their work.[65]

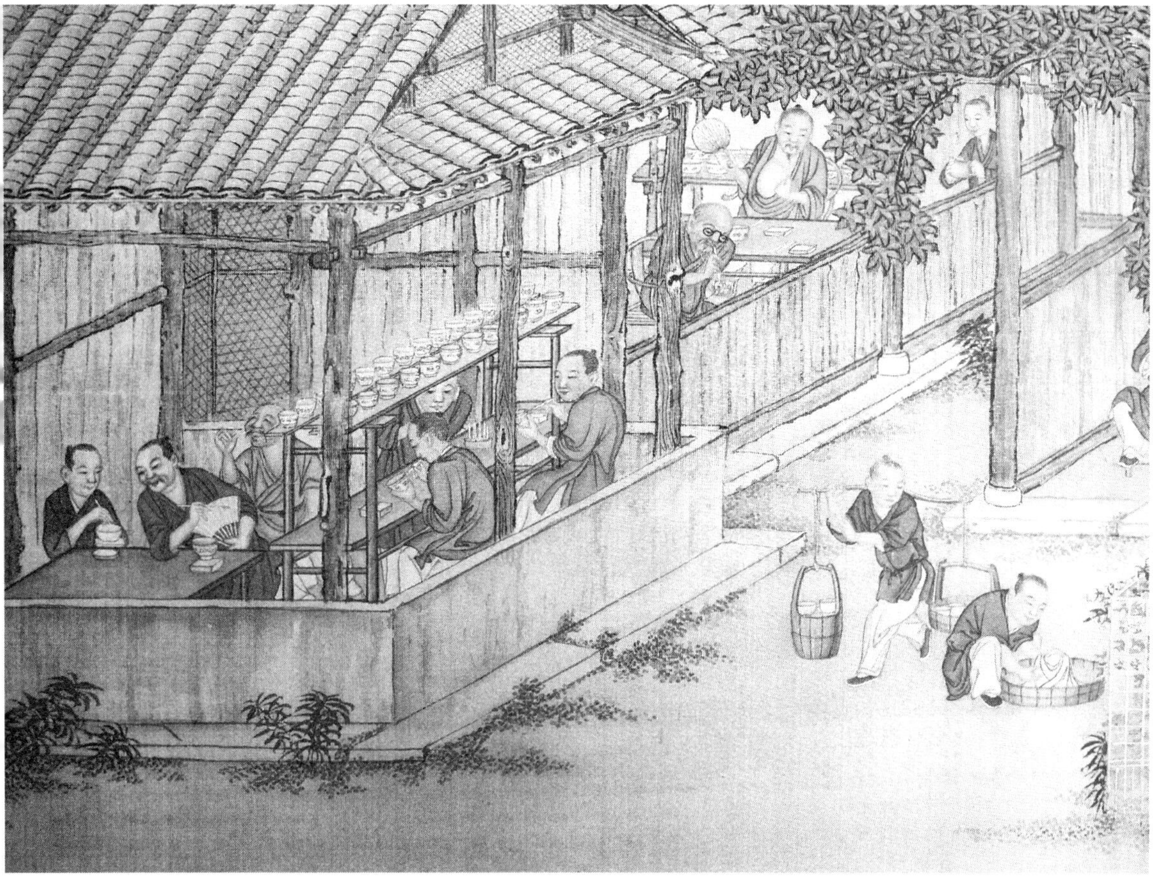

FIG. 3.6. Details from the painting illustrating entry 11, "Painting the Round Ware in Blue and White" (Yuanqi qinghua), from the Qingwan album, *Illustrated Manual of Ceramic Production*, color on silk, 25 × 29 cm, private collection

Some divisions were so demanding that only a handful of experts in the whole town were qualified for them, but the lower end of the labor pyramid mainly required quantity, so it provided opportunities for low-skilled manual workers.[66]

The division of labor increased efficiency in several aspects of porcelain production. It stressed dedicated training and ensured thorough mastery of a particular skill, and the stratification of groups according to their skills maximized the efficient mobilization of labor. This had an impact not only within the circuit of technological production but also in the town's general social organization, because the division of labor in porcelain production extended its structuring force in the wider market economy. Besides the craftsmen, this system of labor division also integrated traders and small business owners. In the eighth entry about collecting cobalt blue, the author points out that merchants (*fanzhe*) carried raw materials from the mountains to the manufactory. In other words, the supply and transport of raw cobalt blue was commercialized, just like many other links in the production chain. There were specialized households to pick and rank cobalt blue, as explained in the ninth entry: "After the cobalt blue is collected, it needs to be graded. The household of cobalt color [*liaohu*] is specialized in this."[67] The fifteenth entry notes, "When porcelain bodies are finished, they are put into saggers and dispatched to households equipped with kilns." This signifies that the owners of private kilns were contracted by the Imperial Porcelain Manufactory to fire imperial wares. Thus the imperial kilns' operation was enmeshed in local society and economy. As mediated by Supervisor Tang, the production of imperial porcelains was an enterprise that mobilized local resources and labor while taking advantage of technological and mercantile exchange networks.

QUANTIFYING FLUID GLAZING AND MARKING

The textual descriptions of the paintings also provide crucial information about quantity. The thirteenth and fourteenth entries, about the final fashioning of the porcelain bodies, include numerical measurements.

Before firing the decorated porcelain, workers needed to apply glaze on the surface. This layer of liquid would vitrify into a glass-like surface and protect the underglazed decoration from shedding, while also strengthening the overall piece. The content and evenness of the glaze would determine the level of transparency or translucency and affect the symmetrical form of the entire body. Tang Ying gives descriptions of three techniques used to improve evenness when glazing, one of which, "glaze blowing," contains some quantitative information:

> The larger round vessels are glazed by blowing. A bamboo tube is cut to one inch thick and some seven inches long, the mouth is covered with a fine gauze, which is dipped into the glaze, then this is blown through the tube from the other end.[68]

The numbers are sparse, but they help the reader imagine the length of the bamboo straw and the numerous rounds of effort required to even out the liquid's application. Tang Ying uses numbers economically but practically, compared to the fastidious enumeration in the archival documents and lists in *Works of Heaven and the Inception of Things*. Each number in his *Illustrated Manual* helps the reader understand a certain standard in the procedure. A good example, on how to make liquid glaze, is given in the third entry, "Burning the Ashes and Preparing the Glaze" (Lianhui peiyou). The glaze is composed of porcelain clay and a kind of ash made from a mixture of burned green-white (*qingbai*) rock, phoenix-tail fern (*fengwei cao*), and water. Tang Ying provides numerical proportions to clarify the recipes for products of different quality:

> A curved wooden stick is passed through the ears of a little iron pot called a *pen* to pour a quantity of the material. The best glaze is made of 10 *pen* of paste and 1 *pen* of ashes. Medium glazes are made of 7 or 8 *pen* of paste and 2 or 3 of ashes, and inferior glazes are made of equal parts of each or with excess ashes.[69]

The little iron pot (*pen*) thus becomes a measuring unit. Unlike contemporaneous European porcelain manufacture, which was fascinated with quantitative arcana and detailed recipes, the craftsmen and supervisors in Jingdezhen recorded the proportions of materials via units of the local standard measuring pot.

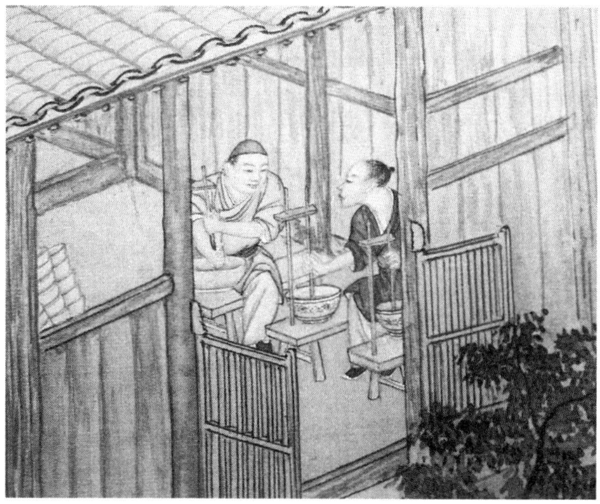

FIG. 3.7. Details from the painting illustrating entry 10, "Molding the Body and Grinding the Colors" (Yinpi ruliao), from the Qingwan album, *Illustrated Manual of Ceramic Production*, color on silk, 25 × 29 cm, private collection

Tools carry technical information and help illustrate the productive process, so the technocratic description of the structure of tools always stresses them in action—that is, in the context of the craftsmen's postures and gestures. Tools are a quantifying standard. For instance, the first half of the tenth entry, "Molding the Body and Grinding the Colors" (Yinpi ruliao) explains how to calibrate the shape of porcelain bodies:

> After the paste has been thrown into a body and been dried, [the craftsman] covers the finishing mold over it and presses gently with his hand until the clay body is regular and even. It is then taken out and dried in the shade, so as to be ready to be finally smoothed with a knife.[70]

The author employs a wide range of verbs to describe how the workers operated their tools. The workshop in the upper left corner houses two craftsmen working on a mortar system to grind the minerals (fig. 3.7).

The text points out that the mortar is placed on a low bench, and the pestle is

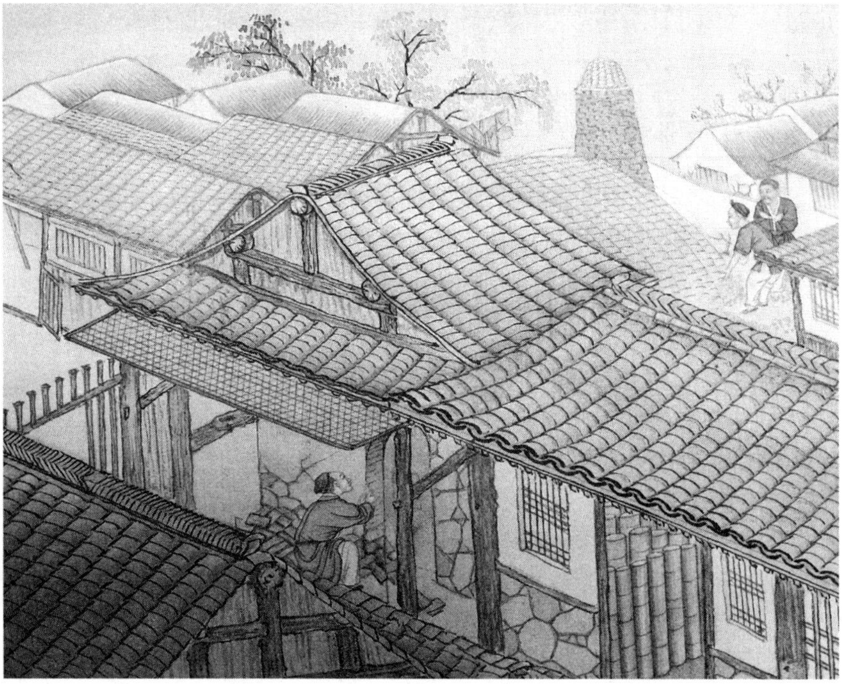

FIG. 3. 8. Detail of chimney, kiln, kiln shed, and bricks, from the painting illustrating entry 15, "Putting the Finished Wares into the Kiln" (Chengpi ruyao), from the Qingwan album, *Illustrated Manual of Ceramic Production*, color on silk, 25 × 29 cm, private collection

attached to a horizontal piece of wood, which is supported by an upright wooden pole fixed on the bench.[71] This textual description alone could be too abstract for a reader to visualize the tools. The pairing of text and image in this album affirms the illustrative power of painting.

IMAGINING THE STRUCTURE OF THE KILN

Painting is particularly effective for articulating the spatial relations between parts of tools or auxiliary settings such as the kiln site. The fifteenth and sixteenth painting leaves in the Qingwan album record the beginning and the completion of the firing procedure. The fifteenth leaf, "Putting the Finished Wares into the Kiln," depicts a detailed kiln complex with a chimney and "kiln shed" (*yaopeng*), a building that has a tiled roof like that of a house covering the kiln (fig. 3.8). The kiln is shaped like an upturned water jar. All of these components, painted on the upper part of this leaf, are described in the treatise.

Without looking at the pictorial portrayal, it would be hard to imagine the actual spatial relations, which are missing from the textual description. The treatise describes the kiln's interior in use:

> When loading the kiln, the wares are packed in saggers and placed in lines, leaving a space between them for the flames to pass through. The fire is distinguished as front, middle, and back. The front fire is fierce, the middle less intense, and the back fire gentle. According to the character of the glaze, porcelains are put in appropriate positions in the kiln.[72]

Tang Ying explains both the layout of the porcelains contained in saggers and the spatial distribution of heat inside the chamber. Among the three texts addressing the firing process, only Tang Ying's treatise discusses the appropriate positioning of specific kinds of glazed ware. The section about firing in Jiang Qi's *Notes on Ceramics* is primarily concerned with taxes:

> The length of the kiln is measured by *yong*. The government measures the size to decide its tax. . . . After the clay shapes are put into saggers, they are stacked and sorted out. The craftsmen properly arrange their placement in the kiln. This is called "loading the kiln" [*zhangyao*].[73]

The section in *Great Gazetteer of the Jiangxi Province* prioritizes the distinction between the official kiln (*guanyao*) and private kilns (*minyao*), and only describes the arrangement inside private kilns. The difference between these texts is that Tang transcribes a more comprehensive and detailed observation. He also addresses details specific to regional manufacture. For example, the painting depicts a pile of bricks used to seal the kiln. The treatise points out that "the entrance of the kiln is bricked up except for a square hole. [The craftsmen] keep throwing in firewood without pausing until the saggers in the kiln turn silver red." This was how workers estimated the temperature inside the kilns. Tang observed production techniques, because such specificity showed his mastery and control. Tang repeatedly referred to local craftsmen as "native of the land" (*turen*), acknowledging their embodied knowledge and their specific geographical region.

Tang Ying did not write about finances for production as he documented accounting details in his memorials and regulation standards, which are worthy of a study on their own. In this sense, his writings are thematically specialized. The illustrated treatise exemplifies his archival and quasi-ethnographical approach.

CEREMONY

The last entry in the treatise records the theocratic conflation of local craftsmen's worship of a ceramic deity and the imperial sanction, reflecting a unique organizational aspect of manufacture. The twentieth entry, "Worshipping the Deity and Rewarding the Fulfilled Wish," starts by introducing the porcelain town of Jingdezhen from a bird's-eye view.[74] In fifty-six words, this entry summarizes the town's geopolitical position, natural environment, scale and dynamic of local industry and commerce, and labor force. Tang Ying points out that "for the success of production, [local people] are keen to worship."[75] Because of the unpredictability of kiln firing, local craftsmen held rituals to plead for kindness from the deity and made offerings to him after successfully completing production. The ritual that took place in Jingdezhen was not a general sacrifice to a Buddhist or a Taoist god, as the deity of trade came into being through a specific event and was consecrated in the previous dynasty. The entry briefly narrates how a certain potter, Tong Bin, immolated himself in the kiln to protect his townsmen from a eunuch-supervisor's punishment for their failure to produce an imperial commission.[76] The legend states that the self-immolation of the brave potter led to successful production thereafter. Then, the official manager of the manufactory (*sishi zhe*) built a shrine inside thc imperial manufactory and gave the deity a title. In the next sentence, Tang Ying justifies this ritual practice: "Up till now, [the deity] has shown his efficacy a couple of times. The potters reverently make offerings to him without fail. They even hire theatrical troupes and musicians to celebrate him together."[77] This official sanction of Tong Bin strategically claimed regulative power for the artisanal organization and prevented social unrest. In other words, the ceremony, composed of worshipping ritual and theatrical performance, was the major venue for ensuring the solidarity of the laborers in Jingdezhen. It provided an occasion for craftsmen to convene and mark the end of a production cycle.

INSTEAD OF ABSORBING INFORMATION from previous texts, Tang Ying preferred to observe techniques and communicate with craftsmen *in situ*. He used numbers selectively, along with texts and images, in a generic convention known as "pictures and explanations" (*tushuo*), which could broadly include illustrated treatises ranging from explanations of metaphysical diagrams to discussions of flowers in poetry since the Song dynasty. In the late imperial period, a few eminent treatises of this *tushuo* genre seem to have used historical or ethnographic information to serve a didactic purpose.[78] A comparable example is the contemporary ethnographic exposition *Illustrated Treatise on Yi Barbarians* (Dianyi tushuo), compiled by a similar bannerman technocrat, Gao Qizhuo (1676–1738), who played a vital role in the bureaucratization of local ethnic chieftains on the southwest frontier.

Tang Ying's treatise on porcelain production took advantage of the media channels of texts and images, yet it was bounded by imperial ideology and available categories of earth, fire, shapes, and numbers before these subjects became geology, pyrotechnics, geometry, and arithmetic in our modern epistemic framework. The major narrative strategies used to construct this narrative derive from the ethnographic and archivist approaches common to the technocratic way of making knowledge. Tang deployed texts, images, and kiln tools to absorb regional knowledge of production and arranged the relevant materials, products, and labor types in order by ranking and quantifying them. The comparison with earlier documentary texts and contemporary albums about porcelain production reveals how Tang collected local knowledge and organized it within the apparatus of the Qing empire's intelligence service.

In the strictly controlled Imperial Porcelain Manufactory, what kind of technical change could technocrats engage in, and how would that be accommodated or rejected by the system? What happened when the supervisors and emperors disagreed? The next chapter explores these questions by considering the negotiation of decorum that took place in technical experiments of porcelain production.

FOUR

Innovations and Experiments in Porcelain Manufacture

THE INSTITUTIONALIZATION of technical expertise in the Qing court merged technical implementation with political control by appointing technocrats to proactively intervene in industrial production and extract local knowledge in the process. Apart from the shared technical language among technocrats, the court judged the appropriateness of artistic forms, which delimited technocrats' technical and aesthetic choices, thus shaping a unique knowledge culture. The sheer number of imperial commissions of porcelain for everyday use, ceremonies, and diplomacy posed unprecedented demands on artistic forms, the realization of which depended not only on the efficient communication of design but also on the shrewd handling of raw materials, tools, and firing procedures. When the court was the largest client in the market, bannermen technocrats exerted political dominance in local society.

Imperial control did not necessarily lead to a shrinking inventory of artistic forms; in fact, the opposite appeared to be the case in the stylistic development of porcelain in the Qing court. Yet both the imperial design system and the technocratic experimentation undertaken to achieve such designs aimed to reduce uncertainty in yielding the desired products. Examination of extant porcelains sheds light on the technocrat's work in visualizing imperial power through manufacturing porcelain. The porcelains and related archival documents exhibit the extent to which the political control and mastery of technique could shape aesthetic forms, and how one technocrat monitored thousands of workers to manufacture tens of thousands of porcelains according to imperial decorum.

This impersonal, massive production evokes the issue of complex authorship. In most cases, we cannot decisively attribute specific pieces to the chief supervisor, since they were made by a system where different makers assumed agency. Yet among thousands of local craftsmen, the supervisor took the lead. Tang Ying's intensive hands-on experience in manufacture distinguished him from late Ming literati taste-makers who mainly wrote about art and spread their opinions through their communication networks.[1] Porcelain supervisors as designers were similar to artists like Chen Hongshou (1599–1652) and Xiao Yuncong (1596–1673), who were simultaneously poets and painters, and also worked in the design of woodblock prints.[2] As hands-on polymaths, the porcelain supervisor and these artists shared experience in extracting images and moving them across media, though they infused drastically different political meaning into their designs.[3] The difference between the late Ming designers and those in the high Qing era lies in the central institutionalization in the latter period.[4] Tang Ying's articulation of manufactured categories and related experiments showcases the substantive intervention of the imperial state in industrial production.

By matching extant porcelain pieces with specific archival documents referring to Tang Ying, we may reconstruct the industrial process used to manufacture specific categories of porcelain. These categories were conveniently inventoried in Tang Ying's *Report on the Accomplishment of Porcelains* (Taocheng jishi bei ji; 1735) for the Yongzheng reign, and *Regulation and Precedents of the Production Cost* (Zhijia zeli zhangcheng ce; 1747) for the Qianlong reign, as well as mentioned in the *Illustrated Manual of Ceramic Production.*[5] Compared to the governmental documents on porcelain manufacture of the Song, Yuan, and Ming dynasties, the number of categories and the types of categorization dramatically increased in these two important inventories as well as in the supervisor's treatise, the budget plan, and numerous managerial memorials of the mid-Qing period. The first type of porcelain classification in Tang Ying's reports is technical—that is, usually based on glaze, but sometimes on forms, decoration techniques, or the reign period when a particular design excelled. Tang Ying's *Report on the Accomplishment of Porcelains* lists fifty-seven categories of designed porcelain successfully produced during the Yongzheng reign.[6] The list predominantly focuses on the technology of glaze and the surface decoration of porcelain pieces, rather than whether they were round wares or molded wares. Yet the categorization of technical innovations is by no means only technical.

The categorization of technical innovations is also inherently value laden, since ceramic production included the imitation of archaic and foreign styles to legitimize the current rulership. Classification involving imitation of old styles (*fangjiu*) versus new designs (*zhaoxin*) included crucial categories within which the supervisor summarized accomplishments in porcelain design and experimentation in the early to mid-Qing periods.[7] "Imitation of the old should follow the classic and elegant styles. To create new styles one must investigate the source. The vessel is made of pottery. All of the measurements honor the ancient standard. . . . Color brushes bring life to flowers. The production of porcelain can attest to civilization."[8] This statement expressed the principles of imitating the old and initiating the new: ceramic replicas aimed to duplicate both the symbolic status and the proper virtuoso skill of the imitated wares. The word *dian* (classic) originally meant "laws" or "canon," and therefore to "follow the classic" means to follow imperial decorum closely. However, as the archival documents and extant pieces show, such replication hardly aimed to produce an exact copy. In order to emulate but surpass the porcelain of previous dynasties and to distinguish themselves through their own excellent vessels, the emperors commanded Tang Ying to make modifications in the process of appropriating old styles. The imitation of old styles almost never led to recovering a lost technique. Rather, the goal was to appropriate extant forms, glazes, and decoration through trials of new techniques. On the one hand, replication of the old styles might indeed have required technological innovation, just as the imitation of foreign styles does. On the other hand, the inception of the new (*zhaoxin*) in form and glaze was not viewed as an unprecedented creation of genius, but rather emerged from archived experiments based on an existing repertoire, the "source" of the old and foreign styles. This historicized notion of innovation provides an antidote to the modern innovation myth.[9] Some of the new forms and decorations showed spectacular Eurasian cultural encounters and indispensable technical experiments. That technical and artistic changes took place in a tightly controlled institution challenges us to reexamine historicized concepts of innovation and experiment.[10]

New Design: Selection and Combination

New colors of glazes and overglaze palettes were the most important innovation in the Qing Imperial Porcelain Manufactory. Dozens of previously unseen colors and decorative styles resulted from the introduction of European art pigments and painting styles. One stunning example is the pink or "rouge" color, which had never been used to decorate porcelain in China but appeared in the late Kangxi reign.[11] It is also listed as "vessels in Western red color" (*xiyang hongse qimin*) in the 1735 *Report*.[12] The pink glazed cups in the National Palace Museum exhibit tiny gold sprinkles if magnified two hundred times under a microscope, and it is plausible that this colorant was connected to a recent European technique (plate 11).[13] The Qing emperors' interest in incorporating European materials, techniques, and styles was integral to their ambition to masquerade—to present themselves in the cultural identities of all ethnic groups in the empire, an empire they considered to be universal.[14] Among their myriad art patronage, Qing emperors' sustained fascination with the production of local *falang* enamel—pigments based on melted glass frits to imitate European enameling technique—is the most telling example of their ambition to control and retool regional resources as well as emulate the foreign.[15]

The category of *falang* enamel on porcelain has been mystified by a century's connoisseurial terminology, which has caused much confusion about essentially a kind of low-fired overglaze pigment carrying glass frits in it.[16] However, publication of the imperial archive in 2005 allowed scholars to identify the commission and production process of quite a few extant enameled porcelains, some of which even had their type names inscribed on the original containers.[17] Further assisted by modern scientific analysis, scholars now can, to some extent, distinguish the subcategories of these enameled porcelains and use their names, such as *falangcai*, *yangcai*, *fencai*, and *famille rose* while being aware of the historical circumstances under which these terms were used.[18] For the purpose of examining Tang's and other supervisors' role in the technical experiments, only the difference between *falangcai* and *yangcai* is relevant. Both terms appear in the archive, and the difference between them implies the development and geographical distribution of this technique.

EXPERIMENTS ON *FALANG* ENAMEL AT THE QING COURT

Three generations of Qing emperors—Kangxi, Yongzheng, and Qianlong—were extremely interested in the technique of painted enamel and the related glass industry. To emulate painted enamel artifacts imported from Europe, they competed in experimenting and boasted about Qing products.[19] As a limited but critical part of the history of this technique in the Qing dynasty, Supervisor Tang Ying mediated between the court and the regional manufactory in Jingdezhen in the development of *falang* enamel technique and the transfer of this technique into the *yangcai* (lit., "foreign colored") enamel technique, which flourished primarily in Jingdezhen.

The experiments with *falang* enamel started in the Kangxi reign. Many Jesuit missionaries, like Jean de Fontaney (1643–1710), Joachim Bouvet (1656–1730), and Jean-François Gerbillon (1654–1707), reported the imperial demand for

European enameled wares and European technicians skilled in this decorative technique.[20] A glass factory inside the Forbidden City built with the assistance of Jesuit missionaries was pivotal for the early stages of the regional production of the glass-like enamel technology, because the glass frit in the pigment of *falang* enamel fundamentally differentiated it from other mineral pigments.[21] Although the Qing court could import pigment, many procedures required for enameling—including determining the right medium, application, and kiln firing—had not yet been mastered. By the late 1710s, with imported enamel pigments as well as the help of artisans visiting from overseas who were recruited in Guangzhou, the court claimed to have achieved considerable success.[22] However, Kangxi and his son, Yongzheng, did not stop seeking European experts in this technology. It took several more years before the court workshops could produce pigment for enameling on their own. Tang Ying was closely involved in the trials that led to this breakthrough.

These experiments and enameled ware production were probably being carried out from the 1690s in the Imperial Workshops within the framework of the Imperial Household Department.[23] Tang Ying started work in the department in 1698, so he might have already participated in this research during the late Kangxi reign. The imperial archive attests to his service in the Imperial Workshops at the very beginning of the Yongzheng reign. He was already a skilled designer and oversaw several commissions of *falang* enameled wares and glass between 1723 and 1727.[24] In contrast to a worker in the regional workshops, a bannerman technocrat followed the entire process of carrying out commissioned projects, to acquire experience with a certain material or technology rather than narrowly focusing on a single technical procedure. In Tang Ying's case, he gradually obtained knowledge related to different aspects of *falang* enamel. First, he was given the opportunity to handle and observe the raw primary materials:

> On YZ 4/11/1 (1726) . . . the bureau director Haiwang carried out four pieces of *falang* [pigment] in four colors (weight 116 *liang*) and gave it to vice director Tang Ying to make *falang* [pigment] according to the imperial order.[25]

These chunks of *falang* pigment were imported. Second, he kept track of the flow of funding and materials used in the experiment to create indigenous *falang* enamel:

> On the YZ 6/1/22 [1728], vice directors Shen Yu and Tang Ying said that the funding and raw materials that Prince Yi had ordered to try to make *falang* pig-

ment should be recorded separately. Archive the [use of funding and materials] after the experiment is accomplished and reported![26]

Like many other archival records, this indicates that a technocrat's apprenticeship involved engagement with commissioned projects, especially their fiscal and logistical aspects. After he left court, fiscal management continued to be a dimension of his career.[27] The record also confirms that he actively participated in the experiments to make enamel materials at the Qing court.

The application of enamel is anything but straightforward, so Tang Ying must have acquired knowledge through trial and error. A designer of enameled patterns should have some knowledge of the firing process. Since the enamel pigments transform under several rounds of firing, they require a proper medium when painters apply them. The temperature of 600–800°C, though not as high as the first firing, still affects a porcelain body and its interface with an enamel pigment. As a designer instead of a *falang* specialist or ceramic expert, Tang Ying must have accumulated knowledge when he was ordered to revise or remake some *falang* enameled pieces in the first six years of the Yongzheng reign (1722–28). On the 3rd day of the 5th month in the 8th year during the Yongzheng reign (1727), Tang Ying and his colleague Shen Yu were ordered to oversee production of a golden statue of Avalokiteśvara Bodhisattva and two bronze statues of the attendants Sudhanakumâra and Dragon Girl. Both attendants were decorated with enamel. Prince Yi, the head of the entire Imperial Workshops, complained that "Avalokiteśvara Bodhisattva's face is slightly joyless. The drapery on the clothes is not properly painted. Redo it accordingly."[28] He also ordered them to use ivory to make the attendants instead of bronze—not an easy task. Prince Yi passed away three years later, but the institutional mechanism enforced the plans until the commission was accomplished and recorded in a clear paper trail in 1736. This is one case among at least a dozen commissions for *falang* enameled wares that Tang Ying oversaw for this short period during his years as an apprentice. The variety of material production in which Tang Ying was involved at court allowed him to experience different production methods, in contrast to the repetition that strengthened strict specialization among local craftsmen in Jingdezhen.

The breakthrough in making local enamel pigment at court was recorded in the 6th month of the 6th year during the Yongzheng reign (1728), when Tang Ying was still working in the Imperial Workshops in the Forbidden City. On the 12th day of that month, the artisans in the Imperial Workshops successfully im-

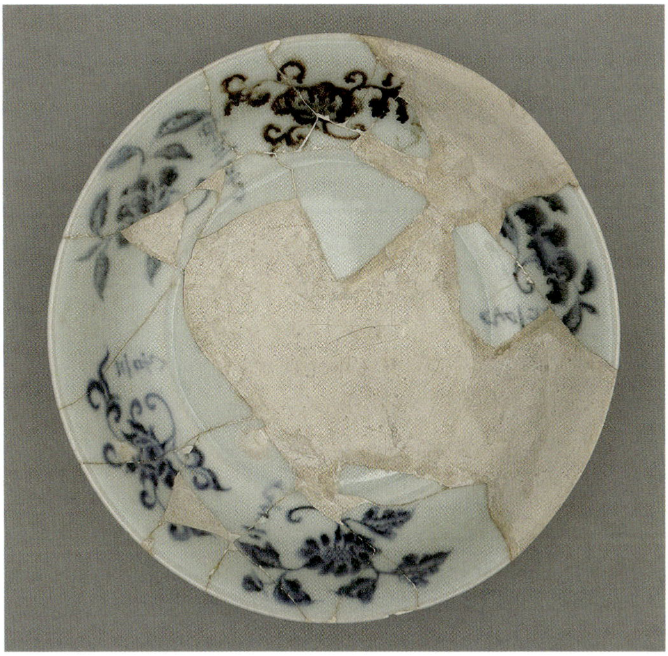

PLATE 1. Blue-and-white porcelain shards, decorated with floral patterns and inscriptions in different shades of cobalt color, dated to the Xuande reign (1426–35), height: 3.9 cm, diameter of mouth: 17.6 cm, diameter of foot: 11.2 cm, excavated from Pearl Hill (Zhushan) in 1993, in Jingdezhen, in Ceramic Archaeological Institute, Jiangxi province

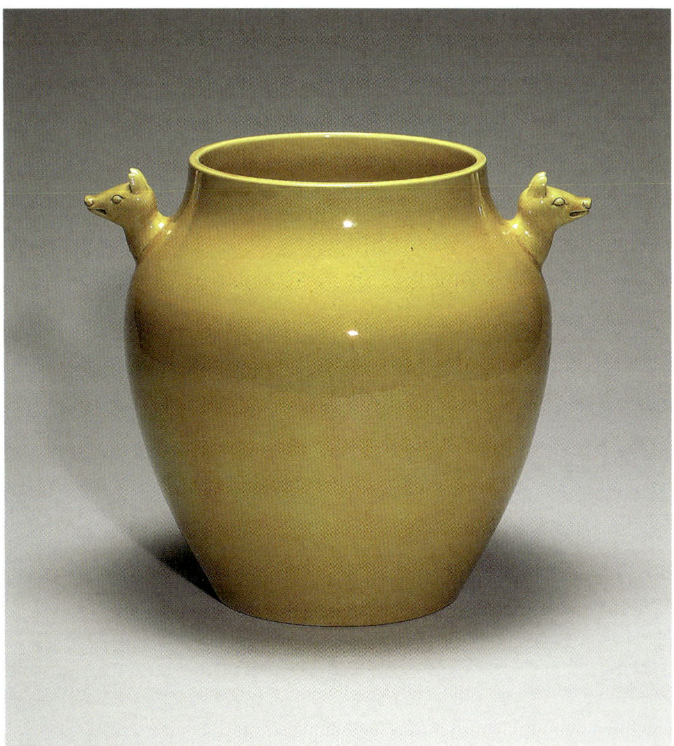

PLATE 2. *Zun* porcelain vase in yellow glaze, dated to 1736–48, height: 28.3 cm, diameter of mouth: 19 cm, diameter of foot: 15.8 cm, in National Palace Museum, Taipei

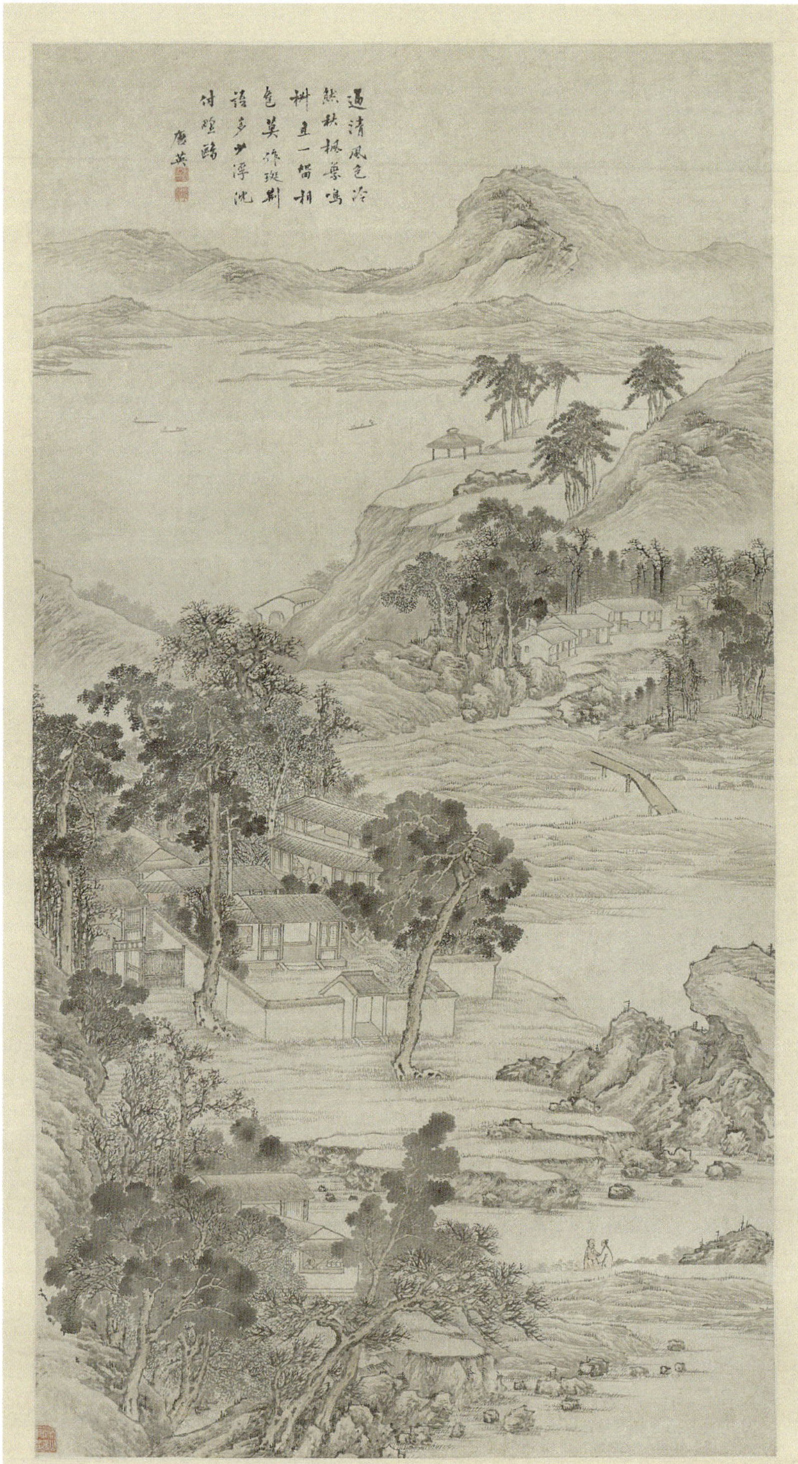

PLATE 3. Landscape painting, hanging scroll, ink and color on paper, inscribed with Tang Ying's poem, signature, and seals, 165 × 89 cm, in Palace Museum, Beijing

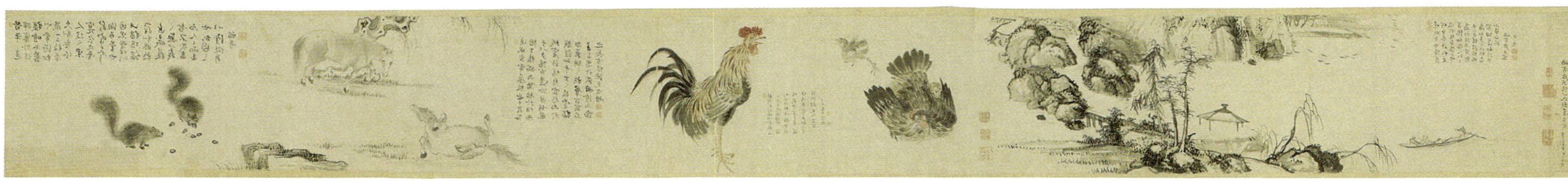

PLATE 4. Handscroll painting of miscellaneous subjects, ink and color on paper, inscribed with Tang Ying's poem, signature, and seals, 29.4 × 288 cm, in Palace Museum, Beijing

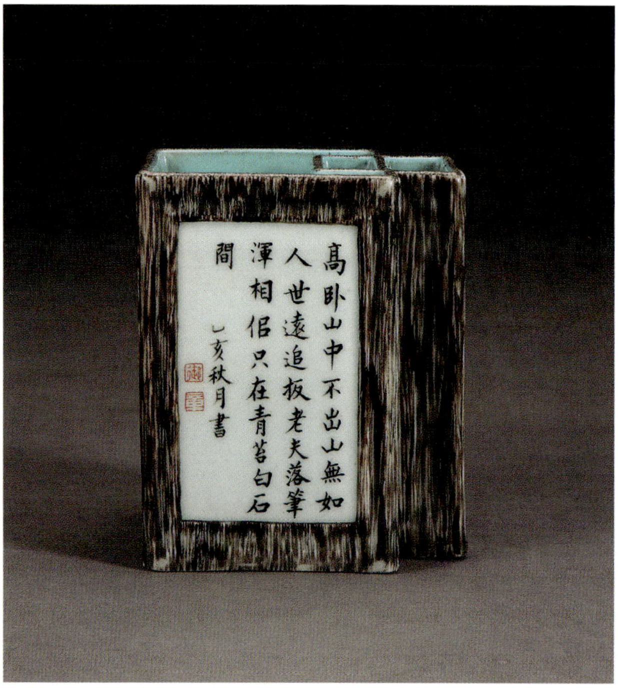

PLATE 5. Porcelain writing-brush holder fashioned by interlocking two square holders (*above*), decorated with black enamel and black calligraphy in cartouche, dated to the Qianlong reign, and bottom mark (*right*), height: 11.5 cm, diameter: 7.5 cm, diameter of foot: 4.5 cm, in Palace Museum, Beijing

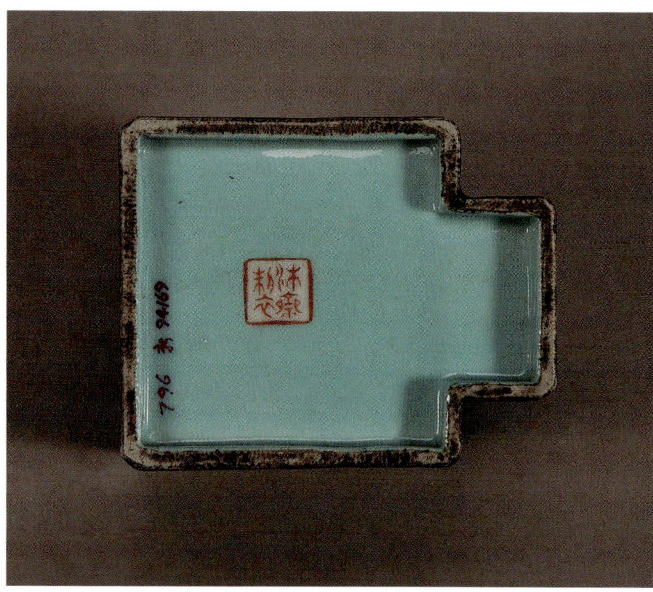

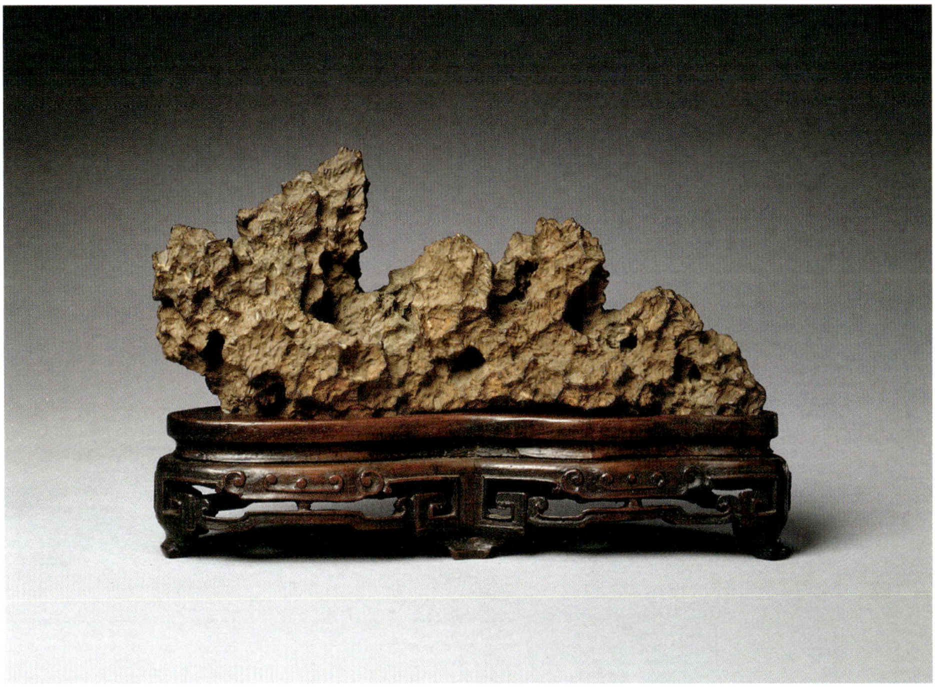

PLATE 6. Porcelain brush rest in the shape of a fancy rock, porcelain on wooden stand, with Tang Ying's signature, 4 × 12.3 cm, in Palace Museum, Beijing

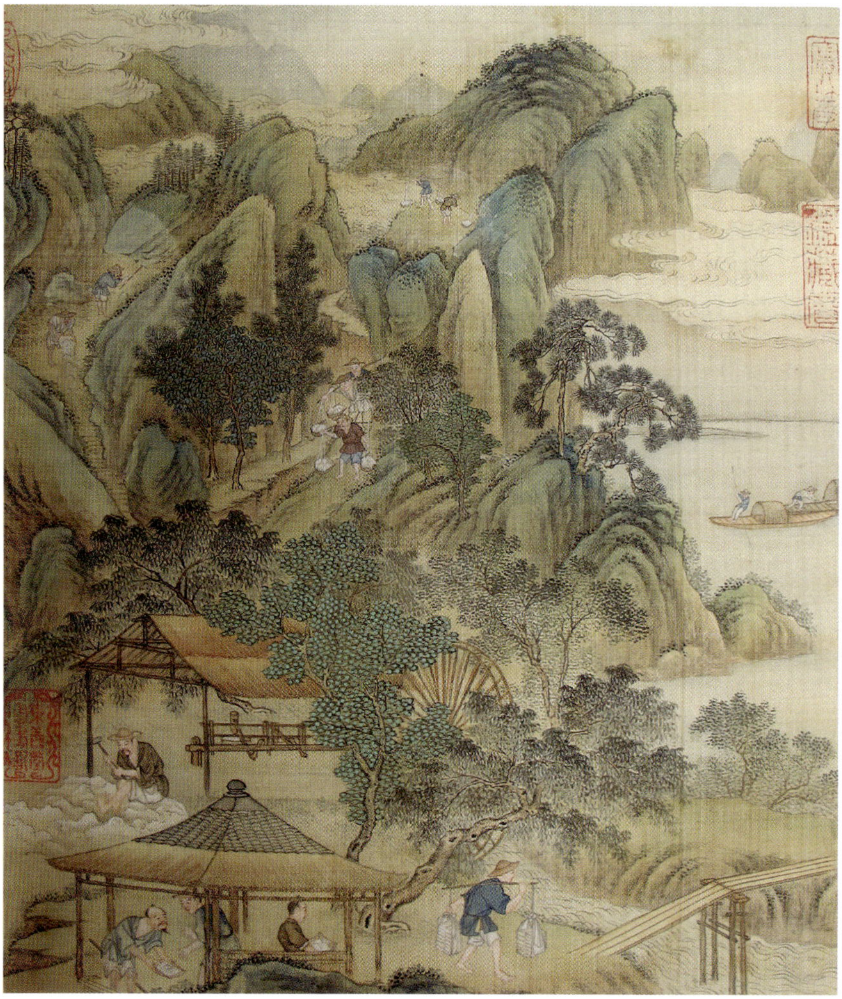

PLATE 7. Painting illustrating entry 1, "Collection of the Stones and Fabrication of the Paste," (Caishi zhini), from the Qingwan album, *Illustrated Manual of Ceramic Production*, color on silk, 29 × 25 cm, private collection

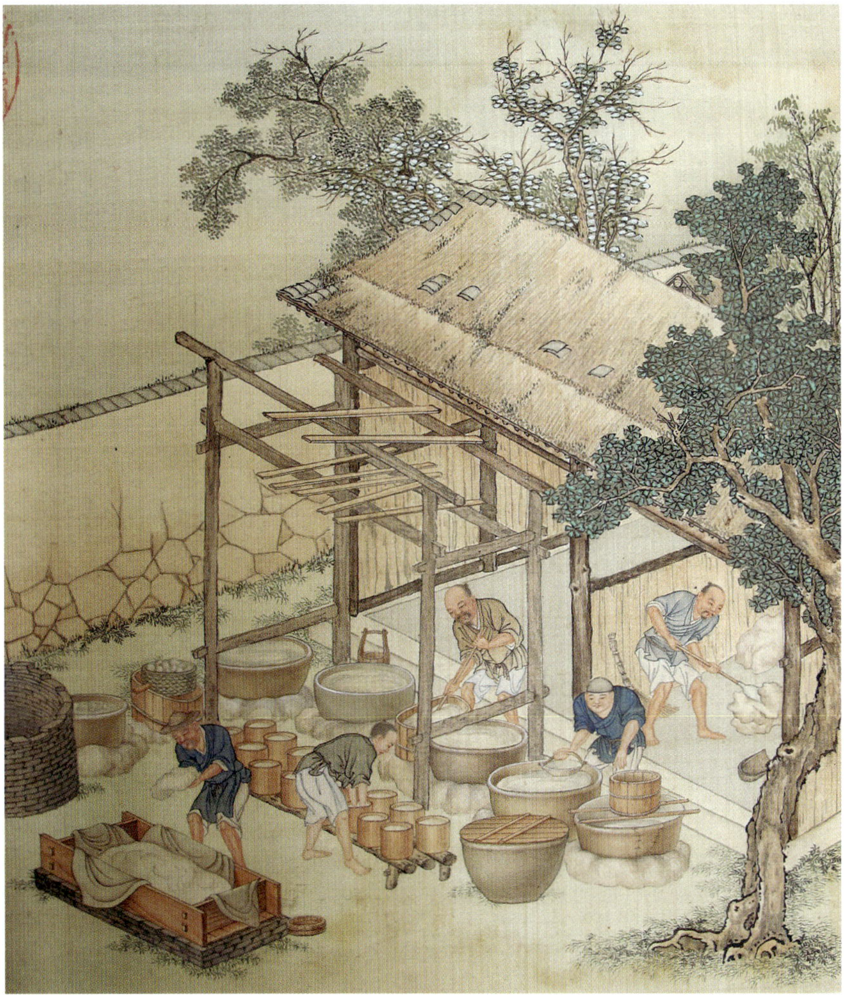

PLATE 8. Painting illustrating entry 2, "Washing and Purification of the Paste" (Taolian nitu), from the Qingwan album, *Illustrated Manual of Ceramic Production*, color on silk, 29 × 25 cm, private collection

PLATE 9. Porcelain Covered Globular Jar with Decoration of Flowers, Butterflies, Rocks, and Lingzhi Fungus, height: 10.9 cm, diameter: 13.2 cm, reign mark: *daming chenghua nian zhi* (made in the Chenghua reign of the great Ming dynasty), in Harvard Art Museums / Arthur M. Sackler Museum, Bequest of Samuel C. Davis

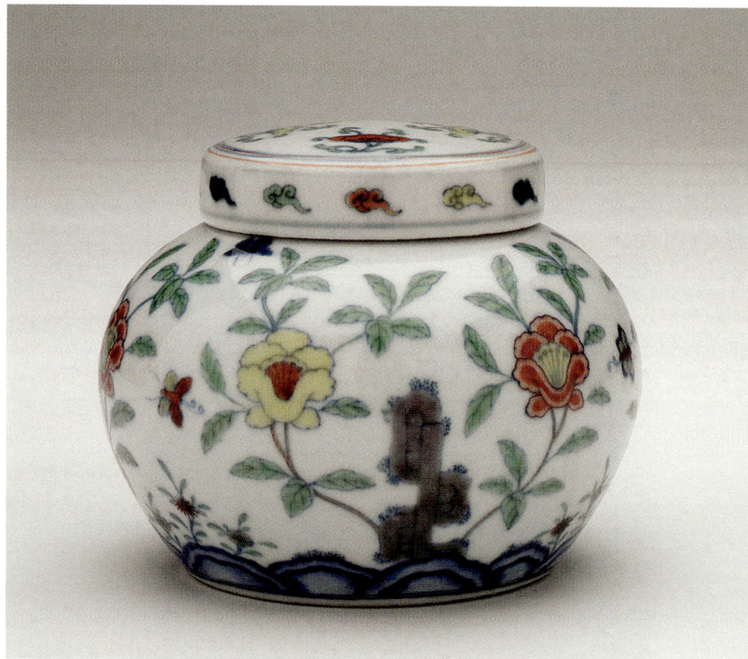

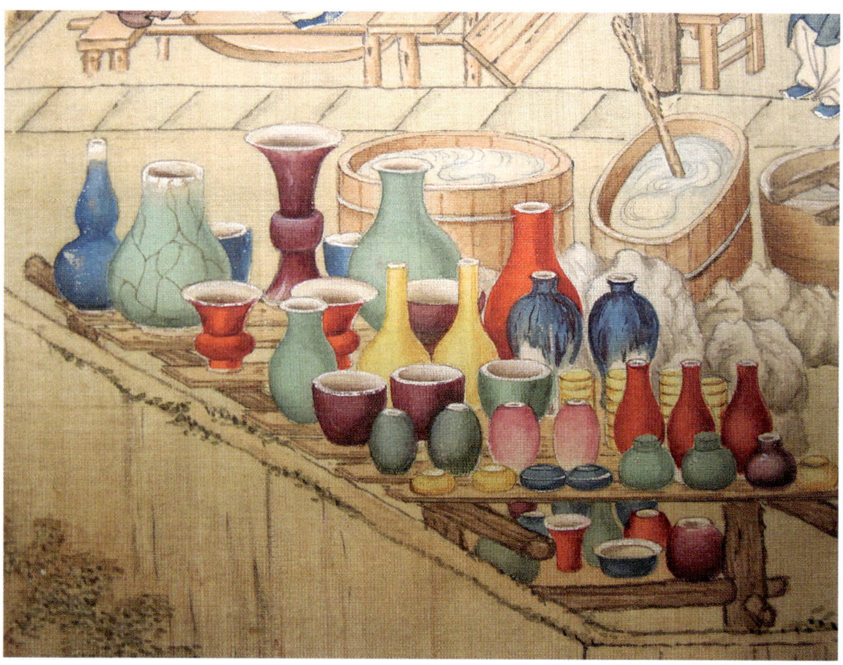

PLATE 10. Details from the painting illustrating entry 7, "Fabrication of the Molded Ware" (Zhuoqi zaopi), from the Qingwan album, *Illustrated Manual of Ceramic Production*, color on silk, 25 × 29 cm, private collection

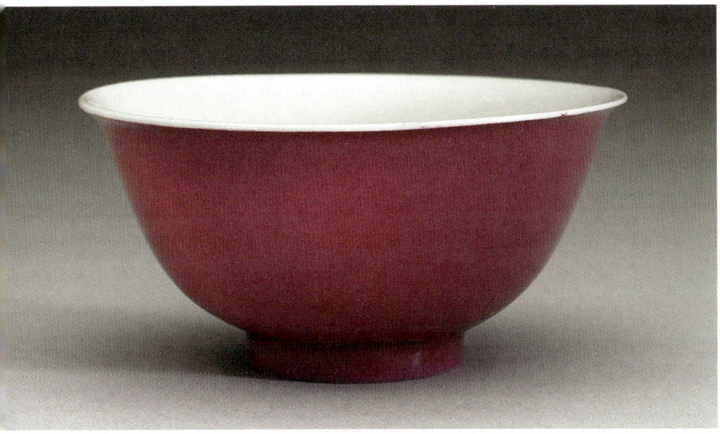

PLATE 11. Porcelain teacup with dragon pattern in rouge red glaze, Qing dynasty, Yongzheng reign (1723–35), height: 5.9 cm, diameter of mouth: 9.2 cm, diameter of foot: 3.5 cm, in National Palace Museum, Taipei

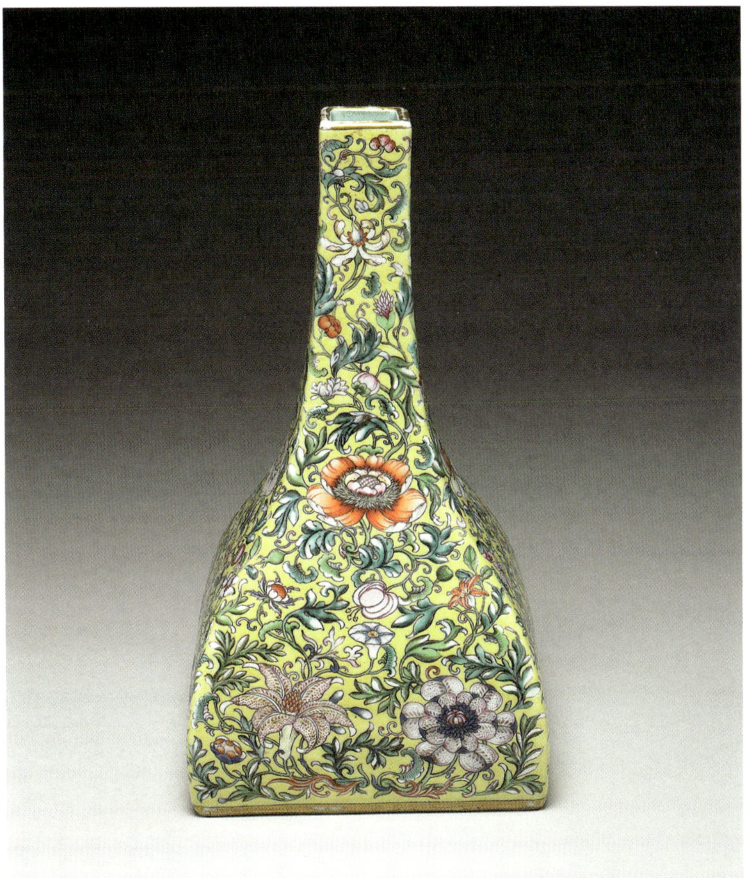

PLATE 12. Square porcelain vase in *yangcai* enamel, decorated with foreign flowers, dated to the early Qianlong reign (1736–1740s), height: 26.4 cm, side of rim: 3.7 cm, side of foot: 14.1 cm, in National Palace Museum, Taipei

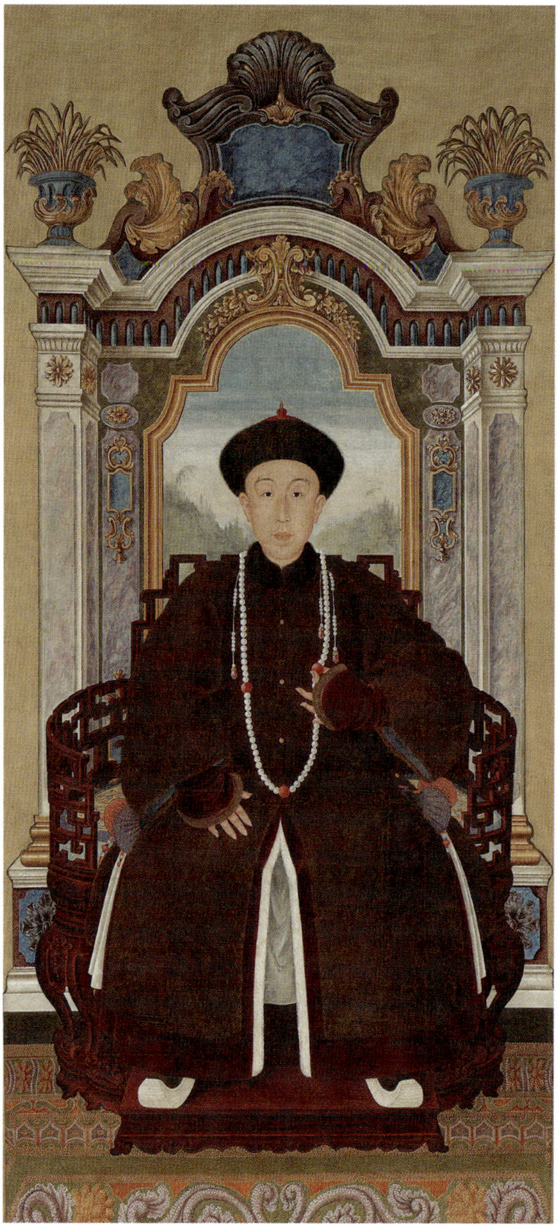

PLATE 13. Detail of a portrait of Prince Guo (1733–1765), dated to the late eighteenth century, 221.1 × 103.7 cm, in Arthur M. Sackler Gallery, Smithsonian Institution, Washington, DC: Purchase—Smithsonian Collections Acquisition Program and partial gift of Richard G. Pritzlaff, S1991.47

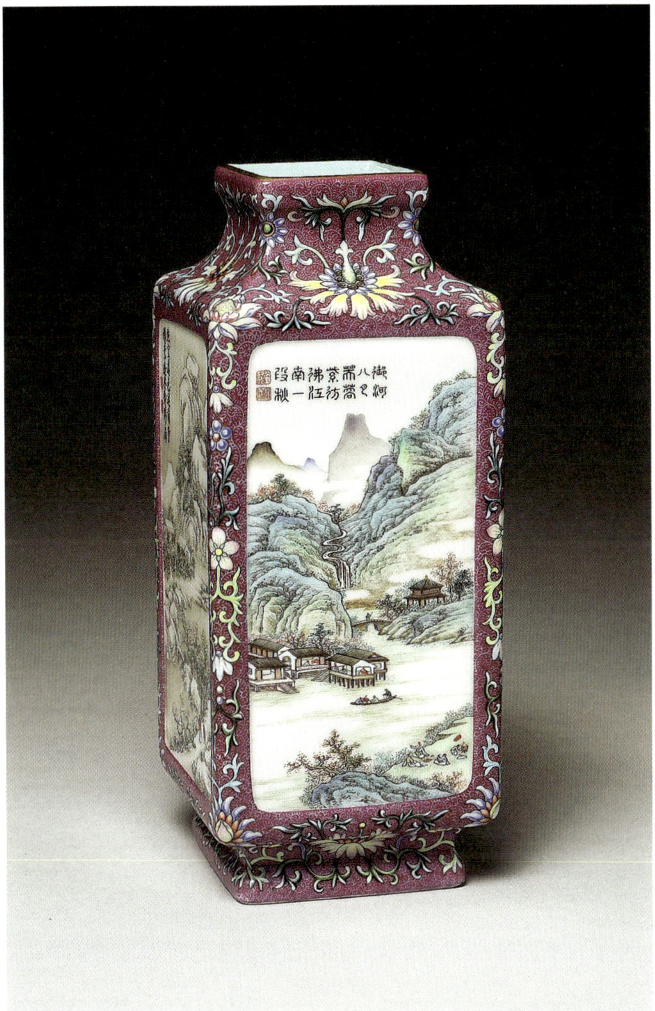

PLATE 14. Square porcelain vase in *yangcai* enamel with incised pattern of flower brocade and landscape in square cartouches, inscribed with imperial poems, dated to 1745, height: 19.8 cm, sides of foot: 5 x 6.8 cm, in National Palace Museum, Taipei

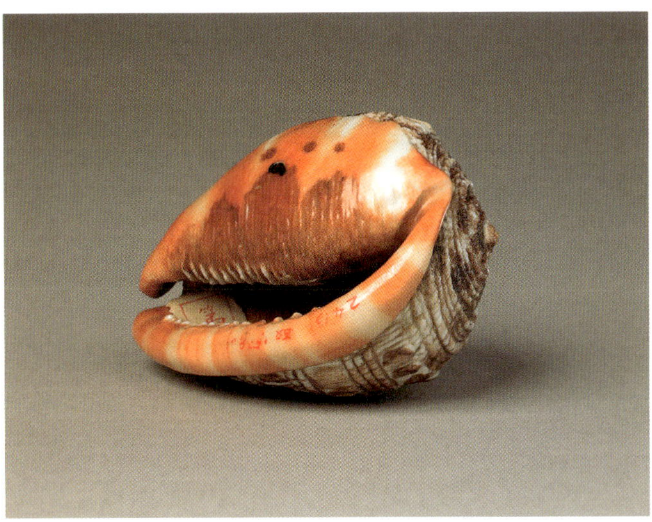

PLATE 15. Porcelain in the shape of a seashell, height: 5.3 cm, length: 9 cm, width: 6 cm, dated to the Qianlong reign (1736–95), in Palace Museum, Beijing

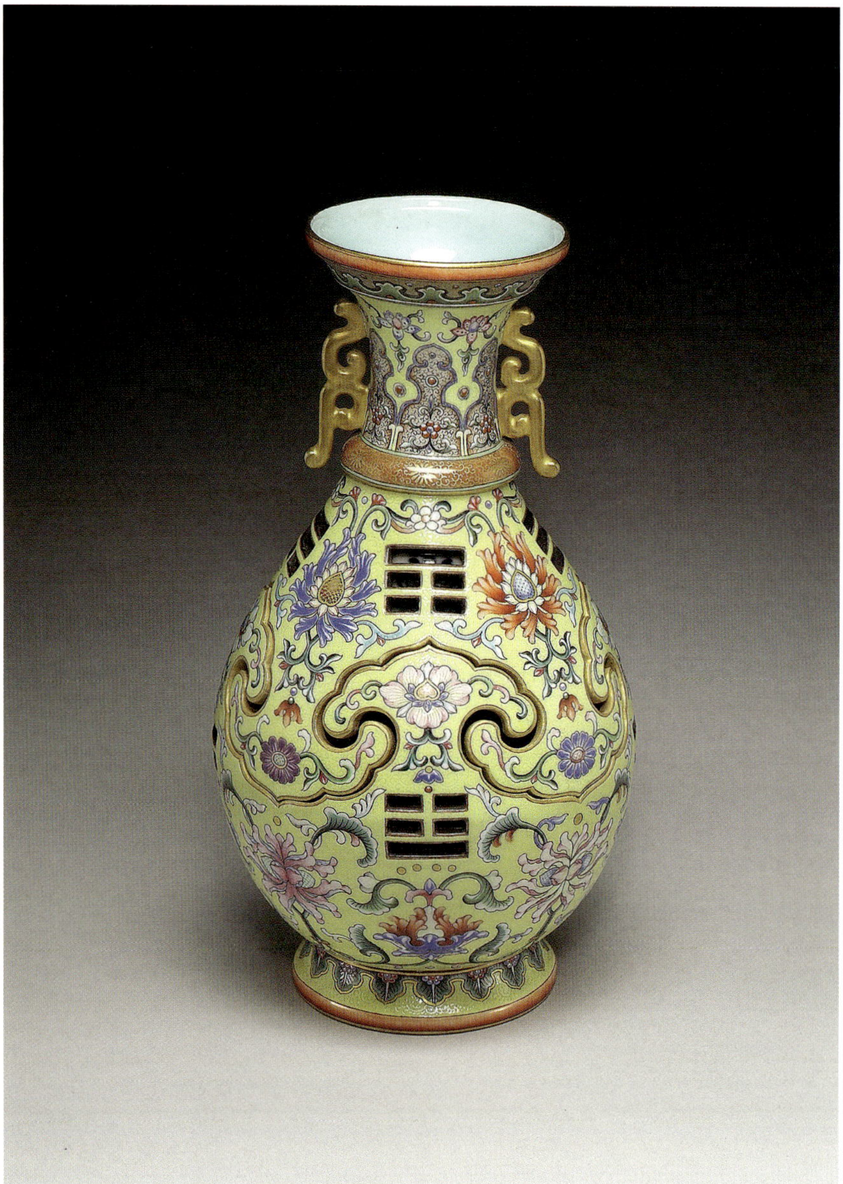

PLATE 16. Revolving openwork porcelain vase in *yangcai* enamels with incised pattern of flower brocade on yellow ground and eight trigram decoration, dated to the early Qianlong reign (1736–1740s), height: 19.6 cm, diameter of mouth: 6.4 cm, diameter of foot: 6.8 cm, in National Palace Museum, Taipei

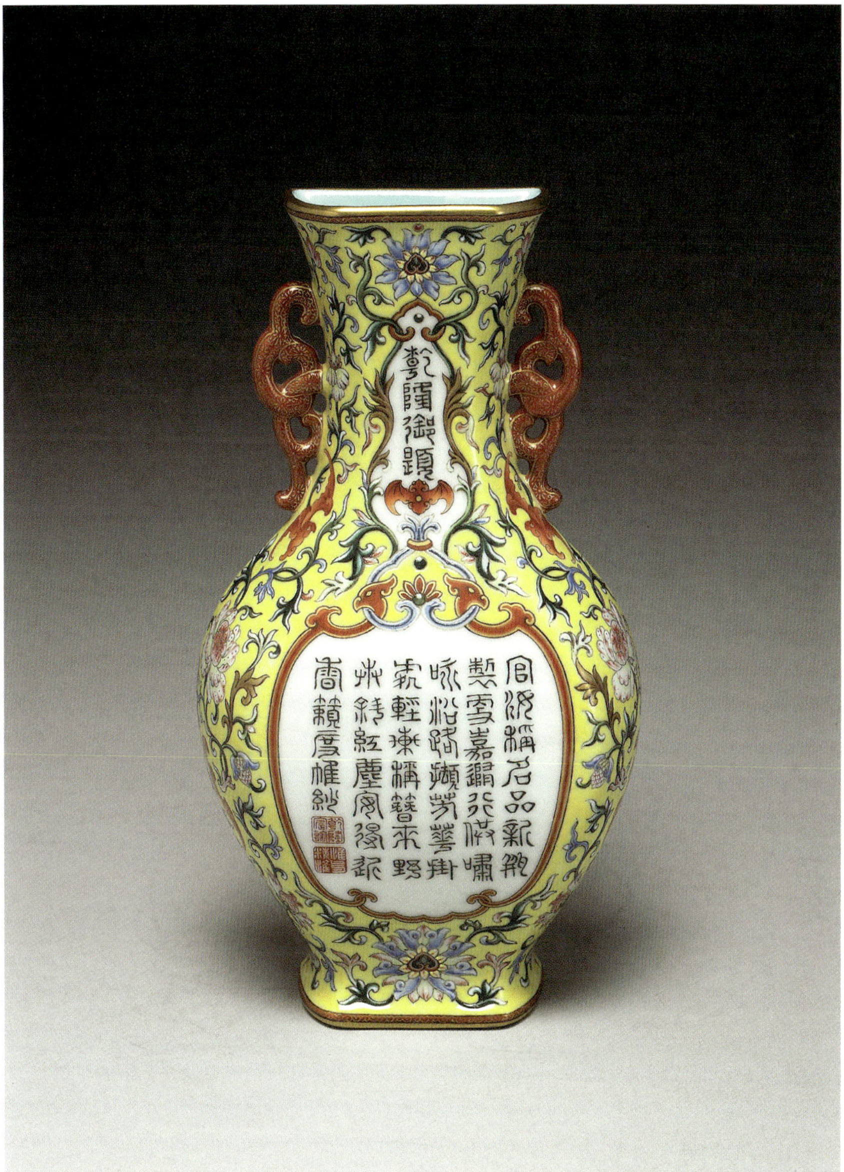

PLATE 17. Porcelain vase for sedan chair or wall, in *yangcai* enamel, inscribed with an imperial poem, dated to 1742, height: 19.2 cm, sides of rim: 6 x 2.9 cm, sides of foot: 5.9 x 2.7 cm, in National Palace Museum, Taipei

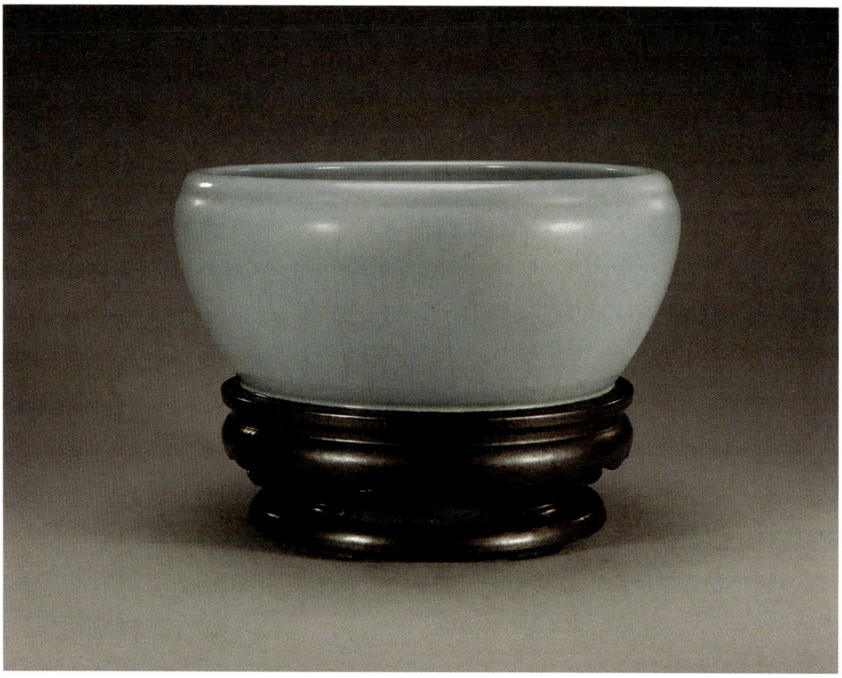

PLATE 18. Porcelain alms bowl in Ru glaze (*above*), with joined brown-colored porcelain stand in imitation of wood, dated to the Yongzheng reign (1723–35), and bottom reign mark (*right*), "Yongzheng nianzhi" (made in the Yongzheng reign), height: 21.5 cm, diameter of mouth: 26 cm, diameter of foot: 15.8 cm, in Palace Museum, Beijing

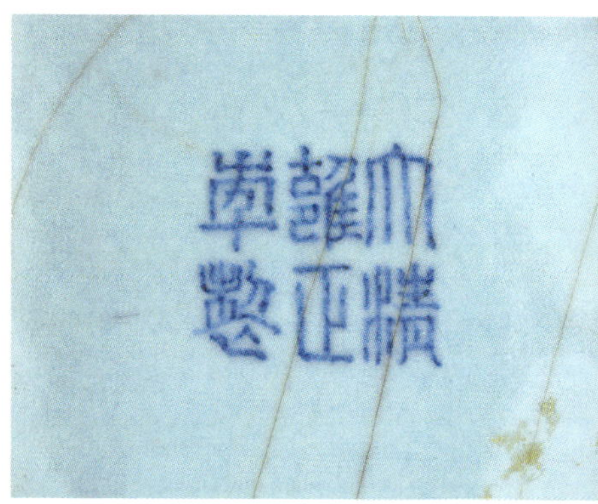

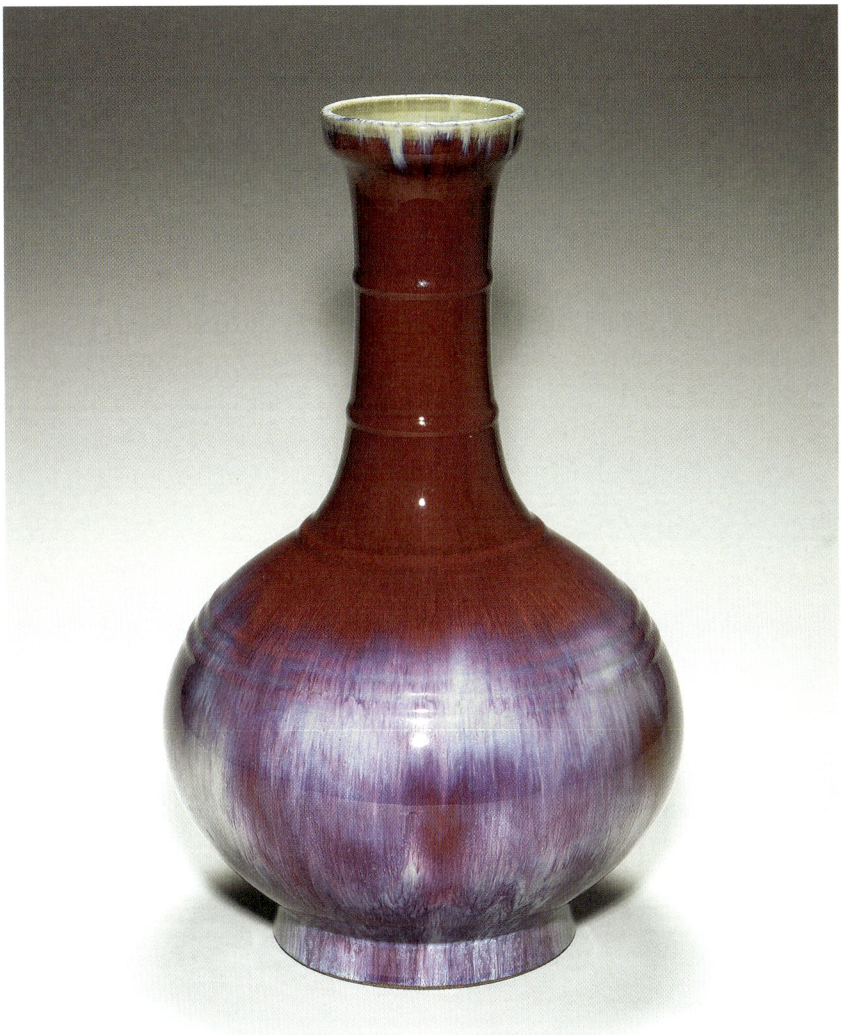

PLATE 19. Flambé glazed porcelain vase with bowstring pattern, dated to the Yongzheng reign (1723–35), height: 45.7 cm, diameter of mouth: 11 cm, diameter of foot: 17.4 cm, in National Palace Museum, Taipei

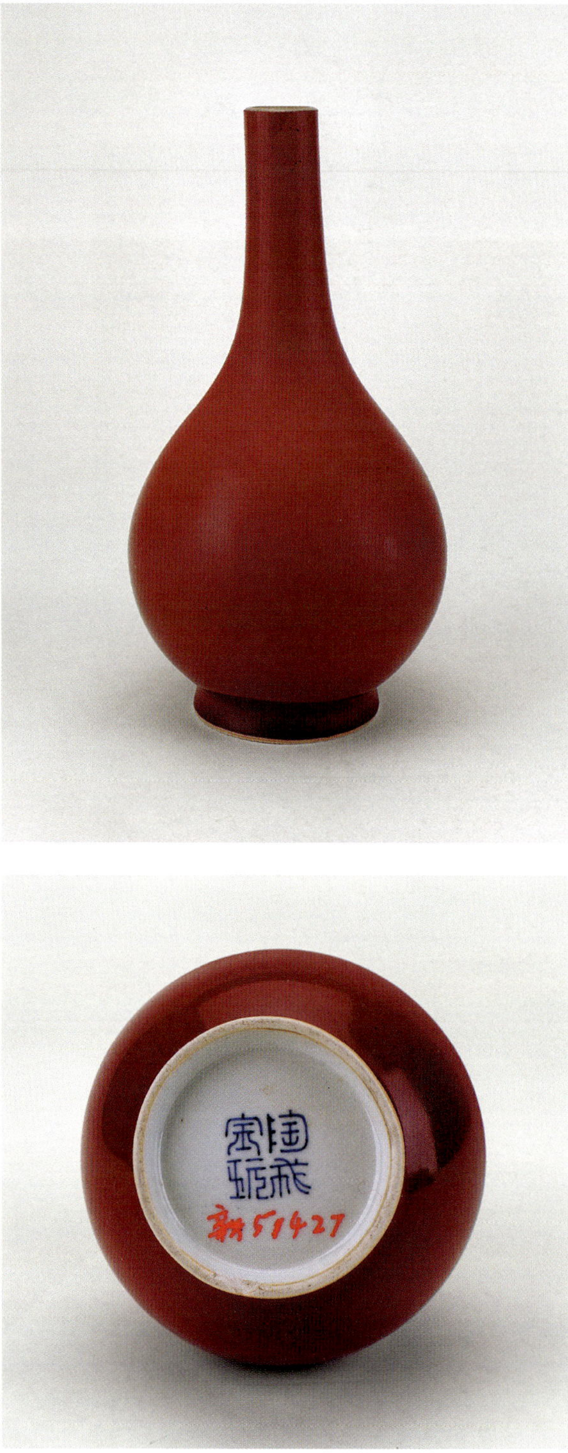

PLATE 20. Porcelain vase in sacrificial red glaze (*top*), dated to the Qianlong reign (1736–95), and bottom reign mark (*bottom*), "Accomplished pot to be cherished" (*taocheng baowan*), height: 21.3 cm, diameter of mouth: 2.5 cm, diameter of foot: 6.8 cm, in Palace Museum, Beijing

itated nine kinds of enamel pigment, each with a minor difference, and derived another nine kinds of color:

> Western *falang* pigment: moon-white, white, yellow, green, deep bright green, light blue, pine yellow, soft bright green, black. Nine kinds in all.
>
> *Falang* pigment [locally] made: moon-white, white, yellow, light green, bright blue, blue, pine green, bright green, black. Nine kinds in all.
>
> Additional kinds of *falang* pigment: soft white, tawny yellow, light pine yellowish green, color of lotus roots, light green, caramel, deep purple, bronzy, pine yellow. Nine kinds in all.[29]

Prince Yi ordered these pigments to be stored as models in the Imperial Workshops, explaining that when they needed to produce glass, he would send the artisan Song Qige to make three hundred catties (*jin*) of pigment for each of these model colors. When they were to make enameled plaques, they should mark characters and numbers on the backs. Most significantly, we see the evidence of painting materials spreading from the court to the porcelain town. As the archival document records, Prince Yi asked Tang Ying, "How much pigment of moon-white and pine yellow color have the Imperial Workshops received? Look into it and inform me. Give them to Nian Xiyao for making the porcelains. Follow this."[30] This important archival document indicates that by 1728 at the latest, *falang* enamel was no longer painted only in the Beijing workshops but at the Jingdezhen kilns as well.[31]

BETWEEN *FALANGCAI* ENAMEL AT COURT AND FOREIGN (*YANGCAI*) ENAMEL IN JINGDEZHEN

Tang Ying resided and worked in Jingdezhen after his appointment by the Yongzheng emperor to the porcelain manufactory in 1728, while his superior, Nian Xiyao, the nominal supervisor of porcelain manufacture appointed in 1726, was preoccupied with tax collecting at the Huai'an custom house and only occasionally visited the porcelain manufactory. Although Tang seldom appears in the archival records between 1729 and 1736, he was not idle. For the first three years after his appointment to Jingdezhen, he was learning ceramic technology by living with local artisans.[32] One can reasonably assume that he played a seminal role in adopting local *falang* enamel techniques for mass production. Correspondingly, the advancement of *falang* technology in Jingdezhen soon picked up so vigorously that the court had to hire local artisans from Jingdezhen to work in the capital.[33] The earliest record for this reverse flow of talent was 1729, when Nian Xiyao sent enamel painters and other specialists from Jingdezhen to the court:

> On the 8th day of the 7th month, Prince Yi dispatched the *falang* painters Zhou Yue and Wu Shiqi, and the *falang* glaze blower Hu Dayou. Nian Xiyao had sent them in together with a short memorial regarding their identification.[34]

Tang Ying made his most tangible contribution to *falang* enameled wares, including overseeing the production of a large quantity of porcelain bodies in "sweet-white" glaze, in Jingdezhen. The sweet-white pieces would provide the base for further enameling decoration at court. In the 2nd month of the 7th year during the Yongzheng reign (1729), Tang Ying's boss, Nian Xiyao, submitted to the court 406 pieces of high-quality porcelains coated in sweet-white glaze. Artisans at court continued to make *falang* enameled pieces out of them over many years, until the end of the Yongzheng reign.[35]

From the beginning of the next reign—that of Qianlong—in 1736, Tang Ying assumed his mentor's full responsibility and replaced Nian Xiyao as the porcelain supervisor, including taking on the job of tax collecting. The Qianlong emperor lost no time in commissioning "the white porcelain for *falang* enameling" by sending a message to Tang Ying, including many precise directions.[36] For instance, the emperor specified when and how many "boneless" (*tuotai*) porcelain bodies he wanted.[37] Tang Ying kept producing vessels for large-quantity commissions until 1743, when the Qianlong emperor decreed, "We no longer need to ask [the manufactory in] Jiangxi for more sweet-white porcelain to produce *falang* [wares]. And inform them that they don't need to send it in."[38] To make *falang* enameled porcelain, the Imperial Workshops could use stored white porcelain bodies, because they had accumulated a sufficient quantity. The artisans at court selected excellent pieces for specially commissioned production. Gao Xiaoran, a scholar from the Palace Museum in Beijing, identified several such stored white porcelain bodies. According to Gao, a pair of boneless wine cups was stamped with decorative lotus patterns inside.[39] The hidden pattern resembled that on a finished *falang* enameled bowl housed in the National Palace Museum, which proves the use of white porcelain bodies as the base of *falang* wares, exactly as textual evidence indicates.[40]

DIFFERENCE BETWEEN *FALANGCAI* AND *YANGCAI* ENAMELED PORCELAIN

The enameled porcelains made at court and in Jingdezhen became increasingly indistinguishable, especially after the successful pigment production at court in 1728.[41] However, Tang Ying's report in 1735 confirms the categorical distinction between *falang* and *yangcai* enamels, while admitting the technical similarity:

> The *yangcai* enameled vessels imitate the new painting technique of Western *falang* enameling. The figures, landscapes, flowers, and birds are all exquisitely painted and vivid.[42]

There are apparently no archival records about *yangcai* enameled porcelain from the Yongzheng reign.[43] However, as the court started to send *falang* pigment to Jingdezhen in 1728, the year Tang Ying was appointed there, he was responsible for developing the production of *yangcai* enameled wares in Jingdezhen since as early as the 6th year of the Yongzheng reign.

In 1743, Tang Ying further refined the definition of *yangcai* enamel in section 17 of his *Illustrated Manual of Ceramic Production*: "Painting round ware and vases of white porcelain with designs in the five colors in imitation of the style of Western foreigners is called 'foreign coloring' [*yangcai*]." The entry then explains the crucial part of production, skilled labor, and experimental tools:

> Highly skilled painters should be selected. They grind and mix different pigments and try to fire them on a white slab of porcelain. They must become familiar with the properties of pigment and fire so that they can be promoted from coarse work to refined work. Practice makes perfect. A clear eye, attentive mind, and precise hand are the best.[44]

Thus, the skilled painters should also be experienced with the physical and chemical changes pigment undergoes during firing in order to prevent colors from overlapping or blurring. The "white slab" is a test tool used by the craftsmen in Jingdezhen to register the interaction of the pigment and the atmospheric environment inside the kiln before formal firing. Then, since there was no thermometer to measure the temperature in the kiln, potters needed to place testers smaller than palm-size next to vessels for simultaneous firing; they took out the testers with a hook to determine the progress of bodies with comparable thickness, glaze, and pigment. Such testers were called "fire testers" (*huozhao*) in the thirteenth century in Jingdezhen:

> When the firing is near completion, no tool can indicate it. We need to probe the kiln with a test piece [*pi*] through the eye of the kiln [*yaoyan*] in order to estimate the level of firing [lit., "between raw and cooked"]. This is how the fire tester comes into play.[45]

Tang Ying also used a variety of fire testers in experiments on glazes and pigments other than *falang* enamels. The careful dates and names on extant testers again show his attentive archiving effort. For example, one inscribed and dated tester probably indicates that Tang Ying was trying to replicate the Ding glaze on a particular kind of clay: "The 7th day of the 3rd month, plain glaze of Ding ware, *wen xiu* clay."[46] The milky white Ding glaze, which had been produced in Dingzhou prefecture in northern China since as early as the Tang dynasty, was not recorded as hard to produce in the Qing, but experimentation may have been required to apply it to this particular clay. In brief, Tang Ying used different kinds of testers to confirm whether porcelain body, glaze, and pigment were properly fired. And to bind these experimental glazes and pigments, especially enameling colors, Tang Ying spelled out the difference of medium for *falangcai* and *fencai* enamels.

Tang indicated that "the color pigment [of *yangcai*] employed is the same as those used on *falang* enamels." Three kinds of media were used for the pigment, namely *yunxiang you*, glue, and water. *Yunxiang* oil was a substitute for the imported *doermen* oil (doermendina).[47] This kind of oil gradually replaced the imported solution, again indicating the nativization of the technique.

YANGCAI ENAMELED PORCELAIN FLOURISHES IN JINGDEZHEN

During the Qianlong reign, the production of *yangcai* enameled porcelains picked up momentum in Jingdezhen under Tang Ying's supervision, and the *yangcai* designs became more distinct and varied, in contrast to the designs of the *falang* enameled pieces produced at court. In the 10th month of the 2nd year in the Qianlong reign, the emperor was so satisfied with the bowls decorated with foreign flowers on a yellow background in *yangcai* enamel that he ordered Tang Ying to produce porcelain boxes and *zun* vases decorated the same way.[48] One outstanding example that showcases the painting style of *yangcai* enamel during the early Qianlong reign is a vase with Western floral decoration on a yellow background (plate 12).[49] The black outline of all motifs probably results from black enamel rather than the traditional Chinese use of black paint. The color gradation on petals and leaves is stressed to create the impression of volume, and white touches produce the illusion of a reflection. Such an imitation of chiaroscuro is not seen on the examples of *falang* enameled porcelains made at court during the Yongzheng reign. The intertwined, crowded floral composition, though highly mannered, covers a rich variety of species seen in European rococo ornamentation. The designer, very likely Tang Ying himself, added many more types of flowers than the usual peony, lotus, and orchid, with intricate arabesque vines. Borrowing European floral patterns and imitating chiaroscuro are specific to *yangcai* enameled porcelains. The same illusionistic technique—that is, the white touch—was used by court painters, who were often Western missionaries and their disciples, to depict rosary beads or other round accessories, especially in portraits of the royal family (plate 13). *Yangcai* enameled porcelains were primarily made in Jingdezhen, while court paintings were created in the Imperial Workshops at court. Their shared visual details indicate an exchange of designs, which must have been facilitated by Tang Ying, who had experience in both production environments.

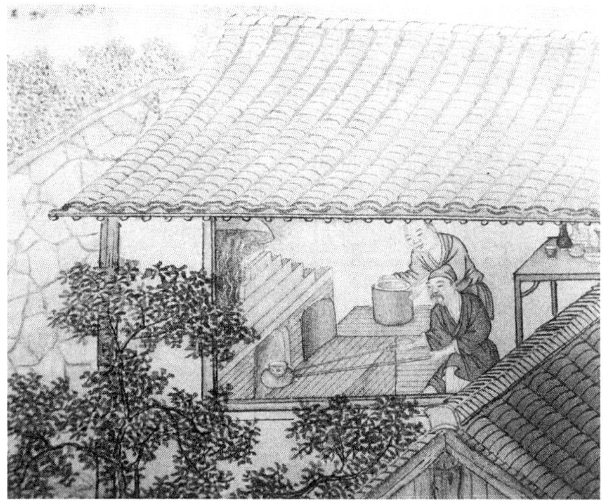

FIG. 4.1. Depiction of a stove for overglazing porcelain, in entry 18, "The Open Stove and the Closed Stove" (Minglu anlu), from the Qingwan album, *Illustrated Manual of Ceramic Production*, color on silk, 25 × 29 cm, private collection

Despite high demand, *yangcai* enameled porcelain was not easily mass-produced. Once designs had been approved, it was challenging to realize them due to the unpredictable transformation of materials in kilns. Tang Ying devoted entries 17 and 18 in the *Illustrated Manual* to explaining the multiple rounds of firing needed to produce *yangcai* enameled wares: "The white porcelain is first fired in kilns before it is decorated in colors. After decoration it needs to be baked again to fix the color."[50] Entry 18 describes two kinds of kilns used to bake the enamel coloring at a relatively low temperature (fig. 4.1):

> So there are two kinds of stove for this purpose, the one open, the other closed. Small pieces are fired in the open stove, which is similar to the stove used for *falang* wares. The door opens outward. The stove is surrounded by a charcoal

> fire. The vessel is put on an iron wheel supported on an iron fork, on which it is passed into the stove. [The craftsmen] turn the wheel with an iron hook to even out the heat. They judge [the firing] by the clarity and brightness of the pigment [on the vessel].[51]

This kind of open kiln is similar to the European muffle kiln depicted in Denis Diderot's *Encyclopédie* and, in turn, the muffle kilns used in enamel workshops in Guangzhou.[52] The *Encyclopédie* was in the collection brought to the Jesuit church in Beijing.[53] Because Guangzhou was the first stop for many European goods and technologies before they entered the hinterland, it is possible that the open muffle kiln as part of enameling technology was introduced to China from Europe. However, Tang Ying probably introduced the muffle kiln from the court to Jingdezhen and conducted many experiments with it to improve the quality of products.

Trials or experiments (*shi*), as Tang Ying stressed in entry 17, were crucial for training artisans and testing enamel pigments as well as kilns. After the initial high-temperature firing, *yangcai* enameled porcelain required several rounds of painting, carving, and firing at a lower temperature. The procedural order and appropriate temperature were crucial to avoid overfiring previous images. The court instructions paid close attention to the landscape paintings in the cartouches on top of the flower brocade background (plate 14). The use of cartouches to frame narrative scenes or landscapes on porcelains dated at least to the Yuan dynasty, yet the coupling of cartouches and a flower brocade background during the Qianlong reign further played with the effect of embroidery on a brocade textile.[54] The design of this kind of work almost treated porcelain surfaces as paper or silk for full-fledged paintings. And the composition left enough space for the inscription of imperial poems.

The polychrome landscape painting drastically complicated the technical order of coloring and firing, because each pigment needed the correct atmosphere (level of oxidation) and temperature to produce the intended color. Some remote mountains, for example, might have been painted with an underglaze of cobalt blue, which meant that the artisans had to follow a precise drawing to paint on the bare white vase. The rest of the painting—the cartouches and floral decorations—were not in place when the craftsmen were painting the mountains. The process must have been carried out with many attempts, some of which may have resulted in pieces bearing Tang Ying's private seals.

The sophisticated enameling and firing technique made possible these inscribed polychrome landscapes. These pieces do not necessarily show the foreignness of *yangcai*. Western images were more often depicted on *falang* enameled porcelains produced in the Imperial Workshops at court instead of in Jingdezhen. In other words, the Western enamel technology disseminated in Jingdezhen was more concerned with pigments and chiaroscuro on decorative patterns rather than any direct use of European motifs. In general, this curiosity about new material possibilities and the politically conservative use of visual symbols characterized technocrats' experiments and constituted an important part of the knowledge culture they sustained.

NEW FORMS: CERAMIC STILL LIFE AND KINETIC VASES

Compared to the intense interest in enameled porcelain among modern scholars, ceramic professionals, and collectors, the sculptural achievement in porcelain under Tang Ying's supervision and his proactive role have not received due attention. It is true that the formal inventory of high Qing ceramics harnessed shapes from all previous periods. Forms of vessels made during the Yongle reign (1403–24) and the Xuande reign (1426–35) of the Ming dynasty provided many models for the mid-Qing manufacture. Following these models, initiated in the founding era of the Imperial Porcelain Manufactory, vessels continued to be made to strengthen Manchu relations with Mongolian and Tibetan allies. For example, the Qianlong emperor commissioned altarpieces and high-stem cups as gifts for Mongolian princes.[55]

More unprecedented innovation that Tang Ying initiated in porcelain forms resulted from the competition with European sculpture and mechanics. Tang Ying drew on his exposure to goods from overseas and voluntarily experimented with ceramic shapes. "Vessels imitating life modeling on Western sculpture and bronze" is listed in the *Report on the Accomplishment of Porcelains*. This "imitation of life" (*xiangsheng*) covered a wide spectrum of sculpted forms, ranging from life-size porcelain fruit and animal objects to shapes reminiscent of animals. Later in the Qianlong reign, Tang Ying submitted twelve porcelains imitating oceanic trumpet shells.[56] The record notes that the model copied was a trumpet shell made of foreign porcelain (plate 15). Such a shell might be similar to the ceramic sculpture made by Johann Kändler (1706–1775), one of the founding members of the Meissen Porcelain Manufactory. I call attention to the year of this production, because in the 9th month of that year, Tang Ying had just completed his appointment in Guangzhou and moved back to the porcelain manufactory in Jingdezhen. Thus, the supervisor may still have had a fresh memory of some sort of shell in a European sculptural medium that he had handled while inspecting European goods in Guangzhou.

The production of porcelain deer illustrates Tang Ying's motivation to experiment with a certain form and the imperial reception of it. Before the 5th month of the 7th year of the Qianlong reign (1742), Tang Ying had been making porcelain cranes and deer. The Qianlong emperor provided specific directions: "Regarding the porcelain cranes and deer that Tang Ying made, the cranes should stand face to face when they are produced in the future. The deer's neck should be straight."[57] The irregular shape of these porcelain animal figures tended to contract during firing in unpredictable ways. A porcelain master sculptor like Kändler had been struggling with this issue all his life. Tang Ying was so thrilled with his experimental success that he wrote four quatrains to celebrate it, titled "To the Joy of the Accomplishment of Porcelain Deer." However, the Qianlong emperor ordered production to stop in 1745.[58] Though Tang was excited about his technological feat, he had little power to decide what styles were produced. Nevertheless, he did retain the power to mobilize labor and tax receipts to enlarge the repertoire of porcelain types.

Indeed, his experiments could take place only with permission from the court, but Tang Ying showed extraordinary enthusiasm for new designs.[59] The knowledge culture of the Qing court nourished the tension between technical curiosity and political limitation. Tang Ying's efforts in technological development, as encouraged or even dictated by the court, exceeded those necessary to fulfill his responsibilities. His lasting dedication to the industry suggests a kind of professionalism. Such professionalism drove him to request that the Qianlong emperor free him from the official task of collecting taxes to let him focus on the craft of porcelain production.[60]

Tang Ying's designs for openwork porcelain vases consisting of several interlocked layers that revolved reveal his creativity and interest in mechanical structures—a prevalent fascination in early modern courts across the globe.[61] He briefly mentioned topologically intricate porcelains in section 7 of the *Illustrated Manual of Ceramic Production*: "As for those bodies that should be engraved or carved in openwork, when sufficiently dried, together with the draft, they are handed to the specialized workers to make."[62] This treatise was written just a few months after Tang Ying and his assistant had designed nine new kinds of openwork, multisection, revolving porcelain (plate 16), as recorded in a report dated the 21st day of the 4th month in the 8th year of Qianlong reign (1743): "Your servant has nine new designs of multilayered openwork and *jiaotai* vases."

Interestingly enough, the report also reveals that Tang Ying engaged in innovation without the emperor's direct commission. These test pieces were based on his own tentative creations (*zixing chuangzao*):

> The new designs come from my own mind. I create them by myself. I am afraid that they might be inappropriate and cost too much. So I dare not make too many. I humbly beg for correction from Your Majesty so that I can continue and produce them in pairs.[63]

It is no coincidence that Tang Ying initiated many new designs at his own expense in 1743.

A VERY BUSY YEAR FOR IMPERIAL PRODUCTION: 1743

The year 1743 was particularly eventful for the imperial porcelain industry. Manufactory operation that year reveals coordination between the court and the local manufactory, showing Tang's negotiations on matters of finance, design, and production.

First, a critical fiscal burden weighed on the local manufactory, as this was the year the court ceased paying for inferior-quality products and required that they be sold locally to recoup their estimated cost. Tang Ying constantly worried about deficits. He notes that because of the political sensitivity of yellow wares and pieces decorated with five-claw dragons, symbols of the emperor, they could not be sold on the commoners' market. The Qianlong emperor agreed to accept the yellow wares but insisted that the rest be disposed of in accordance with the decision.[64]

Second, since the 4th month, Tang Ying had been writing his treatise on porcelain production, arranging his own experience with the twenty pictorial representations by court painters. At the same time, he tackled new designs, including openwork and pieces with complex mechanical structures. However, in the 6th month, he received a harsh reprimand from the chief supervisor of the Imperial Household Department:

> The glaze and decoration of the porcelains produced during the first and second years of Qianlong's reign are much worse in quality than before. And many are broken. Order Tang Ying to pay the fine of 2164.53353 taels of silver.[65]

From this point on, he was required to provide detailed accounts of production, yet Tang Ying claimed that his obligations as a tax collector in the custom house two thousand *li* away distracted him from his management of porcelain production.

Third, in the 9th month, Tang Ying was permitted to spend more time overseeing porcelain production each year. In the last three months of the year, he directed the manufactory to produce a considerable amount of high-quality porcelains. Three kinds of porcelains produced in these last three months of 1743 show three forms of the supervisor's engagement in the industry. In the last month, the porcelain manufactory in Jingdezhen submitted 5,045 pieces of routine products and 170 pieces of *yangcai* enameled pieces decorated with a flower brocade pattern.[66] Though the amount of ordinary wares did not fluctuate much, the amount of *yangcai* enameled pieces was almost triple that of the previous year. Production of the *yangcai* enameled pieces steadily increased, with the annual yield eventually reaching about two thousand pieces.[67]

In the 11th month, the court sent an order for snuff bottles imitating the pattern, glaze, and color of hanging vases (wall bottles; plate 17). The kiln was closed for the winter, but Tang Ying tried to make these small pieces:

> I dispatched clerks to gather artisans to my bureau by Jiu River. I directed them by myself. I designed several forms of bodies and decided on the color and pattern and went to the manufactory before the New Year. I carried out the production in the private kilns that usually used inferior firewood to make coarse ceramics and had the porcelain decorated overnight.[68]

He produced forty pieces for the court, marked with the trademarks of Tang Ying's design. Most of the attributes are consistent with his designs for *yangcai* enameled porcelain; the difference is in scale. The inside of each bottle was glazed with a lake-green color. The combination of visual motifs follows a familiar scheme, showing the consistency of Tang Ying's conceptual craft. The most frequent pattern includes a landscape or birds and flowers—even European figures—framed with a cartouche that was either round or square, depending on the overall shape of the piece. The background dividing the cartouches is decorated with mannered vines and flora. Or the cartouche might frame lines from imperial poetry. The calligraphy of some inscriptions may have come from Tang Ying's own hand.[69] The supervisor showed considerable flexibility in fulfilling this special commission for snuff bottles. Based on his extensive experience in the manufactory and accumulated knowledge, he was able to quickly design new kinds of decorations and forms. But remarkable as his snuff-bottle designs were, such pieces were too small and simple to allow Tang Ying to express the

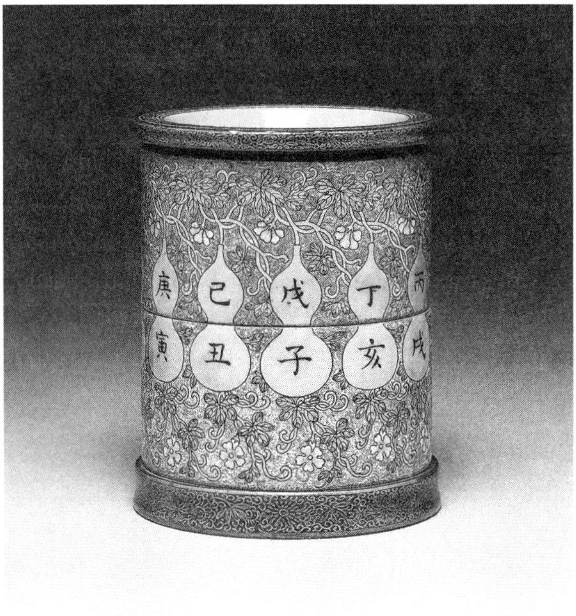

FIG. 4.2 Porcelain revolving writing-brush holders in *yangcai* enamel, decorated with heavenly stems and earthly branches, dated to 1743, height: 12.3 cm; diameter of mouth: 9.9 cm; diameter of foot: 9.8 cm; in National Palace Museum, Taipei

full range of his creativity and formal innovation, as openwork and revolving vases allowed him to do.

In the 10th month of 1743, Tang Ying gathered the craftsmen in the manufactory to make a special brush pot that showcases the symbolic significance and technical prowess of his porcelain design (fig. 4.2). The brush pot consists of four cylindrical parts. Putting them together, the user could turn the upper half and lower half to match the gourds painted at the edge of these two parts. The half gourds were inscribed with a notation system in Chinese. Each of ten numerical characters called "heavenly stems" could match each of twelve characters called "earthly branches." Each pair of two characters denotes a year, and therefore all the combinations of the ten to the twelve characters allow the user to denote sixty years. Tang chose the end of a cycle of sixty years to submit this vessel to the emperor so it could celebrate the beginning of another cycle. From bottom to top, the main body of the bottle is decorated with melon vines and flowers over a background of hand-painted vine patterns. Tang explains the significance of the decoration, which symbolizes "perpetual fulfillment of wishes as constantly as rolling wheels." The conventional symbol for the prosperity of a lineage was turned into the wish for a lasting cycle of imperial rule. Just like his rhetorical discourse in many other reports, Tang attributed this success to an auspicious occasion during the reign.

> At the beginning of the new spring of a *jiazi* of ten thousand years, all the craftsmen are in high spirits. Moreover, it is warm and fine. The body, kiln firing, coloring, inscription, and painting were all smoothly done. In short, the mission is accomplished.[70]

It is hard to tell whether Tang Ying used the role of the imperial auspice as conventional rhetoric to please the emperor or if he seriously believed that technological success relied on a cosmological economy in which a virtuous ruler and benevolent governance were vital. The technocratic way to explain prowess always referred to imperial legitimacy, and many of the nine kinds of new designs made in early 1743 were intended to manifest the state's prosperity and capacity in mobilizing skilled labor.

What happened in the hectic year of 1743 could be regarded as a synopsis of the overall mediation that Tang Ying carried out between the court and the porcelain manufactory in Jingdezhen. His experiments with new openwork designs and revolving pieces again prove how his culturally pluralistic craft appropriated the techniques he had learned from court, from Western artifacts, and from local artisans. These intricate and mobile, even machine-like, pieces synthesized time-worn Chinese motifs and newly imported European mechanical structures. The successful fulfillment of special commissions out of season shows his flexibility in managing the manufactory. The most important articulation of porcelain technology took place in that year, when Tang Ying explained his embodied knowledge of porcelain production in words while organizing the texts according to pictorial representations. Last but not least, after that year, Tang Ying was forced to sell inferior-quality products to repay what the emperor had spent from the Grand Storage Office. No records suggest how and to whom Tang Ying sold them. Given the thriving domestic and international market, it is plausible that domestic and international merchants purchased these products and sold them around the world.

The innovative impetus in porcelain design and technology, and the contrasting close regulation of production, capture the character of knowledge culture during the Qianlong reign, when Tang Ying was experimenting with more new ideas and formulating his treatise on productive knowledge. The aggressive expansion in handicraft production during the Qianlong reign did not consist only in fabricating new forms. A significant part of this cultural production, including porcelain manufacture, was about emulating the past. A successful replication of the past in a specific form symbolized cultural inheritance and implied political legitimacy, and demonstrated the technological prowess of the current ruling house.

Emulating the Past

Although the imperial power wanted to manifest and perpetuate itself in established material forms, the techniques devised by technocrats were often new. A noteworthy example of this occurred when Tang Ying's team attempted to replicate famous old glazes and accidentally invented new monochromes and colors.

We can divide the documented imitation of old glazes into three kinds, based on Tang Ying's *Report on the Accomplishment of Porcelains*: Song dynasty wares, Ming dynasty wares, and undated wares. In order to replicate traditional styles whose formulas were missing, the emperors needed experts to conduct experiments. Tang Ying was a leader among this expert workforce, and he was fully aware of the ideological significance of porcelain manufacture: "Colorful brush gives life to flowers. . . . Porcelain from kilns can testify to the phenomena of civilization."[71] The once imperially favored forms, glazes, and decorations carried symbolic capital that Qianlong expounded in his more than two hundred poems.[72] Because Tang Ying had to follow designs favored by the emperors, the artistic styles of his products were inevitably derivative. Innovation lay in the techniques he developed to achieve the effect of the old wares under new material conditions.

RU AND GE GLAZES

The Imperial Porcelain Manufactory replicated more glazes from the Song dynasty than from any other era, according to the *Report on the Accomplishment of Porcelains*, 1735. Tang Ying specified some of the categories he had imitated with the help of model pieces sent from the imperial storage. He uses the expression "imitation of the color of Song wares sent from the inner [court]" (*fang neifa Songqi seze*).[73] Ru and Guan wares enjoyed great prestige during the Yongzheng and Qianlong reigns, and the cost of the clay, glaze, and even fuel needed to replicate these categories was among the highest.[74] In the Palace Museum in Beijing, there is one vessel shaped like an alms bowl and covered with Ru-style glaze dated to the Yongzheng reign (plate 18).[75] The visual trick in this artifact is that although the stand and the urn are actually one conjoined piece of porcelain, the lower part is covered with a glaze that mimics lacquered wood. When reproducing established styles, the Qianlong emperor gave directions about the modification of forms, usually changing the size of a certain part of an item. Supervisor Tang Ying always obeyed, at least on paper.

Tang Ying was rigorous about dating pieces sent from the court. He carefully described the "imitation of Ge glaze over iron bone" (*fang tiegu Ge you*) by saying they were "imitating the color of the glaze on the *old* ware sent from the imperial storage" (*ju fang neifa jiuqi seze*) instead of imitating "Song wares" (Song *qi*).[76] Tang Ying might have been aware that many pieces of so-called Ge ware might not date from the Song dynasty, and that the "old wares" in the "Ge style" that he received might be replicas from the Yuan or Ming dynasties.[77] Tang Ying had researched the nebulous origin of Ge ware, as he copied the following entry into his journal:

> Investigation of the Porcelain from the Ge Kilns
>
> There was a Zhang family in Longquan county during the Southern Song period. The elder brother [*ge*] was called Shangyi while the name of younger one was Sheng'er. Each of the brothers ran a kiln. Shangyi made better products so people distinguished his kind as Ge ware. There are many cracks on the Ge ware. Now local people in Wenzhou and Chuzhou still call [that kind] Zhang ware.[78]

Although this fragment of a legend does not offer many clues to modern scholars who are still facing the thorny issue of Ge ware, Tang Ying's notation shows his awareness of the complexity in dating the Ge wares.

To replicate the effect of ancient glazes, Tang Ying conducted quasi-archaeological investigations on ceramic fragments by collecting shards from Song kiln sites near Jingdezhen and imitating them. "Imitation of Song glaze in the color of rice is based on the form and color of shards found in the Song kiln site in Lake Xiang, which is 20 *li* to the east of Jingdezhen."[79] Tang Ying must have sent his assistants on this kind of mission more than once. The location he found, now known as the Hutian kilns archaeological site, in southeast Jingdezhen, housed the prosperous Song kilns that produced the renowned Qingbai wares.[80] Learning from these shards may have been common practice among craftsmen and dealers long before their official supervisors did it, but the significance of Tang Ying's empirical approach is threefold.

Tang actively sought local knowledge. He toiled and lived with craftsmen to learn about porcelain technology. This physical closeness not only led to a temporary transgression of the social hierarchy; it also guaranteed the observer more information about the wares and the production process, such as colors, the measurement of details, the appropriate duration and force of a procedure, or even the right smell. Holding the shards unearthed from the specific site of Lake Xiang, Tang Ying was able to learn straight from the artifact itself and constantly compare the results of his experiments with the desired effect.

Tang Ying conducted his work amid the Jesuit presence in China. He may have directly interacted with Jesuit missionaries during his early apprentice years at court (1699–1728), though they may not have strictly discussed ceramics. We know that he successfully begged the emperor for one of Guiseppe Castiglione's disciples to be retired back to Guangzhou. That disciple was very likely a specialist in painted enamel technique, because the archive records before and after this entry show intensive work on enamel.[81] It is not impossible that Tang Ying had learned the empirical methods of Jesuit missionaries at Kangxi's court. On the other hand, several generations of chief supervisors of the porcelain manufactory may have exchanged methods of research about porcelain production with the Jesuit missionaries. When the French priest François d'Entrecolles was preaching Christianity in the region around Jingdezhen, he sent two long letters to Father Orry in Paris, in 1712 and 1722, describing porcelain technology.[82] The "Mandarin" mentioned in the first letter could be Lang Tingji (1663–1715), who was chief supervisor of the manufactory at that time.[83] They must have been well acquainted, since the two packed French wine together for the Kangxi emperor.[84] Coincidentally or not, Lang Tingji compiled an extensive treatise on various aspects of the culture of liquor.[85] Nian Xiyao, the next chief supervisor of the porcelain manufactory between 1726 and 1735, collaborated with Castiglione to compile *The Study of Vision* (Shi xue). Tang Ying may well have continued this interaction with the Western missionaries and learned from their border-crossing fieldwork experiences.

Tang Ying's record is an example of the official impetus to carefully accumulate empirical knowledge.[86] When attempting to reproduce the so-called sacrificial red glaze, the emperor sent broken pieces of old wares to Nian Xiyao and asked him to explain the difference in thickness between the old and new glazes. The research work fell on Tang Ying, as he was working closely with the craftsmen in Jingdezhen at that moment. Similar fieldwork was conducted during experiments with the Jun glaze during the Yongzheng reign. This fieldwork was documented in both official memorials and Tang Ying's poems.

JUN GLAZE

The multiple experiments to replicate Jun wares during the Yongzheng reign reveal that this imitation (*fang*) required many innovations in technology in order to achieve a surface effect similar to the original artifacts. Moreover, rhetorical discourses further helped justify the unexpected results of experiments. Based on modern scholars' analysis and Tang Ying's own inventory entries, we know that the technique and recipe Tang Ying finally used were different from that of the original piece:[87]

> Jun glaze imitates the old vessels sent from the court. Besides the five colors of rosy purple, cherry-apple red, violet of the garden eggplant flower, plum blue, and the color of a horse's lung, I achieved four new glazes, namely new purple, rice color, sky blue, and flambé glaze.[88]

By using the expression "imitates the old vessels sent from the court" (*fang neifa jiuqi*), Tang Ying again implies that the dates of the Jun ware models were unknown.[89] He seems to have received demanding tasks just a few months after his appointment to Jingdezhen. Though we can find only Yongzheng's orders to Nian Xiyao in the archive, we can assume that Tang Ying took much responsibility for this research and experimentation, as he resided in the manufactory between late 1728 and 1735, while Nian was mainly busy collecting custom taxes and thus oversaw production from afar. During those years, the Yongzheng emperor was apparently very interested in Jun wares. In an archival record dated to 1733, he commanded: "Make some Jun wares, Guan wares, . . . and send them here. The Jun wares are the most important."[90] Before and after this, the archive records a couple of commissions. In the first spring after Tang Ying arrived in Jingdezhen, he was still unfamiliar with the complicated ceramic technology, especially the Jun glaze, so he sent his private secretary (*muyou*) to Junzhou to investigate the formula of the glaze in the 3rd month of the 12th year during the Yongzheng reign (1729). This mission is recorded in a poem titled "Seeing Off Wu Yaopu to Junzhou in Late Spring":

> The success of the ceramic production depends on this trip.
> Bells, tripods, wine goblets, and urns are the state's treasure.
> If rosy and emerald glazes still pass down,
> We seek relics, search for books, and pursue elderly people.
> Oh, don't you see,

> Great travelers like the Grand Scribe [historian Sima Qian],
> Cherish great landscapes in their bosoms.
> The ceramic alchemy reveals the secret of the cosmos.
> The supernatural craftsmanship stuns people with its mighty talent.
> Although the languages and institutions may differ,
> Imitation of the antique with a modern source makes them rivals.[91]

Thus, three channels of information were established. Tang Ying directed his assistant to gather artifacts, search for related textual records, and question older potters. To emphasize the value of the fieldwork, he evoked Sima Qian (145–90 BCE), the eminent historian of the Western Han dynasty, who claimed to have traveled extensively to collect geographical and historical information. Tang Ying compared the investigation of ceramic technology to intelligence collection for historiography. By regarding Sima Qian's study of antiquity as an effort to model antiques rather than clarify material qualities of historical objects, Tang Ying revealed the significance of "imitation of the ancient." To reproduce the ancient wares meant communicating with talented people in the past rather than simply replicating an old object. His approach to imitation highlights field investigation and innovative experiments rather than faithful copying.

FLAMBÉ GLAZE, OR TRANSFORMATION INSIDE THE KILN *(YAOBIAN)*

While trying to replicate old glaze colors, Tang Ying's experiments unexpectedly generated some new surface effects that diverged from the old ones. Winning imperial approval for these creations depended on his rhetorical flair. *Yaobian* (transformation inside the kiln), sometimes translated as "flambé glaze," was one such radical derivation. During the Yongzheng and Qianlong reigns, glaze usually referred to a random mixture of red, blue, purple, brown, and white patterns.[92] The colors freely dissolved into each other by degrees, like a cascade pouring over the piece or a dynamic flame flickering. Inside a kiln at a high temperature, the coloring agents, especially copper, iron, tin, and lead, went through unpredictable interactions and generated spectacular effects.

The term *yaobian* during the early Qing actually denotes two surface effects, produced in different experiments during the Yongzheng and Qianlong reigns, that were intended to replicate two kinds of old glazes. Tang Ying listed *yaobian* glaze as a new achievement under the category of Jun glaze in his *Report on the Accomplishment of Porcelains* (plate 19). In fact, this *yaobian* glaze was a failed attempt to produce the Jun glaze. Then, during the Qianlong reign, Tang Ying again accidentally encountered the phenomenon of *yaobian* during production of the "sacrificial red" (*jihong*) glaze:[93]

> In the 11th month of the 8th year (1743), your servant was making porcelains in sacrificial red glaze in the manufactory and achieved several kinds of round wares in glaze transformed in the kiln. They amount to twenty-six pieces. Though they are not of the upright color of sacrificial red, I have not seen this transmutation of glaze for more than ten years. Human effort cannot make it. So when kiln workers create the flambé glaze by chance, they regard it as an auspicious sign and cherish it as a rare curio. As for [previous] production of sacrificial red, when we took the vessels out of the kiln, except for those in the upright color, the rest were all utterly dark. There has never been such a transformation of glaze to a fresh and bright color. Now that we have achieved several kinds of sacrificial red and flambé glazes, I ought to report them together.[94]

The report explained the difficulty of producing the sacrificial red glaze. Very likely because of overfiring or too much coloring ingredient filling in the glaze, the surface of the failed pieces appeared dark. The successful red color carried some moral-cosmic quality, so Tang Ying called it an "upright color." The production of sacrificial red was itself an effort to recover the similar lost glaze initiated in the early Ming dynasty. An extant specimen shows us Tang Ying's experiment with sacrificial red before he submitted it to the court (plate 20). His private seal, "Accomplished pot to be cherished" (*taocheng baowan*), appears again on the experimental sacrificial red piece. Though the emperor did not sanction the mass production of these *yaobian* wares, the local manufactory gradually made use of this unpredictable part of the productive process, as the following pictorial and textual evidence indicates.

Tang Ying must have already been able to exercise some control over the seemingly unpredictable *yaobian* glaze, since he noted it as one of the subcategories of Jun glaze that he had newly mastered during the Yongzheng reign. As for the Qianlong reign, the leaf titled "Fabrication of the Molded Ware" (Zhuoqi zaopei) from the *Illustrated Manual of Ceramic Production* (c. 1743) depicts a pair of *meiping* vases in the flambé glaze, which are close to an extant example. A slightly later source mentioning ceramic production during Qianlong's reign also confirmed the workers' intervention in the production of *yaobian* glaze, confirming that it did not depend entirely on chance.[95] The author of *Notes on the Southern Kilns* (Nanyao biji), Zhang Jiuyue (1722–1803), provided a technological description of this "human ingenuity" (*renqiao*). By manipulating the coloring compound and the firing temperature, the factory workers were able to reduce the risks and channel the dynamic process in the desired direction:

> Jun glaze. . . . Nowadays the method to make it is to use white glaze as a base and add some pigment, often used for underglaze red. Then coat them with the glaze of glass or ruby frit. Paint them on the surface of the body. Let them flow in firing and leave the color as it transforms instead of intending a planned color. Those fired a couple of times may be better.[96]

Though the description could be exaggerated and inaccurate at certain points, it shows the human intervention in the process. Tang Ying's appropriation of the *yaobian* technology followed a strategic logic, which aimed to contain an unpredictable process and benefit from the dynamic energy of limited disorder. The imperial decorum incorporated this dynamism as a way to strengthen and renew itself.

IMITATION OF PORCELAINS MADE IN THE MING DYNASTY

Porcelains made in the early and mid-Ming dynasty were endowed with significantly less cultural capital at the Qing court than those of the Song, but their replication attracted no less sustained enthusiasm. Supervisor Tang Ying's technical advice about Ming wares continued the research and experiments of his predecessors, Nian Xiyao and Lang Tingji, and therefore shared their technocratic approach. Lang, who was active in the porcelain industry in 1705–12, had imitated blue-and-white and monochrome red vessels made in the Xuande reign, as well as vessels of the Chenghua reign (1465–87), called "joined color" (*doucai*) for their combination of overglaze polychrome motifs with underglaze cobalt-blue outlines.[97] All of these categories from the Ming dynasty reappear in Tang Ying's list of successful experiments. Archival documents prove that the court sent many original pieces to Nian Xiyao, under whose scrutiny Tang Ying was working in the manufactory in situ:

> Director of the bureau Haiwang took out a bowl with a dragon painted in cobalt blue on a white background in the style of the Jiajing reign [1522–66] . . . [and] gave it to Prince Yi so he could order Nian Xiyao to produce some according to this design.[98]

The successfully reproduced category is listed simply as "blue-and-white imitating the style of the Jiajing reign" on Tang Ying's list.

Much more technical discussion is preserved in the archive about imitating the blue-and-white, red underglaze, and joined-color wares of the Ming dynasty. Although Tang Ying often took the initiative to experiment with new designs, the Qianlong emperor usually curbed his enthusiasm and enjoined further production. In addition, the emperor often commanded Tang Ying to authenticate old vessels and restore them using his own hands-on experience. On the 11th day of the 5th month in the 8th year of the Qianlong reign (1743), when Tang Ying was ordered to fix the glaze of a jar signed with the character *tian* (heaven) from the Chenghua reign, he was able to negotiate the order. On the 13th day of the 7th month, he replied, first confirming that the chipped vessel did indeed date to the Chenghua reign of the Ming dynasty. He explained that the jar had been made a long time ago, and therefore its "ambience of fire [?]" (*huoqi*) had diminished. To add glaze, he explained, it must be fired again, which would damage the vessel. Thus, he ended up producing three pairs of new pieces instead.[99] The Chenghua joined-color decoration is known for its fine cobalt-blue outline around polychrome floral motifs (plate 9).[100] Local (non-European) cobalt pigment, which is low in manganese, was widely used during the Chenghua reign to produce thin and clear outlines. Section 9 of the *Illustrated Manual of Ceramic Production* (1743) describes a particular kind of cobalt mineral called "chive sprouts" (*jiucai bian*), "which makes very clearly defined strokes and does not 'run' in the fire" and which "must be used for the most delicate pieces."[101] The need to restore, replicate, and even improve extant styles thus forced the technocrats to conduct experiments on technical details and, to various extents, channel technological knowledge from the local artisan community for imperial use. The systematically archived experiments and the operation of the Imperial Porcelain Manufactory across a generation of porcelain supervisors were a key part of the Qing court's encyclopedic effort to culturally integrate the empire's multiethnic populations within the confines of imperial decorum.

ADAPTING THE WESTERN *falang* enamel technique to the indigenous variety, Tang Ying introduced the *falang* technique to production in Jingdezhen. The form and decoration of revolving and openwork vessels and new monochrome porcelains show his interaction with Western designs. The commissions of vessels in old styles required Tang Ying to examine old shards and wares so that he could reproduce their effect using new techniques. In that sense, replication was never exact repetition but rather a reproduction of techniques and style. Tang selected from what he had learned through interaction with Western technicians, local artisans, and old artifacts, reshuffling existing templates to combine them anew. This reshuffling was a process of negotiating with material constraints through experiments, since imperial regulation permeated the design system as well as the manufacturing process. The technical and artistic inventions were based on an inventory of preestablished designs.

CONCLUSION

BETWEEN HIS VISITS to hectic kiln sites, the inviting theatrical spectacle in Jingdezhen sometimes led Tang Ying's mind to wander far and wide in both time and space. As one of his poems attests,

> The Chongyang Festival is the talk of the town.
> For twenty years, my heart soared when imagining I traveled beyond the pass.
> Under tents made of animal skins and pine-tree supports, we poured yogurt.
> A song on the pipa painted the ten thousand mountains yellow.[1]

This memory hails from the days when Tang Ying accompanied the Kangxi emperor to the northern borderland. In his acoustically innovative play *Song of the Foreign Flute* (Jia sao), Tang uses music played on a pipa to evoke the image of a shelter of pine trees, buttered tea, and a mountainous golden landscape. Above all, the play evinces his homesickness for the northeast. The diet, clothing, and the humid weather of southeast China must have constantly elicited in Tang Ying a sense of displacement, which was closely linked to issues of ethnic identity in a sensual way. Although the play is a rewriting of the eminent woman poet Cai Wenji's "Eighteen Songs of a Nomad Flute," the fact that Tang Ying chose to refashion the original narrative poem and the distinct way he transformed it enrich the classical piece with experiences of geographical and ethnic displacement that were common to thousands of fellow bannermen appointed across the empire.[2]

Tang Ying colors the dilemma of the protagonist, Cai Wenji, in the play with his own awareness of displacement. Cai Wenji, the elite woman poet who had been married to a Xiongnu prince residing north of China proper in the early third century, is first portrayed as having a deep longing for her southern hometown in Jiangnan: "In the stern coldness of ice and frost on the bleak plain, the beacon fire is frightening. Heaven has eyes but does not see me. If the gods allow it, when can I go home?"[3] After Cao Cao, a hegemon general from the Han region, successfully negotiates her return, Wenji suffers from the expectation that she will have to abandon her two sons, who were born in the steppe kingdom.[4] The geographical alienation Wenji faces is further complicated by her ethnic ambiguity. Apparently, she and her southern-born servants had become accustomed to steppe customs:

> *Chou* actor [clown role in Kun-style drama], performing the maid serving tea: Your servant saw you sitting playing a zither [*qin*]. You must be thirsty. I have prepared some milky tea to quench your thirst.
>
> *Dan* actor [heroine role]: Perfect. Bring it in. [She drinks the tea.][5]

The southern servant's words and deeds display an ethnic ambiguity. He joyfully provides her with gifts brought by colleagues from the steppes: "I have a sack of butter for you to use with your tea. I have a glass of *a-la-tie* [araqi liquor] for you—drink a cup to keep out the cold on the way." The most telling detail is that the servant calls his townsmen in Suzhou "barbarians":

> [The servant is delighted, carrying the books and the zither.] I am so happy! I am so happy! I have performed like a dog for my Mongol uncle all these years. Now I am returning to Suzhou. When I get there I can bully those barbarian neighbors.

Eventually the scene culminates in an awareness of displacement in time:

> [All sing] In my ear, I hear the local dialect approaching noisily. Plum blossoms and human faces! I feel shy seeing the plum blossoms and human faces. I fear having to talk about the past years with neighboring maids when I return home.

In the long preface to this play, Tang Ying claims a unique insight into Wenji's situation because of his own cultural and geographic experience: he is a man from the area of Yan and Zhao displaced to the south.[6] He suggests that Wenji would appreciate his reading of her mind—that is, the dilemma of ethnic ambiguity. Moreover, he contrasts the musical styles with Wenji's living situation. At the beginning of the act, he employs southern-style flutes and strings.[7] In the middle of the play, he shifts to flutes (*di*) and clappers when Wenji is about to leave for the south, giving these stage directions: "From now to the end of the eighteenth song, all use flutes and clappers."[8] Southern music envelops Wenji while she is in the steppe kingdom; northern music accompanies her all the way back home and keeps haunting her together with her memories and blood ties in the north. Had he not experienced displacement himself, Tang Ying would not have been able to capture the psychological depth of Wenji's perpetual alienation.

Being thousands of miles from the emperor and having his technical business under control, Tang Ying achieved a kind of professional independence. The success of the Imperial Porcelain Manufactory in Jingdezhen owed much to the stability he maintained as a result of his give-and-take with regional resources. Coming from the far north both geographically and culturally, he managed to absorb the local culture, including regional theater and technological knowledge; thus, he adopted the cultural persona of a local person. In his dialectical interaction with the local culture, he formed a technocratic identity within a social and material world that he actively created and shaped.

Theatrical practice and management of porcelain manufacture partook of the same epistemic shift, which began in the early Qing dynasty. This shift was made possible by the unprecedented geocultural diversity of the growing empire in the eighteenth century and a court culture that was increasingly interested in integrating this geocultural diversity. This epistemic shift was effected through a self-conscious appropriation of literati and local knowledge.

Through rare fissures in Tang Ying's play, we can glimpse his otherwise covert concern with ethnic complexity and a sense of displacement. Who was Tang Ying, this bannerman elite and technocrat, and what was to be his place in history? Tang Ying and his bannermen peers were obviously not the loyal yet frustrated literati scholar-official type that populates Chinese history books. As the court assumed more and more weight in producing, applying, and validating technological knowledge and artistic forms, Qing emperors and bannermen became more secure and confident, expressing themselves as central producers of a growing cultural pluralism.

Tang Ying was not at all the last hands-on technocrat. Per the court's orders, his successors continued to oversee the manufacture of porcelain. However, their decreasing technical expertise testified to the court's loosening control of the industry, or at least a switch in focus to industries other than porcelain. In 1741, another bannerman, Laoge (c. 1704–1768), succeeded Tang Ying in the manufactory. This succession mirrored Tang Ying's earlier replacement of Nian Xiyao, as both successors started to oversee production in situ while the predecessors were relocated to nearby custom houses and visited the manufactory for inspection only twice a year. Like Tang Ying, Laoge had worked on handicraft projects at court from 1729 until 1741. Upon arriving in Jingdezhen, like Tang Ying, he also went through an apprentice period for three years to learn porcelain technology.[9] However, what distinguished Laoge's career trajectory, and suggests the changing role of bannermen in the porcelain industry, was the fact that he was never appointed to nearby custom houses but resided in the manufactory in Jingdezhen until 1768, the end of his career. Laoge's exclusive service in the porcelain manufactory for twenty-eight years indicates not the court's sustained intervention in porcelain affairs, but rather a critical break in the line of trained technocrats available to take up the baton.

After Laoge retired, the failures of several incompetent potential successors led the court to retreat from hands-on control of the porcelain industry. After Tang Ying's death in 1756, a few bannermen took on his positions in custom houses near Jingdezhen and communicated with Laoge to keep the Imperial Porcelain Manufactory running. However, these "supervisors" were no longer involved in any detailed technical experiments in the manufactory.[10] Moreover, alleged fiscal corruption or straightforward embezzlement, as was besetting technocratic supervision in other fields of production, further disqualified bannermen elites from monitoring porcelain manufacture. From 1786 on, Qianlong ceased to appoint bannermen technocrats to directly oversee the Imperial Porcelain Manufactory. The manufactory was moved under the jurisdiction of the nearby Jiujiang custom house and the local magistrates of the Rao prefecture. Local magistrates and officials at the local custom house were no longer obligated to participate in any technological research.[11]

The shrinking budget for porcelain production and the disappearance of official specialists in the manufactory reflected the court's constant redistribution of resources and its shift in attention to emerging fields of technocratic control, in line with the changing focus of statecraft in the late Qianlong era. Constrained by natural resources and consumers' needs, porcelain manufacture for the court leveled off after more than six decades' expansion. The waning presence of technocrats in porcelain manufacture, though seemingly caused by a string of personnel accidents, actually may suggest a relatively successful cultural integration in the greater Jiangnan region, with the porcelain town Jingdezhen at its margin. The integration is evidenced by the popularity of the so-called court style in art of the region—*yangcai* porcelains, for example—facilitated by decades of inflow of court designs.

Bannermen technocrats were called upon to collect newly available natural resources such as jade from Inner Asia and to manage information in industries other than porcelain manufacture. As records of ceramic experiments drastically decreased after the mid-1750s, the focus of the cultural industry at court seemed to move to a series of large, encyclopedic projects. These compilations focus on flora and fauna and ritual vessels, and culminate in the Library of Four Treasures in the 1770s.[12] Imperial control of decorum moved from the mastery of material arts to the categorization and interpretation of the imperial collections and other literary projects. For instance, Yiling'a, the distant porcelain supervisor stationed in the Jiujiang custom house between 1768 and 1772, who should otherwise have been responsible for the quality of porcelain products, instead became deeply versed in Chinese drama in connection with an empirewide campaign to censor potentially seditious theater.

Annexation of new territory at the northwest border in the 1760s facilitated the imperial extraction of jade and attracted the Qianlong emperor's enthusiastic exploitation of this mineral as a symbol of military prowess and virtuous legitimacy. For instance, bannermen such as Dekui (c. before 1761–1778) from the Grand Council, together with officers in the region, worked with local Begs and Muslim laborers to fulfill Qianlong's craving for jade from the Khotan and Yarkand.[13] More bannermen of various ranks in the Imperial Household Department, especially vice directors and foremen in the Imperial Workshops, collaborated with master artisans to invent special tools to fashion the unprecedented gigantic jadestones from the New Territory into monumental symbols of military and technical achievement.[14] Like supervisors of porcelain manufacture, bannermen supervisors in the jade industry combined fiscal management with technological involvement in their mediation between the court and the regional centers of production. One salient proof of the similarity across technocrats' fields of engagement is their financial downfall. The fact that innumerable bannermen elites were accused of embezzlement or fiscal mismanagement in their supervision demands a structural rather than moralistic explanation of Qing governance.[15]

What distinguished bannermen technocrats, such as porcelain supervisors Nian Xiyao and Tang Ying, from Chinese bureaucrats and scholar-officials or literati was not their ethnic identity in a modern etic sense but a socially and culturally constructed ethnic categorization based on historical allegiance to the conquering group. Thus, it was not mandatory for allied technocrats to be exclusively Manchu bannermen. In the early Qing, plenty of Chinese officials entered governance from a military background, and many Chinese scholars, such as Confucius's descendant Kong Shangren (1648–1718) and the literary and artistic entourage in the Kangxi emperor's Southern Study (Nan Shufang), served the court without taking the civil service examination. In the second half of the Qing dynasty, a large number of bannermen, such as Wanggiyan Linking (C: Wan-yan Lin-qing; 1791–1846), chose to start their careers with the civil examination rather than a role as a bodyguard/scribe, although Linking's various positions in his long career are characteristic of a typical bannerman technocrat.[16] In the long Qing dynasty, instead of strict ethnic grouping, officials' distinct skills, career patterns, and function in government may show us how technocratic they were. The technological prowess of bannermen elites also ranged across a wide spectrum, from a perfunctory knowledge of terminologies to deeply embodied technical skills. Nevertheless, the ethnically marked Imperial Household Department and a large number of official posts reserved for bannermen institutionalized a technocratic way of knowing and making, as an alternative to classical Confucian learning, by appropriating regional resources and mobilizing local labor.

Tang Ying's career exemplifies the administrative, technological, and literary work of a bannerman in the context of his peers, shedding light on the hitherto little studied knowledge culture of the Qing empire. Technocrats' footsteps between the court and regional society reveal how their craft of porcelain making and their mastery of technological knowledge were integral parts of statecraft. Subverting modern disciplinary divisions between institutional, technological, and cultural history, this account privileges our protagonist's vantage point to display an institutional basis, primarily the Imperial Household Department, and an unfolding technocratic culture evinced in both knowledge production and art making.

Material governance in the printing industry, textile industry, salt monopoly, animal husbandry, and hydraulic industry, where the Qing state attempted to exert control over ateliers and factories in regional societies, could be similarly investigated. Understudied textual and artifactual evidence left by technocrats allows us to see the persistence of imperial power shaping technological knowledge and material forms, one object at a time. The study of technocracy not only complements the well-explored fiscal, policy, and legal regulations of the Qing state, but also foregrounds an expert officialdom working closely with artisans, merchants, and technicians, rather than with the men of letters previously regarded as the pillars of statecraft and intellectual history in dynastic China. The Qing porcelain industry foreshadows the modern "made in China" factory regime in its emphasis on state intervention in industry. From its inception, industrialization in China was driven by cadres associated with state interests and not by profit-seeking capitalists. This positioning of specialized experts in political decisions in a centralized political regime invites consideration of the effects in early modern China and other parts of the world of equipping political elites with technological skill and of the shaping force of a political agenda on the making of knowledge and art.

GLOSSARY

alatie / 阿拉貼 / raqi liquor

baidun / 白丕 / white clay bricks
bangzi xi / 梆子戲 / clapper drama
banyan qimen ao / 搬演奇門奧 / perform the magic military alignment called mysterious gate
baoyi / 包衣 / bondservant (M: booi)
beiwu zhaocheng / 備物昭誠 / preparation of sacrificial offerings to show piety
bian / 匾 / placards
bitieshi / 筆帖式 scribe (M: bithesi)

caoyan / 操演 / exercise
chai / 差 / running errands (M: baita)
chailiao / 柴料 / fuel
Changshengdian / 長生殿 / *Palace of Lasting Life*
"Chengpi ruyao" / 成坯入窯 / "Putting the Finished Wares into the Kiln"
chijin, chichu / 持進 持出 / carrying valuable artifacts in and out
chongyi / 重譯 / repeated translations
chuanyi jing / 穿衣鏡 / dressing mirror
chuanzuo / 傳做 / commission
Ciju / 瓷局 / Porcelain Bureau
Cining Gong / 慈寧宮 / Palace of Compassion and Tranquillity
ciqi jiangren / 瓷器匠人 / craftsmen specializing in porcelain
Ciqu Ju / 詞曲局 / Bureau of Songs

Da Qing Kangxi Nian Zhi / 大清康熙年製 / Made in the Kangxi Reign of the Great Qing
da shipian / 大石片 / large stone slab
daochui lian / 倒垂蓮 / possibly tiger lily, *Lilium tigrinum*
dayang / 大樣 / big yang

di / 笛 / flutes
dian / 典 / classic
diangu / 典故 / literary anecdotes
Dianyi tushuo / 滇夷圖說 / *Illustrated Treatise on Yi Barbarians*
dibao / 邸報 / capital gazette
ding yuanzi / 頂圓子 / pigment of top quality
ditan / 地壇 / altar of Earth
doucai / 斗彩 / joined color
duizhen gunpai zhizhu / 對陣滾牌之助 / assist the performance of the exercise
duo'ermen you / 多爾門油 / doermendina oil

falang / 琺瑯 or falangcai 琺瑯彩 / painted enamel with pigments based on melted glass frits
Falangzuo / 琺瑯作 / Workshop of Painted Enamel
fang / 仿 / imitation
fang neifa jiuqi / 仿內發舊器 / imitation of old vessels sent from the court
fang neifa Songqi seze / 仿內發宋器色澤 / imitation of the color of Song wares sent from the inner [court]
fang tiegu Ge you / 仿鐵骨哥釉 / imitation of Ge glaze over iron bone
fangjiu / 仿舊 / imitation of old styles
fanglue / 方略 / military campaign history
fanzhe / 販者 / merchants
fengwei cao / 鳳尾草 / phoenix-tail fern

gewu / 格物 / categorizing things
geyao / 哥窯 / Ge kiln; sometimes refers to Ge wares
gong / 工 / artisan; craft; regulated
gongdan / 貢單 / list of tributes
gongdiao / 宮調 / music modes
gongyi / 工役 / clerks
guang / 光 / brightness or luminosity
Guangchusi / 廣儲司 / Grand Storage Office
guanyao / 官窯 / official kiln
guchen / 孤臣 / solitary subject
guniang qiang / 姑娘腔 / tunes of the lass
guoni xiabo / 過泥匣缽 / earthenware vessels for sedimentation

hepai yang / 合牌樣 / bundle of cardboard
Hezihao shi / 和字號十 / 10 under the He group
huabu / 花部 / flowery sector
Huai'an guan / 淮安關 / Huai'an custom house
huan xingtou / 換行頭 / change costumes
huangci zun / 黃磁尊 / yellow porcelain *zun* vessel

huaya banshi / 畫押辦事 / manager with seal
huayang / 畫樣 / copy the design
Hubu / 戶部 / Board of Revenue
Huidian / 會典 / *Collected Statutes*
huiqing / 回青 / cobalt-blue pigment
Hujun Xiao / 護軍校 / commandant in the Palace Guards Brigade
Huolangdan / 貨郎擔 / *Peddler's Carrying Pole*
huoqi / 火氣 / ambience of fire
huozhao / 火照 / fire tester

Jia sao / 笳騷 / Song of the Foreign Flute
jiangyi / 匠役 / artisans
jianzao / 監造 / production supervisor
jianzhi / 建置 / institution
jiaoqiang / 交槍 / Western firearm
jiazi / 甲子 / sixty years
jieyun / 解運 / transport
jihong / 霽紅 / sacrificial red
jin / 斤 / catty
Jingdezhen / 景德鎮 / the town where porcelain wares were manufactured
Jingshan / 景山 / Prospect Hill
jingxi / 精細 / exquisite
jitang / 集唐 / assembling lines from Tang dynasty poetry
jiucai bian / 韭菜邊 / chive sprout
Jiujiang guan / 九江關 / Jiujiang custom house
Jiuzhou Qingyan Shangxianlou / 九州清宴上仙樓 / mansion known as the Celestial Immortals' Banquet over Nine Regions
ju fang neifa jiuqi seze / 俱仿內發舊器色澤 / imitating the color of the glaze on the old ware sent from the imperial storage
jue / 爵 / beaker
Junjichu / 軍機處 / Office of Military Strategy

kaozheng / 考證 / evidential scholarship
ku / 枯 / economy (of brushstrokes and washes)
kuanshi / 款識 / style
Kun / 崑 / a southern place name; the name of a style of drama

li / 禮 / rite
li / 里 / miles; a sense of withinness, in opposition to graphic flatness
lian / 蓮 / lotus or other species from a separate genus conventionally called by the same name in premodern China
liaohu / 料戶 / household of cobalt color
liaojia / 料價 / price

Lifanyuan / 理藩院 / Ministry for Ruling Outer Provinces
luantan / 亂彈 / tunes of miscellaneous play

mao / 毛 / rough incompleteness, encouraging participatory viewing
mawei xiluo / 馬尾細蘿 / fine horsehair sieve
meiping / 梅瓶 / sometimes translated as prunus vase
mingtang / 明堂 / Hall of Light
minyao / 民窯 / private kilns
mise ci / 秘色瓷 / a kind of celadon
mulian hua / 木蓮花 / wooden lotus
mupa / 木耙 / wooden prong
muyou / 幕友 / private secretary
Muzhai Zhi / 沐齋製 / Made by [the owner of] the Mu Studio

Nan Shufang / 南書房 / Southern Study
neiting gongzao shiyang / 內廷恭造式樣 / honorable style of the inner court
Neiwufu / 內務府 / Imperial Household Department
niaoqiang / 鳥槍 / muskets
nijiang / 泥匠 / worker handling clay

pen / 盆 / iron pot
pi / 坯 / preliminary base

qi / 啟 / inform
qi zhi pinshu / 器之品數 / kinds of vessels
qianli jing / 千里鏡 / telescopes
Qianlong yuzhi / 乾隆御製 / made by Qianlong's imperial commission
qin / 琴 / zither
qingbai / 青白 / green-white
Qinqiang / 秦腔 / tunes of the Qin region

renfu / 人夫 / labor
renqiao / 人巧 / human ingenuity
run / 潤 / lustrous effect
Ruyiguan / 如意館 / Hall of Self-Fulfillment

shang / 商 / merchant
Shangxiaolou / 上小樓 / *Ascending a Small Pavilion* (name of an aria)
shanpan / 山叛 / mountain rebels
shatu / 砂土 / clay
sheguan / 設官 / office
shejitan / 社稷壇 / altar of grain

Shengmu / 聖母 / Immortal Mother
shi / 試 / trials or experiments
shiba tan / 十八灘 / eighteen rapids
shifang / 試放 / testing
shiyang / 式樣 / copy for reference
shuangceng juandai / 雙層 / bag made of double layers of silk
shuigang / 水缸 / earthenware jar
sishi zhe / 司事者 / official manager of the factory
Song qi / 宋器 / wares made in the Song dynasty
suiyi huayang / 隨意畫樣 / improvise some yang
suqi / 俗氣 / vulgar

Tang Ying / 唐英
Tao ji / 陶記 / *Notes on Ceramics*
taocheng baowan / 陶成寶玩 / accomplished pot to be cherished
taocheng jushi / 陶成居士 / Buddhist layman who made pottery
"Taolian nitu" / 淘練泥土 / "Washing and Purification of the Pastes"
Taoren xinyu / 陶人心語 / *Words from a Potter's Mind*
Taoye tushu / 陶冶圖說 / *Illustrated Manual of Ceramic Production*
tianbai / 甜白 / sweet white
tiangan / 天干 / celestial branches
Tianhou Gong / 天后宮 / Temple for the Queen of Heaven
tieluo / 貼落 / paintings pasted onto the walls
tieqiu / 鐵楸 / iron spades
tong / 筒 / cylinders
Tonghui he caoyun tu / 通惠河槽運圖 / *Picture of Transporting Grain to the Capital on the Tonghui Canal*
tongshi / 通事 / interpreter
tongtai huafalang / 銅胎畫琺瑯 / painted enamel over bronze body
tuizhong / 推鐘 / timepieces
tuotai / 脫胎 / boneless
turen / 土人 / native of the land
tushuo / 圖說 / narration by pictures (or illustrated treatise)

Wang Yuanqi / 王原祁 / painter
Wan-yan Lin-qing / 完顏麟慶 / M: Wanggiyan Linking (1791–1846), high-ranking official, hydraulic specialist
Weiyuan / 威遠 / Mighty General
Wubeiyuan / 武備院 / Imperial Armory
wucai / 五彩 / five colors
wudi muxia / 無底木匣 / wooden box with no bottom
wugong / 五供 / five-offering wares

xiangsheng / 像生 / imitation of life
xiangxi / 詳細 / in detail
xiaoyang jiqi tu / 小様祭器圖 / small yang of sacrificial vessels
xibu dadan / 細布大單 / large cloth of fine cotton
xifa / 西法 / Western technique
xifanlian / 西番蓮 / Indian lotus, lit. "lotus of western aborigines"
"Xihu yuchang xu" / 西湖漁唱序 / "Preface to *Fisherman's Song by West Lake*"
xiumo / 修模 / fixing molds
xiyang hongse qimin / 西洋紅色器皿 / vessels in Western red color

yabu / 雅部 / elegant sector
yang / 様 / design drafts
yangben / 様本 / model
yangcai / 洋彩 / foreign enameled
Yangxindian / 養心殿 / Hall of Mental Cultivation
yanse / 顏色 / pigment
yaobian / 窯變 / transformation inside the kiln
yaopeng / 窯棚 / kiln shed
yaoshang ren / 窯上人 / people at the local kiln site
yaotang pao / 藥膛炮 / chamber cannon
yaoyan / 窯眼 / eye of the kiln, holes on kiln walls through which craftsmen observe the color of fire in order to estimate temperature
yaozhi / 窯製 / kiln regulation
yihai / 乙亥 / twelve
yilei midui / 依類覓對 / searching for the couplet according to categories
Yinghe (1771–1840) / 英和 / supervisor-in-chief of the Imperial Household Department
yingqing / 影青 / translucent green
Yingzaosi / 營造司 / Bureau of Works
"Yinpi ruliao" / 印坯乳料 / "Molding the Body and Grinding the Colors"
yinqi / 印器 / molded ware
Yinxiang / 胤祥 / Prince Yi
Yiyong cijin / 義勇辭金 / *Righteous Refusal of a Gift of Gold*
Youtao Lingci / 佑陶靈祠 / Shrine to Protect Ceramic Production
yuanqi / 圓器 / round wares
"Yuanqi qinghua" / 圓器青花 / "Painting the Round Ware in Blue and White"
"Yuanqi xiumo" / 圓器修模 / "Preparing the Molds for the Round Ware"
yuanwailang / 員外郎 / vice director of a bureau
Yuci Chunyitang Zhencang / 御賜純一堂珍藏 / Hall of Purity, Imperially Bestowed
Yue haiguan / 粵海關 / Guangzhou custom house
yugong / 御貢 / tribute
yunxiang you / 芸香油 / local solution for pigment, a substitute for the imported *doermen* oil (doermendina)
Yuqichang / 御器廠 / Imperial Vessel Manufactory

Yuxi meng / 虞兮夢 / *Dream about Yuxi*
Yuyaochang / 御窯廠 / Imperial Porcelain Manufactory
Yuzuo / 玉作 / Jade Workshop

zaju / 雜劇 / northern drama
Zaobanchu / 造辦處 / Imperial Workshops
zeli / 則例 / regulations and precedents
Zhai Gong / 齋宮 / Palace for Fasting
zhangyao / 障窯 / loading the kiln
zhaoxin / 肇新 / new designs
zhaoyang huayang / 照樣畫樣 / draw design drafts according to the model
zhengwei / 正位 / main position
zhenlu / 振鷺 / soaring crane
zhentao yawan / 珍陶雅玩 / ceramic connoisseur's elegant plaything
Zhijia zeli zhangcheng ce / 製價則例章程冊 / *Regulation and Precedents of the Production Cost*
zhilian / 製煉 / burning the color pigment under the furnace floor for three days, then taking it out and washing it carefully again
zhishi / 執事 / foreman (M: baitangga)
zhong / 中 / alignment, overall balance
Zhuandiao huolang'er / 轉調貨郎兒 / *Peddler in Alternating Tunes*
zhuangdiao jiju / 轉調集句 / assembly of lines with alternating tunes
zhuangtong jiang / 裝桶匠 / specialized packers
Zhuantianxin / 轉天心 / *Turning the Mind of Heaven*
zhuanzi kuan ziyang / 篆字款字樣 / design draft of seal script
zhuoqi / 琢器 / molded ware
zidishu / 子弟書 / youth book
zixing chuangzao / 自行創造 / tentative creations
Zouxiao Dang / 奏銷檔 / Archive of Accounting
zuo / 作 / organized workshop of craftsmen
zuoling / 佐領 / companies (M: niru)

NOTES

INTRODUCTION

1. Tang Ying, *Tang Ying ji*, 360. All the translations are my own unless otherwise mentioned.

2. Throughout this book, Imperial Porcelain Manufactory will serve as the translation of Yuyaochang, the name established in the Qing dynasty. The manufactory was there before the Qing dynasty (since the early 1400s), but it was given this name, which literally means "manufactory where the imperial kilns stood," in the Qing. I chose "porcelain" over "ceramic" or "pottery" because the most significant products from this manufactory were fired under high temperature, usually around 1300°C. In both premodern Chinese and modern classification, they are porcelains. However, the imperial manufactory did produce stoneware and earthenware, fired at less than 1300°C, often in imitation of famous products from earlier dynasties. These I refer to as "ceramics." For a recent anthropological study of the entire history of this industrial town, see Gillette, *China's Porcelain Capital*. Gerritsen, *The City of Blue and White*, pieces together a true global history of Jingdezhen to uncover the secret of its sustained productivity and performance on the global market from the tenth century up until the late seventeenth century.

3. D'Entrecolles, "Lettre du Père D'Entrecolles au Père Orry, 1 sept. 1712," 253–357.

4. On the demand for bureaucratic sophistication and technical expertise in Europe in this period, see Ash, "Introduction," 1–24. See also Rabier, *Fields of Expertise*, xi–34.

5. For instance, on the Qing dynasty central government's systematic bookkeeping, see Shi, *Central Government Silver Treasury*. For a study of finance in the Imperial Household Department, see Lai Hui-Min, *Qianlong huangdi de hebao*.

6. On the early history of the Manchus, see Liu Xiaomeng, *Manzu cong buluo dao guojia*. A comprehensive overview of the period under scrutiny is found in Naquin and Rawski, *Chinese Society in the Eighteenth Century*.

7. On the tension between bureaucratization and monarchic power, see Kuhn, *Soulstealers*. On the Manchu court's consolidation of Chinese elites, see Kessler, "Chinese Scholars and the Early Manchu State," 179–200. On the "struggle and compromise

between imperial and literati interests" via civil examinations, see Elman, *Civil Examinations and Meritocracy*, 95–146.

8. For instance, Bartlett discusses in detail the trusted Office of Military Strategy (*Junjichu*), which later expanded into what she translates as the "Grand Council," a powerful privy ministry serving the emperor. See Bartlett, *Monarchs and Ministers*.

9. For studies of technocrats in modern China, who, I believe, bear the legacy of imperial China, see William Kirby, "Engineering China: Birth of the Developmental State, 1928–1937," in Yeh, *Becoming Chinese*; Andreas, *Rise of the Red Engineers*; and Cheng Li, "The Rise of Technocracy," 13–14.

10. Mukerji, *Territorial Ambitions and the Gardens of Versailles*, xix–96.

11. Schlesinger, *A World Trimmed with Fur*.

12. Whiteman, *Where Dragon Veins Meet*; Kleutghen, *Imperial Illusions*; Berger, *Empire of Emptiness*.

13. The development of the sociology of knowledge is summarized by Bloor, "Sociology of Scientific Knowledge," in Niiniluoto, Sintonen, and Woleński, *Handbook of Epistemology*.

14. I draw great insights from the study of early modern artisans as knowledge makers. See Ko, "Entanglements of Body, Text, and Stone," in Anderson, Dunlop, and Smith, *The Matter of Art*.

15. Smith, Meyers, and Cook, *Ways of Making and Knowing*; Klein and Spary, *Materials and Expertise in Early Modern Europe*; Roberts, Schaffer, and Dear, *The Mindful Hand*.

16. Nappi, *The Monkey and the Inkpot*.

17. For a review of the concept of technics and technology in anthropology, see Sigaut, "Technology."

18. Ingold, *The Perception of the Environment*, 315.

19. Bray, "Towards a Critical History of Non-Western Technology."

20. The meaning of "technocrat" here derives from its classical etymology and is not modeled on American engineers advocating scientific governance or the Soviet technological cadres active in the twentieth century. Some reflection on technologically specialized officialdom is also available in recent Chinese scholarship. See Liu Fengyun, "Shiba shiji de jishu guanliao," 17–20; Ding Haibin, *Qingdai "guan keji" qunti de yangcheng yu jiegou yanjiu*.

21. A series of thorough studies on the role of Manchus in the Qing dynasty comprehensively clarify the military origin, institutional expansion, and political significance of the banner system since the founding of the Manchu kingdom before 1644. See Elliott, *The Manchu Way*; Crossley, *A Translucent Mirror*; Rawski, *The Last Emperors*, 61–63.

22. For a study of powerful bannermen clans, see Lei, *Qingdai shehui baqi guizu shijia shili yanjiu*.

23. For a comprehensive introduction to the banner system and how it came into being, see Naquin and Rawski, *Chinese Society in the Eighteenth Century*, 4.

24. *Booi* in the Manchu language literally means "(people in) a household." Depending on the context, *booi* may stand for *booi aha*, which translates directly as household slave.

For a detailed clarification of bondservants (*booi*), see Elliott, *The Manchu Way*, 81–84. For an explanation of the complex situation of multiethnic subjects subjugated as bannermen or bondservants, see Crossley, *A Translucent Mirror*, 45–50, 84–128; Rawski, *The Last Emperors*, 166–71. See also Qi Meiqin, *Qingdai baoyi qiren yanjiu*.

25. Rawski, *The Last Emperors*, 178–81. Royal family members and common bannermen also received their education in specially built schools in Beijing. Bondservants from the upper three banners and their children attended the Prospect Hill Officials' School and Xian'an Palace Officials' School, which were both annexed to the Imperial Household Department. For a detailed explanation of these schools and the official examinations for different circles, see Crossley, "Banner Education and the Conquest State," in Elman and Woodside, *Education and Society in Late Imperial China*.

26. The development of the institute and its actual fluctuating numbers have been systematically—but not exhaustively—surveyed in a few studies. See Qi, *Qingdai Neiwufu*; Torbert, *The Ch'ing Imperial Household Department*; Chang Te-Chang, "The Economic Role of the Imperial Household in the Ch'ing Dynasty."

27. Qi, *Qingdai Neiwufu*, 55–59, 77–85.

28. Torbert, *The Ch'ing Imperial Household Department*, 28–29.

29. Wu Zhaoqing, "Qingdai zaobanchu de jigou he jiangyi."

30. George Loehr, "The Sinicization of Missionary Artists," 795–803.

31. Three textile manufactories were located in Jiangning, Suzhou, and Hangzhou. For more information about these, see Torbert, *The Ch'ing Imperial Household Department*, 111–13; Chou Wen-Hui, "Qingchao qianqi zhizao chutan-yi Suzhou zhizao wei zhongxin."

32. Rawski, *The Last Emperors*, 179.

33. Jonathan Spence has discussed bondservants' wide-ranging missions in different chapters of life of the famous textile commissioner Cao's family. See Spence, *Ts'ao Yin and the K'ang-hsi Emperor*.

34. Technocrats as institutional personnel were not unique to the Qing dynasty. The role of technological specialists in previous imperial governments awaits further examination; the cultural products of this community reveal how imperial states integrated technological expertise. A representative example of the state's integration of architectural expertise in the middle period is available in Feng Jiren, *Chinese Architecture and Metaphor*.

35. For a detailed study of the exclusive communication system of memorials, see Silas Wu, *Communication and Imperial Control in China*.

36. Early scholarship relies on memorials, Jesuit missionaries' letters, and sporadic consultation of the imperial archive to recover information about the Imperial Workshops and their products. See, e.g., Zhu Jiajin, "Qingdai hua falang qi zhizao kao."

37. Chen Kuo-tung, "Neiwufu guanyuan de waipai, wairen yu Qianlong gongting wenwu gongji zhijian de guanxi."

38. Hostetler's study of the *Miao* album uses the concept of ethnography in the early modern context and convincingly shows how ethnographic information was put in order by taxonomy and refined categorization to fulfill an administrative goal. See *Qing Colonial Enterprise*, 6, 45, 96–100, and 127–57.

39. Wu Zhaoqing ("Qingdai zaobanchu de jigou he jiangyi," 84) shows that the

recruited artisans were paid more handsomely than house workers. See also Dagmar Schäfer, *Gongting yu difang*.

40. We can find the history of their introduction in two studies: Pagani, *Eastern Magnificence and European Ingenuity*; Curtis, *Glass Exchange between Europe and China, 1550–1800*.

41. For a summary of the global porcelain network, see Finlay, *The Pilgrim Art*. See also Gerritsen and McDowall, "Material Culture and the Other."

42. Elliot's and Crossley's works investigate the formation and transformation of Manchu identity in the empire. They demarcate the discursive, as well as practical, boundary that the ruling Manchu were able to develop and make effective. On the pivotal role of the Manchu language in political administration, see Crossley and Rawski, "A Profile of the Manchu Language in Ch'ing History."

43. Crossley, "The Banner Elites," in *A Translucent Mirror*, 285–90. Bondservants actively acquired not only martial skills but also the technology of occupation. See also Crossley, "Manchu Education," in Elman and Woodside, *Education and Society in Late Imperial China*.

44. This claim calls for further research and fine-tuning. However, it would be a serious stretch to claim that the evidential scholarship covered in Elman's *From Philosophy to Philology* significantly overlapped with bannermen's inventory of writing, which consists primarily of military journals, geographical studies, and poetry anthologies. For one example, see Hong Wei, "Qingdai Wanqi Baqi Menggu wenren En-Hua, jiqi 'Baqi wenyi bianmu," 1–10.

45. There are some not very detailed exceptions; see Qi, "Qingdai Neiwufu Baoyi dui Qingdai Wenhua de Gongxian."

46. Cicero, *On Obligations*, book I, 93, 95–97. "Decorum, Cicero's attempt to translate πρέπον, is defined as an appreciation of the fitness of things, propriety in inward feeling or outward appearance, in speech, behavior, dress, etc. Decorum is as difficult to translate into English as πρέπον is to reproduce in Latin; here, as an adjective, it is rendered by 'proper,' as a noun, by 'propriety.'" M. Tullius Cicero, *De Officiis*, trans. Walter Miller, 96.

47. For an in-depth analysis of the regulatory force of *li*, see Keliher, "The Manchu Transformation of Li"; and recently his monograph, *The Board of Rites and the Making of Qing China*.

48. Angela Zito analyzes the performance of *li* with texts as well as the grand choreography of artifacts and people in imperial sacrifices in her *Of Body and Brush*. Berger, in *The Empire of Emptiness*, focuses on the Qianlong emperor's multiculturalist integration by means of the eclectic use of Chinese, Manchu, and especially Mongolian and Tibetan Buddhist artistic conventions.

49. Hostetler, *Qing Colonial Enterprise*, 5–6.

50. Mosca has pointed out the important and often overlooked "off-duty" inquiries about frontiers that Manchu, Mongol, and later Han Chinese officials voluntarily conducted without bureaucratic requirement. See Matthew Mosca, "Empire and the Circulation of Frontier Intelligence," 147–207, esp. 149 and 183.

51. Dear, "Mysteries of State, Mysteries of Nature."

52. Historian Mitchell explains how the making of the national economy's knowledge system and scientific discipline was never divorced from multiple agents' exercise of power in the economic reformation of Egypt, which further shaped the political regime. See Timothy Mitchell, *Rule of Experts*.

53. For a conceptual articulation of the embodiment and social embeddedness of skill, see Eyferth, "The Nature of Skill."

54. On the role of Chinese officials in practical statecraft, such as promoting agricultural production and hydraulic management, see Bray, "Chinese Literati and the Transmission of Technological Knowledge"; and Rowe, *Saving the World*. See also Liu Fengyun, "Shiba shiji de jishu guanliao."

55. No comprehensive survey is known to date, but Chen Kuo-tung clearly explains the institutional phenomenon of this exclusive employment of bannermen in the imperial household in his study "Neiwufu guanyuan de waipai, wairen yu qianlong gongting wenwu gongji zhijian de guanxi."

56. Elman, *A Cultural History of Civil Examinations in Late Imperial China*, 460–85.

57. Elman, *A Cultural History of Modern Science in China*, 69.

58. Elman, "The Jesuit Role as Experts in High Qing Cartography and Technology," in *On Their Own Terms*.

59. On the difference between specialists and generalists in the officialdom, see Will, "L'apprentissage du métier de fonctionnaire à la fin de la période impériale." Elman also points out that "banner students could participate in the provincial examinations and become generalist officials," meaning that bannermen could choose to pursue other career trajectories. "The bannermen regarded civil examinations and mathematical training as secondary and complementary to their primary military skills. . . . The Qianlong emperor stopped bannermen from training in mathematics in 1738." Elman, *On Their Own Terms*, 151.

60. For a discussion of the modes of knowledge making, see Smith and Schmidt, *Making Knowledge in Early Modern Europe*, 7. Moreover, my approach to these proficient bannermen technocrats benefits from Pamela Smith's investigation of the polymath alchemist Johann Becher (1635–1682), who engaged in artisanal production and dispensed economic advice at the courts of various electors of the Holy Roman Empire. See Smith, *The Business of Alchemy*.

61. Lenoir, *Inscribing Science*.

62. Leroi-Gourhan, *Gesture and Speech*, 249–63.

63. Lydia Liu, *Translingual Practice*, 1–42.

64. For an analysis of the multiple uses of preparatory sketchbooks and drawings in an earlier period, see Sarah Fraser, "The Artist's Practice in Tang Dynasty China," 1–21, 99–238. She posits several possible functions of preparatory materials. Depending on different formal specifications, they could be used as instructions for an atelier, a design draft for a patron to review, an aide-memoire for a ritual, or a model for ink paintings produced much later.

65. For a theoretical discussion of the general sociality and assemblage, see Bennett,

"Affective Bodies" and "What Is Assemblage?," in *Vibrant Matters*, 20–24; and Bruno Latour's rediscovery of Gabriel Tarde in "Gabriel Tarde and the End of the Social."

66. On the rare conceptualization of choice in the study of Chinese history, see Peterson, *Bitter Gourd*. For an illuminating discussion of the influence or control that a superior in an organization exerts on lower operatives through limiting their choice of alternatives, see Simon, *Administrative Behavior*, 2, 67, 79–80, 123–39.

67. An organized workshop of craftsmen (*gong*) is called a *zuo*. For studies of *zeli* (regulations and precedents) used in managing such workshops, see Moll-Murata, Song, and Vogel, *Chinese Handicraft Regulations of the Qing Dynasty*.

68. For example, the standard size of prefabricated shoe components implies the average size of bound feet. See Ko, *Cinderella's Sisters*, 218.

69. For example, see the work of Tang Dai (1673–after 1751), a bannerman and a premier court painter. See Ju-hsi Chou, "Tangdai."

70. For a discussion of representational strategies in the ethnographic descriptions and depictions of populations in the southwestern territory of the Qing empire, see Hostetler, *Qing Colonial Enterprise*, 45–46, 127–99.

71. Almost all design drafts and models dated before the 1800s are now lost, although some later examples, primarily architectural designs, still remain. See Guo Daiheng and He Yan, *Shenzang jiyi yichan zhong de Yuanmingyuan*.

72. Many splendid exhibitions, along with concurring conferences, have been organized to showcase the taste of the Kangxi, Yongzheng, and Qianlong emperors. See Feng, *Emperor Ch'ien-lung's Grand Cultural Enterprise*; Feng, *Harmony and Integrity*; Feng, *Emperor Kangxi and the Sun King Louis XIV*; Rawski and Rawson, *China: The Three Emperors*. Although the judgment of "decorum" cannot be divorced from emperors' personal taste, I use the term to mean the judgment of a public character, concerning political appropriateness and auspiciousness.

73. My interdisciplinary approach is inspired by historian Anthony Grafton, who has uncovered a steady transformation in the cultural pattern, from the residual medieval to a humanist paradigm, by teasing out the way polymath Leon Alberti (1404–1472) used his rhetorical skill to build up an arena for each of his forms of cultural production, including painting, husbandry, antiquarianism, and architecture. See Grafton, *Leon Battista Alberti*.

74. For a discussion of individuals' "internalization" of influence in an organization, often through training and indoctrination, see Simon, *Administrative Behavior*, 103.

75. The colonial ethnographic approach is obvious from the large number of commissions of painting albums. See Hostetler, *Qing Colonial Enterprise*, 159–99.

ONE Bannermen Technocrats in the Mid-Qing

1. For systematic introductions to the department's institutional structure, see Qi, *Qingdai Neiwufu*; Torbert, *The Ch'ing Imperial Household Department*, for its complex system of ranks and recruitment; Du and Zhang, "Qingdai Neiwufu guanzhi de fuzaxing jiqi tedian." Regarding the civil promotion of bannermen, especially in the second half of the Qing dynasty, see Huang Li-Chun's dissertation, "Huangdi jiqi baoyi nucai," in which her

detailed study of bannermen bondservants' paths of promotion confirms the career channels exclusively reserved for bannermen, especially in the early to mid-Qing period.

2. E'ertai et al., *Baqi manzhou shizu tongpu*, 855.

3. Spence, *Ts'ao Yin and the K'ang-hsi Emperor*, 16n72.

4. People's ages are by Chinese count. Tang Ying, "Preface to the *Manual for Calligraphy*," in *Tang Ying ji*, 274. There are unfortunately few or no records about Tang's life before that.

5. For an explanation of the particular martial career opportunities reserved for bannermen, see Chen Wen-shih, "Qingdai de shiwei," in *Ming Qing zhenzhi shehui shilun*, 623–50.

6. For bannermen's special civil career path, see Chen Wen-shih, "Qingdai de bitie shi," in *Ming Qing zhenzhi shehui shilun*, 599–622.

7. See "Stela Memorandum of Wenchang Pavilion on Zhushan Hill beside the Manufacture": "In the fourth year of Qianlong's reign, Wenbao received the imperial favor to serve at the inner court as a *Zhishi*. Since then he should have had the opportunity to return the favor by working without rest," in Tang Ying, *Tang Ying dutao wendang*, 15.

8. There were some exceptions to this exclusiveness, especially during the Kangxi reign. Probably as a result of political coalitions during early days of the dynasty, Chinese and Mongolians may have been offered positions such as bodyguard, which later tended to be occupied mainly by bannermen.

9. "Announcement of successful candidates took place when I was inspecting Xun Yang. Hearing my son Yin'er passed, I casually composed two poems to encourage him," in *Tang Ying quanji*, 1:1, 202.

10. Famous literati-officials like Yuan Mei (1716–1798) attested to Tang's well-connectedness. See Yuan Mei, *Suiyuan shihua buyi, juan* 1, 443.

11. The fact is recorded in the succinct biography in a poetry collection written by bannermen elites. See Tie Bao, *Xichao yasong ji*, 1283.

12. Sun Yue, "Cuitao Tang Ying yu Qingdai guanyao," 15.

13. Director-in-chief of the Imperial Household Department, in charge of the Imperial Handicraft Workshops; see Hummel, *Eminent Chinese*, 931.

14. Tang Ying, *Tang Ying quanji*, 1:9a.

15. Jonathan Spence, "The Kangxi Reign," in Peterson, *The Cambridge History of China*, vol. 9, part 1, 162–65.

16. Gu Donggao, "Preface to *Taoren Xinyu*," in *Tang Ying quanji*, 1:1, 5.

17. *Taoren xinyu*, in *Tang Ying quanji*, 1:35.

18. "Shufa Zhinan Xu," in *Tang Ying ji*, 275.

19. All these reports are published as part of his journal manuscripts in the *Tang Ying quanji*, 2:444–53.

20. Bartlett, *Monarchs and Ministers*, 51.

21. Hummel, *Eminent Chinese*, 413; Wang Zhonghan, *Neiwufu shijia kao*, 529–30; Torbert, *The Ch'ing Imperial Household Department*, 136–71; Qi, *Neiwufu Gaoshi jiazu kao*, 108–14.

22. *Tang Ying quanji*, 1:3.

23. Gao Bin, *Guzai caotang shiji*, in *Qingdai shiwen ji huibian*, book 273, pp. 583, 596.

24. Wu Zhaoqing, "Qingdai Zaobanchu de jigou he jiangyi," 83–86. Apparently, apprentice bannermen from the upper banners were paid less than skillful artisans recruited from the south or European missionary experts.

25. "Supervisor-designer" in Jonathan Hay, *Sensuous Surfaces*, 36–37.

26. For example, on 4th day of the 1st month of the 4th year of the Yongzheng reign, Tang Ying received an order from Prince Yi to make seven more Baling (Tibetan Buddhist ritual instruments). He was directed to create a design with banded panels (*hepai yang*) to be inspected, and he could not produce them until the design had been agreed on (Record from the Painted Enamel Workshop). *Tang Ying dutao wendang*, 120.

27. Ding and Guan are names of kiln sites for porcelain production. Here these terms indicate kinds of glaze on the surface of ceramics. The Ding wares are matte white, sometimes with a faint yellow. The glaze of Guan wares is covered with an unbroken cracking effect. *Jiajing* is a reign title (1521–67) of the Ming dynasty. Here it refers to the time period when the specific styles of porcelain were produced.

28. "Ask Tang Ying to draw the design [*yang*] based on the model [*yang*]." See records on the 13th day of the 2nd month from the Jade and Ivory Workshops, in *Tang Ying dutao wendang*, 119.

29. Many late *yang* are still housed in the Palace Museum. The earliest *yang* used for ceramic production I can find is in Wang Guangyao and Guo Xingkuan, *Guanyang yuci*.

30. For a thorough study of the appropriation of Western visual techniques in large-scale and often verisimilar paintings pasted onto the walls (*tieluo*) at the Qing court, see Kleutghen, *Imperial Illusions*.

31. For some rare *yang* for textile, furniture, and small tableware, see Zhongguo Guojia Tushuguan, *Qingdai yangshilei jianzhu tudang zhan*, 35–36.

32. Mang-gu-li had the typical career of a bannerman technocrat rooted in the bannermen's political establishment, which extended to various vital regional positions. He worked for the Ministry for Ruling Outer Provinces (Lifanyuan), the Changlu bureau for salt monopoly, the Hushu custom house, and the former version of the Grand Council. See Bartlett, *Monarchs and Ministers*, 107, 330. See also his biographical information, conveniently collated in the Chinese Biographical Database.

33. The Freer Gallery houses the portrait of Yingxiang, and the painting of a palace lady is in the Philadelphia Museum of Art. See also Yu Hui, "Shiba shiji fuwu yu jingcheng wangfu huandi de renwu huajia."

34. Although Tang Dai also claimed to be a disciple of Wang Yuanqi, a master of orthodox brushwork and the paragon of literati painting in the early Qing. See Wang Yao-t'ing, "Yuci huazhuangyuan Tang Dai," 18–29. For a biography of Tang Dai, see Goepper's dissertation, "Tang-tai, Ein Hofmaler der Ch'ing-Zeit"; and Chou Ju-hsi, "Tangdai."

35. Ma Ya-chen, *Kehua zhanxun*, 127–243, esp. 146–48 and 196–214.

36. Bartlett (*Monarchs and Ministers*, 95) analyzes the orderly and secretive nature of such recommendations.

37. *Tang Ying dutao wendang*, 124, 125.

38. *Tang Ying dutao wendang*, 124.

39. *Tang Ying dutao wendang*, 126

40. *Tang Ying dutao wendang*, 123.

41. About the exclusive career opportunity reserved for guards, see Wei Qingyuan, "Neiwufu de jiangyi he yuyong shougongye," in *Mingqing shi xuxi*, 362; Chen Wen-shih, "Qingdai de shiwei," in *Ming Qing zhengzhi shehui shilun*, 636–42.

42. For a brief account of the Bureau of Works (Yingzaosi), Imperial Armory (Wubeiyuan), and Imperial Workshops involved in the military industry, see Wei Qingyuan, "Neiwufu de fuofangmian gongneng," in *Mingqing shi xuxi*, 355–58.

43. On the importance of Hanjun bannermen in the development of the cannon, see Huang Yi-nong, "Hongyi dapao yu Huang Taiji chuangli de baqi Hanjun," 74–105.

44. *Tang Ying dutao wendang*, 121. The mother-and-son cannon is explained in Needham's project: "It fired a projectile which burst and sent forth other projectiles that all fell down upon the enemy. . . . It was rather like a Western mortar." See Needham et al., *Science and Civilisation in China*, 409.

45. *Tang Ying dutao wendang*, 122.

46. *Tang Ying dutao wendang*, 121.

47. The seventeenth scene of *Turning the Mind of Heaven* is "Rebel on the Mountains" (Shanpan). See *Tang Ying quanji*, 3:969–70; see also *Tang Ying ji*, 788.

48. *Tang Ying quanji*, 2:487.

49. *Tang Ying quanji*, 2:683.

50. *Tang Ying dutao wendang*, 122.

51. A relevant but even earlier bannerman ceramic supervisor, Lang Tingji (1663–1715), worked during the late Kangxi reign, when the boundary between private production and imperial kilns was more elusive and underdocumented by the imperial archive.

52. "Jiangxi Provincial Administration Commissioner Chang Deshou's Memorial on An Shangyi's Ceramic Production in Jingdezhen," in *Tang Ying dutao wendang*, 29.

53. Thomas Lawton translated part of *Moyuan Huiguan*, the catalog of An Qi's collection, into English in "An Eighteenth Century Chinese Catalogue of Calligraphy and Painting." See also Arthur Hummel, *Eminent Chinese*, 11–13.

54. For the analysis of this plausible link, see Huang Qinghua, "Lang yao yu Kangxi Guanyao guanxi kaoshi."

55. Nian Xiyao is the older brother of the powerful general Nian Gengyao (1679–1726). See Hummel, *Eminent Chinese*, 587–90; Corsi, "Nian Xiyao de shengping jiqi dui yishu he kexue de gongxian," 156.

56. Gugong Bowuyuan, *Qinggong Neiwufu zaobanchu dang'an zonghui*, 2:456.

57. Giès, "'Perspectiva' ou 'Science de la vision' de Nian Xiyao (?–1739)," 13–33.

58. Kaijun Chen, "Yiwei jishu guanliao de ziwo xiuyang."

59. *Tang Ying dutao wendang*, 145.

60. *Tianbai* is usually translated as "sugar white" or "sweet white," partly due to the choice of character used, i.e., *tianbai* instead of "filling white."

61. These white wares would be painted with overglaze enamel and fired at a low temperature in the Workshop of Painted Enamel (Falangzuo) at court.

62. *Tang Ying dutao wendang*, 145.

63. From either an emic or etic perspective, many studies have expounded on the importance of the Manchu language as an ethnic marker for bannermen and the somehow waning mastery of it since the middle of the dynasty. See Elliott, *The Manchu Way*, 290–304; Crossley and Rawski, "A Profile of the Manchu Language in Ch'ing History."

64. These subjects remained to be communicated in Manchu, although more and more archived documents were written in Chinese during the second half of the Qianlong reign.

65. For brief biographical information on Tie Bao, see Hummel, *Eminent Chinese*, 717–18.

66. Tie Bao, *Weiqing zhai quanji*, 358.

67. Torbert, *The Ch'ing Imperial Household Department*, 37. See also Crossley, "Manchu Education," in Elman and Woodside, *Education and Society in Late Imperial China*, 355–59. Crossley summarizes bannermen's study subjects as "technical competence in military skills, translation, mathematics, and astronomy," in addition to the Confucian curriculum.

68. "Shufa zhinan xu," in *Tang Ying ji*, 275.

69. "Shufa zhinan xu," in *Tang Ying ji*, 275.

70. He was not embarrassed to look for literary correction from a local official at the Education Department in Guangzhou. See "To respond Shanzhang, Mr. Wu Mingpei in prefecture Zhaoqing [the meeting on Dec. 12th] . . . I respectfully submit about ten chapters to your master's place for your correction," in *Tang Ying quanji*, 2:690.

71. Xiang, "Tang Ying jiqi xiqu chuangzuo," 18. Woji was Tang Ying's style name.

72. In the preface to *Bedding Made of Reeds*, Jiang Shiquan signed, "Before the Chongyang [9th day of the 9th month] of the year Wuchen [1748], Jiang Shiquan from Qianshan, composed and inscribed in the barge on River Wen." See Tang Ying, *Gubaitang xiquji*, 46. In his preface to *San Yuan Bao*, he also recorded, "In August of 1744, Jiang Shiquan from Qianshan composed and inscribed in the boat when he passed Jining." Tang Ying, *Gubaitang xiquji*, 15.

73. See "Respond to Jiang Xiaolian's [Jiang Shiquan] ten *lü* poems in the same rhyme," dated to the 2nd month of QL 13. *Tang Ying quanji*, 2:516.

74. *Tang Ying quanji*, 2:519.

75. *Tang Ying quanji*, 2:550 (author's emphasis).

76. *Xin* could be literally translated as "heart," but "mind" foregrounds the intellectual function of this faculty.

77. "Xihu yuchang xu" (Preface to *Fisherman's Song by West Lake*), in *Tang Ying ji*, 222.

78. *Tang Ying ji*, 222.

79. Gao Bin's poems are anthologized in the *Guzai caotang ji* (Poetry from Guzai thatch hut).

80. *Guzai caotang ji*, 519.

81. *Guzai caotang ji*, book 273, 517.

82. From Zhou Xuejian's preface, "On the Reconstruction of Pipa Pavilion," in Tang Ying, *Jike Pipa Ting shi*, 2.

83. D. C. Lau, *Mencius*, 59, with my amendments.

84. *Tang Ying quanji*, 1:7.

85. For a pioneering discussion of merchants' route books, see Brook, "Guides for Vexed Travelers," 32–76.

86. *Tang Ying quanji*, 2:536.

87. *Tang Ying quanji*, 2:658.

88. The portion is signed as "recorded in a boat at Wusuo Rapid on QL 15/5/6 (1750)."

89. For a comparison of merchants' route books, see Huang Bian, *Tianxia shuilu lucheng*, 215.

90. *Tang Ying quanji*, 2:578.

91. Curtis, *Glass Exchange between Europe and China*; Shih Ching-Fei, *Riyue guanghua*.

92. I have not found any record of court interpreters so far, but Tang Ying did note an interpreter (*tongshi*) in Guangzhou in his journal.

93. Near-sighted Kong Shangren (1648–1718) commented on his visual amazement when he put on a pair of glass spectacles. The playwright Li Yu (1611–1680) exaggerated the function of a telescope by imagining its capacity to serve as a matchmaker for talent and beauty. See Li Yu, *A Tower for the Summer Heat*. In the highly acclaimed *Story of the Stone*, the spectacular image created by a large dressing mirror (*chuanyi jing*) significantly contributes to the central trope of illusion in the entire narrative. See Shang Wei, "Truth Becomes Fiction When Fiction Is True."

94. *Tang Ying dutao wendang*, 84.

95. *Tang Ying dutao wendang*, 179–80.

96. *Tang Ying dutao wendang*, 179–80.

97. The specifically stylized rocks were building materials for garden mansions. The practice had been summarized as early as the Northern Song dynasty in Du Wan's *Stone Catalogue of Cloudy Forest*. It is unclear whether these rock models were drawings or small pebbles in specific shapes. See *Tang Ying dutao wendang*, 180.

98. He would mark the transliteration of the names of Western cargoes with a small square to the left of every character.

99. Huang and Van Dyke, "Hoppo Tang Ying."

TWO A New Knowledge Culture

1. McKendrick and Brewer, *The Birth of a Consumer Society*. On the integration of porcelain, especially the chinoiserie style, as oriental taste into British material culture, see Porter, *The Chinese Taste in Eighteenth-Century England*, 115–53.

2. Lai Hui-Min, *Qianlong huangdi de hebao*, 211–56. See also Schlesinger, *A World Trimmed with Fur*, 55–91, 129–66.

3. The extent and nature of intervention in the local ceramic industry by the Yuan court is still open to debate. Some scholars argue about the existence of an "imperial kiln" during the Yuan dynasty while others believe the government only taxed private kilns for their products and did not interfere with production. The latest view can be found in

Shang Gang, "Yuandai taoshi liangti," 48–53. See also Jiang, "Yuanqinghua yu Fuliang Ciju jiqi yaochang"; Shih Ching-Fei, "Mengyuan gongting zhong ciqi shiyong chutan"; Liu Xinyuan, "Jingdezhen Hutianyao geqi dianxing wanlei de zaoxing tezheng jiqi chengyinkao," 50–60.

4. Peng Tao, "Mingdai huanguan zhengzhi yu Jingdezhen de taozheng," 111, 114–20; Sato, "Ming jidai Kanyō ni okeru seika tōsai no ichi," 56–59; Wong, "Zhenzhu de zhuisuizhe," 170–72.

5. Gerritsen, "Ceramics for Local and Global Markets: Jingdezhen's Agora of Technologies," in Schäfer, *Cultures of Knowledge,* 161–84.

6. The Hongxi emperor's reign only lasted for one year, 1425.

7. Fan, "Qingdai feichu jiang ji de lishi yiyi"; Li Qijiang et al., "Mingqing shiji jiangji zhidu de biange dui Jingdezhen jishu fazhan de yingxiang."

8. Chi, "Cong huojidang kan yongqian liangchao de neiting qiwu yishu guwen." She also discusses the recruitment of craftsmen from the south in the second half of the Qing dynasty: Chi, "Qing zhonghouqi (1821–1911) Neiwufu zaobanchu nanjiang jiqi xiangguan wenti," 63–89.

9. For details about a technocrat in the imperial printing industry, see Jin Jian (M: Gingiyan; before 1750–1794), who wrote the definitive manual on movable type printing technology, *Wuying dian juzhenban chengshi* (A Chinese printing manual; 1774), translated by Richard Rudolph in 1954. For Jin Jian's involvement in copper money minting and hydraulic projects, see Xu Kai, "Lun Jin Jian." For a study of Jin Jian's extensive technocratic family, the Jin clan, and their Korean cultural legacy, see Li Dan, "Mingmo Qingchu Chaoxian yimin Jinshi Xindali jiazu yanjiu."

10. For a discussion of the role of emperor as an institution rather than an individual, who had to "follow imperial tradition and conventions in court art production," see Wang Cheng-hua, "Material Culture and Emperorship: The Shaping of Imperial Roles at the Court of Xuanzong 1426–35," 1–10.

11. For instance, Yuwen Kai (555–612), a court architect of the Sui dynasty, made a wooden *yang* of the Hall of Light (Mingtang Muyang) sometime between 605 and 618. See Di Luo, "A Grain of Sand," 192.

12. Feng Jiren, *Chinese Architecture and Metaphor.*

13. Zhu Qiqian pioneered the study of the Lei family of designers. See Wang Qiheng and He Beijie, "Zhu Qiqian 'Yangshi Lei kao' Jiaozhu," 84–87. The latest research on the craft of the Lei family is available in He, "Yangshi Lei shijia yanjiu." The extensive genealogy of the Lei family is available in Yi and Cui, *Qingdai jianzhu shijia yangshi Lei zupu jiaoshi.*

14. Wang Guangyao, "Ciqi xiaoyang yu yuyaochang shengchan zhidu," in *Zhongguo gudai guanyao zhidu,* 179–92.

15. The earliest textual evidence appears in *Kaogong Ji,* but there is not yet any unanimous consensus about the actual date of the text. It is conventionally dated to the Warring States period.

16. Zhang Daoyi, *Kao Gong Ji,* 293; Wenren, *Ancient Chinese Encyclopedia of Technology: Translation and Annotation of Kaogong ji (The Artificers' Record),* 130. Another

recent English-German translation is available, see Guan Zengjian and Konrad Herrman, *Kao Gong Ji*.

17. Liu Xu, *Jiu Tang shu*, *juan* 48, "Shihuo (foodstuff and goods)," *Scripta Sinica*, 2090, quoted in Wang Guangyao, "Thoughts on the Ceramics Inscribed with 'Guan Yang' from Yue Kiln," in *Zhongguo gudai guanyao zhidu*, 40–49.

18. For a study of *yang* used for bronze vessel production during the Song dynasty, see Chen Fang-mei, "Song guqiwuxue de xingqi yu song fanggu tongqi."

19. Zhuang Chuo, *Jilei pian*, quoted in Feng Xianming, *Zhongguo gutaociwenxian jishi*, 118.

20. "Bureau of Painting, the second tier of the eighth rank, is in charge of drawing and making all kinds of designs. In 1278 an official is appointed," from *Yuanshi*, *juan* 88, 2227.

21. Hsieh Yu-chen, "Mingchu guanfang yongqi renwuwen de yihan," 127–32.

22. Wang Guangyao, *Zhongguo gudai guanyao zhidu II*, 1–28.

23. Yu Pei-Chin, "Lang Shining (1688–1766) yu ciqi," 1–37.

24. Many splendid exhibitions along with concurring conferences have been organized to showcase the tastes of the Kangxi, Yongzheng, and Qianlong emperors. For instance, Feng Mingzhu, *Emperor Ch'ien-lung's Grand Cultural Enterprise*; Feng, *Harmony and Integrity*; Feng, *Emperor Kangxi and the Sun King Louis XIV*.

25. From as early as 1701, during the Kangxi emperor's reign, a regulation about the size of a straw mat had already been recorded. See Dalian Tushuguan, *Dalian tushuguan cang Qingdai Neiwufu Dang'an*, 1:435–39.

26. For instance, the Kangxi emperor frequently asked Cao Yin and Li Xu for details about the weather and harvest in the south. See an example in Gugong Bowuyuan Ming-Qing Dang'an Bu, *Li Xu zouzhe*, 2.

27. Lai Yu-Chih, "Images, Knowledge and Empire."

28. McCausland, "The Emperor's Old Toys."

29. Yu Pei-Chin, "Pinjian zhi qu," 133–66, esp. 135–40.

30. Regina Krahl, "The Yongzheng Emperor and the Qing Court Collection."

31. Qin, "Jingdezhen yuyaochang yizhi 2014 nian fajue shouhuo yu xiangguan wenti yanjiu," 69–88.

32. Besides numbered prototypes collected by museums, archaeologists in the Palace Museum in Beijing recently discovered such numbered shards within the palace, which should suggest the storage of prototypes at court. In contrast, according to published researches so far, all the test pieces dated to the Ming dynasty were excavated in the regional manufactory in Jingdezhen.

33. In the mid-eleventh century, officials started to mark archival shelves with characters from *The Thousand Character Classic* to locate correspondingly labeled governmental documents. See "Zhou Zhan . . . created a method for archiving with the *Thousand Character Classic* and order [documents] according to dates," in Zeng Gong, *Longping ji*, vol. 14, p. 18.

34. Peter Lam, "Towards a Dating Framework for Qianlong Imperial Porcelain," 12.

35. *Tang Ying dutao wendang*, 152.

36. Yun Lu et al., *Huangchao liqi tushi*, 18.

37. For several detailed analyses of the intellectual and political agenda around intel-

lectual practice with bronze ritual vessels, see Moser, "Recasting Antiquity"; Sena, *Bronze and Stone.*

38. See also Cai Mei-Fen, "Guanfu yu guan Yang," 321–27; Han, "Songdai fanggu zhizuo de yangben wenti," 288–96.

39. One complete hand-painted color set is housed in the Palace Museum in Beijing. Quite a few chapters of the colored version are kept in the Victoria and Albert Museum and the University of Alberta Museum.

40. Its scale—forty-eight volumes—and its original location mean it is plausible that it could be an album mentioned in an archival log dated to the 18th day of the 10th month in 1764. Following the format of this small *yang* of sacrificial vessels (*xiaoyang jiqi tu*), Qianlong ordered painters to make another small-format album based on the content of the big design draft (*dayang*) and many added painting leaves of the colored *Huangchao liqi tushi* (Illustrated regulations for ceremonial paraphernalia of the Qing dynasty) in the next two years. See *Archive of the Imperial Workshops*, 1:29, 51–52, 54, and 1:30, 119.

41. Tang Ying, *Qinggong Neiwufu zaobanchu dang'an zonghui*, 1:16, 240–41.

42. Chi, "Qianlong shiqi de ruyiguan," 127–52.

43. Qingshi Guan, *Qingshi gao*, book 502, 1:289, 13866.

44. Qingshi Guan, *Qingshi gao*, book 504, 1:291, 13911.

45. "Agora," in Schäfer, *Cultures of Knowledge*, 157–60.

46. Yu Hui, "Shiba shiji fuwu yu jingcheng wangfu huandi de renwu huajia," 63–70; Whiteman, "Creating the Kangxi Landscape," 142–62.

47. *Tang Ying dutao wendang*, 119.

48. *Tang Ying dutao wendang*, 32.

49. *Tang Ying dutao wendang*, 43.

50. Tang Ying never did manage to pay off his fine by selling inferior products at discount. Some bannermen who oversaw the lucrative regional factories and custom houses were able to accumulate private wealth by bypassing local governors, for they were fiscally responsible for the emperor's privy purse in the Imperial Household Department. Yet such wealth often paid for unforeseen fines or imperial expenditure, or was confiscated altogether.

51. The reign mark on this piece is in the style of the early years of the Qianlong reign, which means that it was made during Tang Ying's period of supervision. See Lam, "Toward a Dating Framework for Qianlong Porcelain." For the reproduction of the image of this vessel, see Lam, *Jixia qingshang*, 192.

52. Yu Pei-Chin's dissertation provides data about the annual yield. Yu Pei-Chin, "Qianlong guanyao yanjiu," appendix 1, 325–29. Tie Yuan adds the numbers from archival records and concludes that Tang Ying oversaw the production of 433,868 pieces of porcelain in total. See Jiang Jianxin, *Tang Ying yu Tangyao*, 138.

53. Lam, "Toward a Dating Framework for Qianlong Imperial Porcelain," 9.

54. Two vases (flower beaker) belonging to the National History Museum (Guojia Lishi Bowuguan) and Chinese University of Hong Kong respectively. A broken part of an incense burner was auctioned at Poly in Beijing in 2010. The burner bears the same in-

scription as the previously discussed four pieces. See Geng, "Mantan Tang Ying yu tangyao ciqi," 12.

55. Li Jinlu and Wang Guangyao, "Beijing xinchutu Tang Ying qie Keji ci guihuiguan," 14:41–45.

56. *Tang Ying quanji*, 202.

57. See *Tang Ying dutao wendang*, 52.

58. Soaring Crane (Zhenlu) is also one of Lang Tingji's studio titles, which appears on some extant pieces. See Lu, "Langyao jiqi zuopin yanjiu"; "Langyao xiangguan wenti zaikao"; Lam, "Lang Tingji (1663–1715) and the Porcelain of the Late Kangxi Period."

59. Lü Chenglong, "Kangxi chao Langyao ciqi pinzhong chutan," 74–91.

60. For instance, the eminent painter Yu Zhiding produced portraits as well as visual designs in a variety of media. See Scheier-Dolberg, "Yu Zhiding (ca. 1646–ca. 1716) and the Envisioning of the Early Qing World."

61. For an efficient introduction to the life and work of Liu Yuan, see Dorothy Ko, *Social Life of Inkstones*, 20–36.

62. Lam, "Cangu Yunxin," 11–24.

63. Tong Pengnian's preface to *Lingyan ge Illustration*, reproduced in Burkus-Chasson, *Through a Forest of Chancellors*, 260–63.

64. "Liu Yuan zhuan" (Biography of Liu Yuan), in Qingshi Guan, *Qingshi Gao*, vol. 505, pp. 5488–89.

65. Lam, "Cangu Yunxin," 11–24.

66. Recorded on the 10th day of the 9th month in 1742. See *Tang Ying dutao wendang*, 158.

67. *Tang Ying dutao wendang*, 158. According to the ensuing archival records, the bare wooden models were finished in about twelve days. Then the court ordered them to make paper drafts of landscape paintings in a medallion decoration and dispatch them to Tang Ying for production. Yet it took another twelve days for the bare wooden model to be fully decorated with the flower brocade pattern for Tang Ying to model on. Eventually, Tang Ying finished the products in about three months.

68. Brown, *Great Qing*, 41–43, 61–91; Hearn, "Document and Portrait."

69. Hou, "Keshen qingjin."

70. Berger, "When Words Collide," in *The Empire of Emptiness*, 34–62; Whiteman, "Kangxi's Auspicious Empire."

71. The play was prefaced by Dong Rong (c. 18th century) on the 13th day of the 7th month, according to the lunar calendar, in the Western year 1754.

72. This is a story about Guan Yu's refusal of Cao Cao's attempt to recruit him.

73. Zeng, "Yuan zaju tizhi guilu de yuanyuan yu xingcheng," 218–19.

74. *Tang Ying quanji*, 2:474, 475.

75. For a historical survey of the practice, see Zong Tinghu and Li Jinling, *Zhongguo jiju shi*.

76. Lang Tingji, *Ji Tang yao fa*, 12.

77. *Tang Ying quanji*, 2:400.

78. For an extensive discussion of the discourse on literati painting, see Bush, *The Chinese Literati on Painting*.

79. For studies of the school of Chinese painters whose literati style and theoretical discourse prevailed at the Qing court, see Fong, "The Orthodox School of Painting," in Fong and Watt, *Possessing the Past,* 473–91; James Cahill, "The Orthodox Movement in Early Ch'ing Painting," in Murck, *Artists and Traditions*, 169–81; Chu-Tsing Li, *A Thousand Peaks and Myriad Ravines*, 135–50.

80. On the integrating and canonizing function of Wang Yuanqi's painting and theory in the Kangxi emperor's cultural enterprise, see Whiteman, "Creating the Kangxi Landscape," 162–77; and Shen Wang, "Wang Yuanqi and the Orthodoxy of Self-Reflection in Early Qing Landscape Painting."

81. *Tang Ying ji*, 241. In 1745, when inscribing a friend's album, he recalled his early experience of studying literati painting. I thank Jonathan Hay for his expert suggestions in translating these premodern terms for painting criticism.

82. We cannot claim that his experience with porcelain painting influenced his painting on silk and paper, because the paintings are dated before his appointment to Jingdezhen in 1727.

83. *Tang Ying quanji*, 678.

84. Aohan, now transliterated as Aoqan, is a Mongol banner in Juu Uda League, east of the Greater Khinggan range. I am thankful to Matthew Mosca for identifying this and the term Ba-du-ma, which is a transliteration of "lotus" in Sanskrit.

85. For a typological study of *xifanlian* as a decorative motif on porcelain, see Wang Yiping, *Yuanmingqing guanyao fanlianhua wenshi zhi yanjiu.*

86. *Tang Ying ji*, 141.

87. Geng, *Mingqing ciqi jianding*, 389–90; Geng, "Jiang Qi and Tang Ying," 49–51; Geng, "Mantan Tang Ying yu tangyao ciqi," 1–17.

88. Schäfer, "Inscribing the Artifact and Inspiring Trust."

89. Foucault, "What Is an Author?"

90. This same inscription appears on several ceramic wares related to Tang Ying. And there are several other seals at the end of calligraphic texts on the body: "Taozhu" (Pottery Making), "Tang Ying," and "Jungong shi" (Mr. Jungong).

91. Tang Ying's inscription states, "Written in the fall of year *yihai*."

92. See Liao Baoxiu, *Huali caici*, 177. The date of the very piece can be open to discussion, but a square brush holder was indeed made and submitted to court in 1742. See Tang Ying, *Qinggong Neiwufu zaobanchu dang'an zonghui*, 1:11, 170.

93. For a slightly dated but pioneering categorization of these *chen* signatures, see Nie Chongzheng, "Tan Qingdai chen zikuan huihua."

94. The seal of the studio name Gubai Tang next to the date "Yongzheng jiunian zhongdong" also appears on the aforementioned brush pot in Guan-style glaze.

95. Huang Qinghua, "Beiyiwang de Tangyao jiaqi," 111–12.

96. *Tang Ying quanji*, 420.

97. Wang Yifeng, *Zhongguo Nanfang yuanshici yaoye yajiu*, 185–266.

98. Rawson, "Central Asian Silver and Its Influence on Chinese Ceramics."

99. Guojia Tushuguan, *Qingdai Yangshilei jianzhu tudang zhan*, 35.

THREE Tang Ying's *Illustrated Manual*

1. For the very few exceptional studies on bannermen's literary works, see Suet-Ying Chiu, *Bannermen Tales*; and Stary, "Fundamental Principles of Manchu Poetry." There are a few Chinese surveys of bannermen's Chinese poetry, but the literary analysis tends to focus on the individual poet's style rather than looking into the broad technocratic epistemology and ideology shared among bannermen's literary and other functional writings. See Zhang Juling, *Qingdai Manzu zuojia wenxue gailun*.

2. Ellen Huang's translation of the title, "Explanations of the Illustrations of Porcelain Manufacture," in her dissertation is both literal and accurate, for the textual entries were written temporally after the paintings as explanation. However, I chose a shorter title for convenience. Huang contextualizes this treatise, as the first instance of a theme, in the extensive global dissemination of porcelain manufacturing visual motifs between late Ming and the nineteenth century. See her "China's China," 131–33, 158–61. Her discussion covers profound "artistic, cultural, and political factors which sustained this theme." See also Ellen Huang, "An Art of Transformation."

3. Golas, *Picturing Technology in China*. Golas points out the lack of technical clarity of many premodern illustrated treatises in China and opens up a space for discussing their purposes and functions. See also Golas, "Technical Representation in China."

4. For two exemplar treatises written not for government officials but probably for artisans and businessmen, see Ji, *Yuanye*; and Ruitenbeek, *Carpentry and Building in Late Imperial China*.

5. For English and French translations, see Wenren, *Ancient Chinese Encyclopedia of Technology*; Biot, *Le Tcheou-li ou Rites des Tcheou*, 456–611.

6. An annotated version of the text is available in Jiang Qi, *Taoji jiaozhu*. See also a classic study by Liu Xinyuan, "Jiang Qi Taoji zhuzuo shidai kaobian."

7. Tang Ying, "Ciwu shiyi shiyu gaoxu" (Preface to the Report to the [Yongzheng] emperor about porcelain production), in *Tang Ying ji*, 145.

8. Scholars have pieces of information about this integration from archival documents. See Ye Xiaoqing, *Ascendant Peace in the Four Seas*, 15–127; Zhu Jiajin, *Qingdai neiting yanju shimokao*; Ding Ruqin, *Qingdai neiting yanxi shihua*, 1–160. Based on extensive archival research, some scholars have exercised insightful close reading of court drama cases; see Liana Chen, "Ritual into Play." In 1683, the Kangxi emperor included real tigers, elephants, and horses in the performance of a Mulian play. See Dong Han (1624–1697), *Chunxiang zhuibi*, 96. For an analysis of Earl Macartney's (1737–1806) witnessing of the theatrical spectacle at Qianglong court, see Ye Xiaoqing, "Ascendant Peace in the Four Seas."

9. For the bureaucratic administration of theater, see Wang Zhizhang, *Qing Shengpingshu zhilue*. An enormous archive of the theater bureau has been published; see Zhongguo Guojia Tushuguan, *Zhongguo Guojia Tushuguan cang qinggong shengpingshu dang'an jicheng*.

10. Ye Xiaoqing, *Ascendant Peace in the Four Seas*, 82–83.

11. Gu Pingdan, "Cao Yin 'Taiping leshi' zaju chutan."

12. For a modern translation of the Japanese songs, see Tang, "Woyu zhixi."

13. Some plays can be dated based on the prefaces and forewords written by friends. Chiu Hui-Ying provides a comprehensive survey of Tang Ying's plays, analyzing their literary techniques and narratives, in *Tang Ying xiqu yanjiu*.

14. Andrea Goldman has examined the Qing court's decisive role in the prolonged competition between the elite Kun opera and regional theatrical styles from the late eighteenth century on, a period slightly later than my focus, when the bannermen were just starting to mediate "conspicuous cultural patronage" and the "organization of knowledge for dramatic music." Goldman, *Opera and the City*, 121–23. See also Shang Wei, "The Literati Era and Its Demise," 298; Mackerras, "The Growth of the Chinese Regional Drama in the Ming and Ch'ing," 58–91.

15. Nienhauser et al., *The Indiana Companion to Chinese Literature*, 353–55, 514–16; Grant Guangren Shen, *Elite Theater in Ming China*, 5–10; Mackerras, *Chinese Theater*, 61–77, 92–102.

16. Zeng, "Lunshuo xiqu yasu zhi tuiyi," 249–96.

17. Gugong Bowuyuan Ming-Qing Dang'an Bu, *Li Xu zouzhe*, 4, 127.

18. Zhu Jiajin, *Neiting yanju shimo kao*, 55–67.

19. Per the suggestion of Yiling'a, Qianlong launched an empirewide campaign to censor drama. See Ye Xiaoqing, *Ascending Peace in the Four Seas*, 183–86.

20. This aria musical structure, the so-called *banqiang ti*, was arranged to fit the rhythm of the clapper. See Chang Jingzhi, *Lun bingzi qiang*, 43, 53–76. See also Luo Yinghui, *Bangziqiang changqiang jiegou yanjiu*, 8–84.

21. Nienhauser et al., *Indiana Companion to Chinese Literature*, 515.

22. *Tang Ying ji*, 466–67.

23. In 1856, Stanislas Julien translated the textual treatise into French, heavily editing it and omitting the last entry. A Japanese translation appeared in 1907. In 1910, Stephen Bushell translated *Taoye tushuo* as part of *Tao shuo*, an expanded treatise on ceramics penned by Zhu Yan (c. 1766–69). Bushell's translation is used as my main reference here—*Description of Chinese Pottery and Porcelain*, 7–29. On the international dissemination of several Chinese texts on porcelain production in the nineteenth century, see Ellen Huang, "China's China," 113–20, 158–61.

24. The extant album is published by the Society of Refined Curios (Qingwan yaji). See Hongxi Meishuguan, *Chinese Art*. I assert that the Qingwan album is closest to the versions recorded in the archive. Both the scrutiny of scholars in the Palace Museum and my own comparison of the Qingwan album with other contemporary examples support this claim. See an extensive study of the album in Yu Pei-Chin, "Taoye tuce suojian Qianlong Huangdi de lixiang guanyao."

25. On QL 5/4/25 (1740), an album on porcelain production was commissioned. Tang Dai (1673–after 1751) was ordered to paint trees and rocks. Sun Hu (c. mid-eighteenth century) painted the architecture with a ruler, and Ding Guanpeng (active 1726–after 1770) was required to paint figures.

26. On QL 8/4/8 (1743), a twenty-leaf album depicting porcelain production was sub-

mitted by the eunuchs Hu Shijie and Gao Yu, according to foreman Bai Shixiu's report. See also *Tang Ying dutao wendang*, 160.

27. In the same year, on QL 8/5/21, Tang Ying sent his treatise back, together with the original album. There is one complication concerning the multiple available albums that might have been produced at court. If this was the only album painted, then the whole process lasted for three years, from 1740 to 1743. However, the painters in the archival record are Tang Dai, Sun Hu, and Ding Guanpeng, one of which does not match the signatures on the last leaf of the Qingwan album, Sun Hu, Zhou Kun, and Ding Guanpeng. Thus, in theory, there could be more than one album that was produced at court during or before Qianlong's reign. Moreover, other contemporary albums about porcelain production exist. Percival David mentions a version he glimpsed in Beijing before 1949, which the dealer dated to the Kangxi reign. See Percival David, "The *T'ao shuo* and 'The Illustrations of Pottery Manufacture'"; and *Tang Ying dutao wendang*, 168.

28. Kerr and Wood, *Ceramic Technology*, 20–36.

29. For the study of an illustration of production activities in carpentry, agriculture, and textile production, see Ruitenbeek, *Carpentry and Building in Late Imperial China*; Bray, *Biology and Biological Technology: Part II, Agriculture*; Hammers, *Pictures of Tilling and Weaving*.

30. The first edition of the illustrated *Works of Heaven and the Inception of Things* dates from 1637. On the multiple editions of the book, see Schäfer, *The Crafting of the Ten Thousand Things*, 276–77. The English translation is available as *T'ien-kung k'ai-wu; Chinese Technology in the Seventeenth Century*, trans. E-tu Zen Sun and Shiou-chuan Sun. Golas points out that the illustrations in *Works of Heaven and the Inception of Things* integrate laboring figures into their depiction of tools and raw materials, which reveal the "idea that technology involved human beings employing their skills to make useful the resources provided by nature." See Golas, "Like Obtaining a Great Treasure," in Bray, Dorofeeva-Lichtmann, and Métailié, *Graphics and Text*, 585.

31. Golas and Wagner find it difficult to trace the textual or pictorial sources of *Works of Heaven and the Inception of Things*. Similarly, it is difficult to identify the illustrators and the audiences of the treatises under review. See Golas, "Like Obtaining a Great Treasure," in Bray, Dorofeeva-Lichtmann, and Métailié, *Graphics and Text*, 580; Donald Wagner meticulously analyzes the chapters about iron mining and points out the possibility that the text and illustrations were prepared at different times. See Wagner, "Song Yingxing's Illustrations of Iron Production," in Bray, Dorofeeva-Lichtmann, and Métailié, *Graphics and Text*, 615–32. My analysis draws on Golas and Wagner's methods of such examination of pictotextual relations in order to elucidate the technocratic appropriation of regional information and the articulation of the making process within the ideological frame.

32. *Pictures of Tilling and Weaving* has many more precedents, dating from as early as the Northern Song dynasty. Its first reproduction in the Qing dynasty was attributed to Jiao Bingzhen (active c. 1680–1720). Both the album and the imperial inscription of the painting were immediately reproduced again in woodblock versions and spread to officials

all over the empire. See Hammers, "Perspectives in Early Qing-Dynasty Pictures of Tilling and Weaving and Pictures of Cotton."

33. Bushell's English translation does not include the preface. And the procedural order described in the *Illustrated Manual* is different from the enumeration in *The Great Gazetteer of Jingxi Province* (Jiangxi sheng dazhi). See Feng Xianming, *Zhongguo gutaoci-wenxian jishi*, 83–87; Kerr and Wood, *Ceramic Technology*, 23–24.

34. This literal translation highlights the plausibly Islamic origin (*hui*) *of* the cobalt blue pigment that is believed to have been used during the Jiajing reign, when the gazetteer was compiled.

35. Wang Zongmu et al., *Jiangxisheng dazhi*, 83–87.

36. Anne Gerritsen has thoroughly studied the information in these texts on the ceramic industry of the Ming dynasty in *The City of Blue and White*.

37. Fu Yuhong, "Shaozao ciqi changcheng zhiding hou yuyao jingfei de hexiao."

38. To summarize the budgetary changes, since 1727 the Yongzheng emperor stopped the provincial government from paying for the production and instead allocated eight thousand taels of silver from Huai'an custom house, which was part of the Imperial Household Department. This means that the manufacture was paid for from the emperor's private purse. The budget increased to twenty thousand early in the Qianlong reign but quickly dropped back to ten thousand paid by the Jiujiang custom house from 1739. The budget remained at this level until it further decreased to five thousand in 1799. See Wang Guangyao, *Zhongguo gudai guanyao zhidu II*, 238–44.

39. I keep as much of Bushell's concise and accurate translation as possible and refer to Ellen Huang's translation, making amendments when necessary. Because of the discovery of the album and calligraphy of the *Illustrated Manual of Ceramic Production*, we have important new textual fragments that were not included in the version Bushell used.

40. A sagger is a container made of coarse, refractory clay in which an object is contained during firing.

41. "Body" means the rough form of a product.

42. However, I limit my presentation of the other three albums to a minimum as they are not immediately relevant for illustrating technocrats' collection of information and therefore deserve formal analysis in a separate study.

43. Lam, "Porcelain Manufacture Illustrations of the Qing Dynasty." This is the best study of both the early and later albums on porcelain production to date.

44. The Palace Museum in Beijing acquired the album in the mid-twentieth century. The color plates are published in the exhibition catalog Zheng Xinmiao et al., *Douse zhengyan*, 276–83.

45. The paintings are 30.5 cm high and 35.5 cm wide. This horizontal format is different from the Qingwan album, which is a vertical rectangle. The format of the Beijing album is somewhat in between (34.7 cm x 34.7 cm), shorter than the Qingwan.

46. Although the Sotheby's album is a highly relevant comparison to the Beijing and Qingwan albums, the paintings in that volume are remarkably dissimilar in style from other court paintings attributed to Jiao Bingzhen. Jiao Bingzhen is reputed for employing a "Western technique" (*xifa*) that he learned from Jesuit missionaries; see Cahill, *Pictures*

for Use and Pleasure, 60, 78, 88–90; and Shan, "Style of the Painting of Beauties at the Qing Court." The rocks and trees in his paintings, signed "Respectfully painted by Jiao Bingzhen," are usually conspicuously patterned, and some rocks are painted like blocks of squares. We see none of these in the Sotheby's album. The depiction of porcelain pieces in the Sotheby's album lacks volume. The architecture is devoid of shading. However, these are not technical defects but stylistic choices. Based on its overall style, it could be attributed to painters who were familiar with Wu school techniques. We cannot exclude the possibility that the Sotheby's album was used as a model for later court copies.

47. Scholars have dated the Lund album to the 1730s, even though most exported illustrated manuals about porcelain production are dated later than the Qingwan album. Each leaf in the Lund album is a vertical rectangle, 41 cm high and 31 cm wide, a format similar to the Qingwan album. See Belfrage, "Chinese Watercolours from the 18th Century Illustrating Porcelain Manufacture."

48. The authors of the Beijing, Sotheby's, and Lund albums all chose to use an entire second page to focus on the crushing system powered by waterwheels.

49. *Tang Ying ji*, 954.

50. Bushell, *Description of Chinese Pottery and Porcelain*, 7. Hereafter, when quoting the treatise of *Illustrated Manual of Ceramic Production*, I use Bushell's translation with some modification.

51. *Tang Ying ji*, 954.

52. *Tang Ying ji*, 957.

53. Barnhart, "Figures in a Landscape."

54. *Tang Ying ji*, 957. Cobalt-blue pigment used on porcelain of the Yuan dynasty was imported from West Asia. Due to the closing off of the Ming empire since the middle of the Xuande reign, the imported source was exhausted and the imperial manufactory adopted domestic cobalt pigment. By the Qianlong reign, cobalt pigment was sought exclusively from Zhejiang province. For modern scientific surveys of various kinds of cobalt-blue pigment in Chinese porcelain production across dynasties, see Kerr and Wood, *Ceramic Technology*, 658–88; Li Jiazhi et al., *Zhongguo gudai taoci kexue jishu chengjiu*, 300–332.

55. *Tang Ying ji*, 957; Bushell, *Description of Chinese Pottery and Porcelain*, 17.

56. *Tang Ying ji*, 957; Bushell, *Description of Chinese Pottery and Porcelain*, 17.

57. *Tang Ying ji*, 958; Bushell, *Description of Chinese Pottery and Porcelain*, 27. Although the packing process documented in paintings in the Beijing and Sotheby's albums follows some principles of classification, the depiction does not strictly match the textual description in the treatise.

58. *Tang Ying ji*, 958; Bushell, *Description of Chinese Pottery and Porcelain*, 27.

59. On the evolving policy regarding defective wares since the Imperial Vessel Manufactory (Yuqichang) was established in the Ming dynasty; see Wang Guangyao, *Mingdai gongting taoci shi*, 142–48. The memorials with imperial comments regarding defective wares are published in *Tang Ying ji*, 926–27.

60. *Tang Ying ji*, 955.

61. Tang Ying's text described two other techniques to make the molded wares that are

absent from the pictorial representation. One is how to make angular vases: "The polygonal, square, ribbed, and angular pieces are made from paste wrapped up in cloth and pressed with boards into slabs, which are cut into sections, and cemented together with some of the original paste mixed with water." The other method is called *yinpi*, which uses molds to form vessels.

62. Bushell, *Description of Chinese Pottery and Porcelain*, 13.

63. The Sotheby's album is not clear about this collaborative labor. The vessel maker is shown throwing a bowl alone while another worker is mixing the clay in a distant workshop. The Lund album introduces other techniques to turn the wheel instead of the bamboo staff. A worker uses string around the column under the wheel to turn it. Another worker holds a rope hanging from the ceiling of a pavilion-like workshop and treads on pedals extending around the wheel. The Lund album does not seem to distinguish between the making process of round wares and molded wares.

64. Feng Xianming, *Zhongguo gutaociwenxian jishi*, 82; Liu Xinyuan, "Taoji zhuzuo shidai kaobian"; Zhao Bing, "Erudition, expertise, technique et politique"; Ma Wenkuan, "Ping Jiangqi Zhuzuo shidai kaobian."

65. *Tang Ying ji*, 956–57; Bushell, *Description of Chinese Pottery and Porcelain*, 19.

66. *Tang Ying ji*, 956–57; Bushell, *Description of Chinese Pottery and Porcelain*, 19.

67. *Tang Ying ji*, 956; Bushell, *Description of Chinese Pottery and Porcelain*, 17.

68. *Tang Ying ji*, 956; Bushell, *Description of Chinese Pottery and Porcelain*, 17.

69. *Tang Ying ji*, 954; Bushell, *Description of Chinese Pottery and Porcelain*, 9–10.

70. *Tang Ying ji*, 956; Bushell, *Description of Chinese Pottery and Porcelain*, 18.

71. *Tang Ying ji*, 956; Bushell, *Description of Chinese Pottery and Porcelain*, 18.

72. *Tang Ying ji*, 958. Bushell, *Description of Chinese Pottery and Porcelain*, 23.

73. Feng Xianming, *Zhongguo gutaociwenxian jishi*, 82.

74. *Tang Ying ji*, 959; Bushell, *Description of Chinese Pottery and Porcelain*, 28.

75. This sentence is not included in Bushell's translation.

76. Ellen Huang ("An Art of Transformation," 150) discusses this ceramic deity in her study of the phenomenon of kiln transformation in the Qing.

77. *Tang Ying ji*, 959.

78. See the analysis of an illustrated admonition to Ming emperors in Murray, "From Textbook to Testimonial"; and Li-Chiang Lin,"The Creation and Transformation of Ancient Rulership in the Ming Dynasty."

FOUR Innovations and Experiments

1. I refer mainly to the authors of prolific connoisseurship manuals produced in the second half of the Ming dynasty. Wen Zhenheng is a well-studied example; see Clunas, *Superfluous Things*. An extensive survey of this genre of literature can be found in Mao, *Wan Ming xianshang meixue*.

2. For instance, Chen Hongshou may base his painting composition on the detail of an ink-cake design. See Burkus-Chasson, "Between Representations," 322.

3. For a detailed study of Chen Hongshou's authorial voice in his print work, see Bentley, *The Figurative Works of Chen Hongshou (1599–1652)*

4. If we broaden our scope of investigation or suspend the boundary between decorative art and fine art, meaning painting and calligraphy, we might be able to observe the institutionalizing process of some painters at the early Qing court, too. Such so-called court painters often originated from, and continued to contribute to, regional markets. See Maxwell Hearn's study of Wang Hui and Xu Yang, "Document and Portrait"; Ju-hsi Chou, "Tang Dai"; and Alfreda Murck, "Yuan Jiang: Image Make," in Brown and Chou, *Chinese Painting under the Qianlong Emperor*.

5. The text of *Taocheng jishi bei ji*, gathered from local gazetteers, is available in *Tang Ying ji*, 950–53. A broken stela on which the text was inscribed was discovered in the 1980s and analyzed in Jiang Jianxin, "Tang Ying 'Taocheng jishi beiji' jiqi chutu canbei yiwen jiaoshi." The complete document of *Zhijia zeli zhangcheng ce*, probably finished on the 7th day of the 10th month of 1747, is included in Tie Yuan and Li Guorong, *Qinggong ciqi dang'an quanji*, 3:70–83.

6. *Tang Ying ji*, 950.

7. Section 12; see *Tang Ying ji*, 950.

8. *Tang Ying ji*, 957.

9. For the call for a more historically informed understanding of innovation and a brief critique on a few myths about creation, see Sawyer, *Explaining Creativity*, 3–32.

10. Peter Dear (*The Literary Structure of Scientific Argument*, 135–63) explains the important role of rhetorical articulation in experimental practices in early modern Europe and the relationship between experience and experiment. See also Dear, "The Meanings of Experience," in Park and Daston, *Cambridge History of Science: Early Modern Science*, 106–31.

11. See Kerr and Wood, *Ceramic Technology*, 634–39.

12. *Tang Ying ji*, 952.

13. Wang Chu-p'ing, "Jinhong cailiao zai kangxi shiqi falangcai ci de shiyong qingxing" (The use of gold based pigment in falang enamel during the Kangxi and Yongzheng reigns), in Yu Pei-Chin, *Jincheng xuying*, 298–313.

14. Wu Hung, "Emperor's Masquerade."

15. Enameling as a technique can also be used to apply pigment to bronze, which is called *tongtai huafalang* (painted enamel over bronze body), but this is not relevant to our discussion.

16. For a comprehensive discussion of the nomenclature conundrum, see Shih Ching-Fei and Peng Ying-Chen, "Cong wenhua mailuo tantao qingdai youshangcai mingci."

17. The most helpful effort in matching archival records with extant pieces is found in Yu Pei-Chin, *Jincheng xuying;* and Liao Baoxiu, *Huali caici*.

18. The terms *fencai* and *famille rose* were employed by late Qing and Republican-era connoisseurs based on visual impression; they never appeared in archival documents. See Wang Chu-P'ing, "Cong kexuefenxi wenxian huigu kan falangcai, yangcai yu fencai de fenlei yu mingming."

19. For exchange in the glass industry, see Curtis, *Glass Exchange between Europe and China*. For the development of painted enamel in China, see Shih Ching-Fei, *Riyue guanghua*.

20. Loehr, "Missionary-Artist at the Manchu Court"; Curtis. *Glass Exchange between Europe and China*, 57–79; Xu Xiaodong. "Kangxi yongzheng shiqi gongting yu difang huafalang jishu de hudong," in Schäfer, *Gongting yu difang*, 279–97.

21. Curtis, "European Contribution to the Chinese Glass of the Early Qing Period"; Curtis, "Qingchao de bolizhizao yu yesuhuishi zai Canchikou de zuofang."

22. Regarding artisans from overseas, see Wu Zhuo, "Jesuit Missionaries in China and the Imperial Workshops in the Imperial Household Department of the Qing Court"; Curtis, *Glass Exchange between Europe and China*; Shih Ching-Fei, *Riyue guanghua*, 229. On recruitment in Guangzhou, see Lü Jian, "Kangxikuan huafalang suoyi"; "Memorial on the List of Foreign Ships and Enamel Artisans Sent to Court, by the Governor of Guangdong Province, Yang Lin," *Qinggong yuegang'ao shangmao dang'an quanji*, 1:102. On the success of the endeavor, see Zhongguo Diyi Lishi Dang'anguan, *Kangxichao Hanwen zhupi zouzhe huibian*, 8:342.

23. Wu Zhaoqing, "Qingdai Zaobanchu de jigou he jiangyi."

24. *Tang Ying dutao wendang*, 119–20.

25. *Tang Ying dutao wendang*, 120. The source does not specify what these large pieces of *falang* pigment look like. I have only seen half palm-size scraps or powder-like frits of *falang* pigments in modern Jingdezhen. They are close to glass but opaque or translucent.

26. *Tang Ying dutao wendang*, 124.

27. I explain in chapter 1 that the taxes Tang Ying collected from the custom houses of Huai'an and Jiujiang Rivers went directly to the emperor's Grand Storage Office in the Imperial Household Department.

28. *Tang Ying dutao wendang*, 120.

29. *Tang Ying dutao wendang*, 129–30.

30. *Tang Ying dutao wendang*, 129–30.

31. However, the majority of extant refined enameled porcelains were finished at court, according to the archival records and the inscriptions on boxes made specifically to contain them. Several porcelain pieces decorated with *falang* enamel are suspected to have been produced in Jingdezhen because of their slight differences.

32. Tang Ying, "Preface to the Report to the [Yongzheng] Emperor about Porcelain Production," in *Tang Ying ji*, 145.

33. The central-local exchange in ceramic production can be traced back to the previous imperial reign. A record dating from 1725 mentioned that craftsmen specializing in porcelain (*ciqi jiangren*) be sent back to Jiangxi province, except for one excellent porcelain painter, Song Sanji. The court retained him to paint enameled porcelains. See *Archive of the Imperial Workshops*, 1:678; Shih Ching-Fei. *Riyue guanghua*, 85.

34. Zhongguo diyi lishi dang'an guan, Xianggang Zhongwen Daxue Wenwu Guan, *Qinggong Neiwufu Zaobanchu dang'an zonghui*, 1:4, documented in the *falang* workshop in the intercalary month of 1729, 99.

35. *Tang Ying dutao wendang*, 131–32, in the second month of 1729.

36. *Tang Ying dutao wendang*, 143.

37. "Boneless" porcelain refers to a body that is thrown so thin that it is translucent against light and feels as if the glaze is thicker than the body.

38. See Gao Xiaoran, "Falangcai shaozao guocheng zhong de jjian wuzheng," 103. Except for a large commission in 1753, the Imperial Workshops at court seemed to only need sporadic commissions.

39. Gao Xiaoran, "Falangcai shaozao guocheng zhong de jjian wuzheng," 105.

40. Yu Pei-Chin, *Jincheng xuying*, catalog entry 007, 31.

41. For the confusion of *falang* enamel (*falangcai*), foreign enamel (*yangcai*), and *famille rose* (*fencai*), see Wang Chu-P'ing, "Cong kexuefenxi wenxian huigu kan falangcai, yangcai yu fencai de fenlei yu mingming," 115–66.

42. *Tang Ying ji*, 952.

43. Modern ceramic historian Zhou Sizhong seems to have found a record referring to *yangcai* of the Yongzheng reign. "According to the Imperial order in the 11th month, the Porcelain Manufacture should produce *yangcai* enameled teapots based on the model of the Yixing teapot" (quoted in Shih Ching-Fei and Peng Ying-Chen, "Cong wenhua mailuo tantao qingdai youshangcai mingci," 7). However, another published record for probably the same commission seems to formulate the Yixing teapot differently, "On the 11th day of the 11th month . . . eunuch Cangzhou turned in four Yixing teapots. The exterior is painted with foreign golden patterns." See Gugong Bowuyuan, *Qinggong Neiwufu zaobanchu dang'an zonghui*, 5:336, 342, 589.

44. *Tang Ying ji*, 958; Bushell, *Description of Chinese Pottery and Porcelain*, 25 (modified).

45. Jiang Qi, *Taoji jiaozhu*, 40. Scholars have recently discovered a large group of such tools used in the production of blue-and-white porcelain in the Yuan dynasty. See Zheng Naizhang and Zhang Qingyu, "Jingdezhen yao yizu zhaozi de xingzhi yu gongneng yanjiu."

46. Geng, *Mingqing ciqi jianding*, 284.

47. Wang Chu-P'ing, "Cong kexuefenxi wenxian huigu kan falangcai, yangcai yu fencai de fenlei yu mingming," 146–48.

48. Liao Baoxiu, *Huali caici*, 118.

49. The seal script of the reign mark on the bottom could be dated to the writing style of the early Qianlong reign. By comparing a large quantity of basemarks of the Qianlong reign, Peter Lam was able to narrow down the dates of Qianlong porcelain to a smaller range than the almost sixty years of the reign. Peter Lam, "Toward a Dating Framework for Qianlong Imperial Porcelain."

50. *Tang Ying ji*, 958.

51. *Tang Ying ji*, 958.

52. Shih Ching-Fei and Peng Ying-Chen, "Cong wenhua mailuo tantao qingdai youshangcai mingci," 29–30, fig. 21; Beurdeley and Raindre, *Qing Porcelain*, 35–37.

53. Lazarist Mission Press, *Beitang Tushuguan cang xiwen shanben mulu*, 64, entry 241. See also Mao Ruifang, "Beitang shumu," 112–18.

54. Saitō, "Gen jidai sometsuke sagasu I & II."

55. On the commission of a candlestick for Mongol princes, see *Tang Ying dutao wendang*, 136.

56. *Tang Ying dutao wendang*, 86.

57. *Tang Ying dutao wendang*, 157.

58. *Tang Ying dutao wendang*, 166.

59. Yu Pei-Chin, "Tang Ying jianzao zhuanxinpin jiqi xiangguan wenti," 207–9.

60. Memorial on QL 3/12/6 (1738), "When I resided in the manufactory before, I kept track of the details. Now the custom house of Suqian is more than 2,200 *li* from the manufactory, which is indeed out of reach [i.e., more than one thousand kilometers]." See *Tang Ying dutao wendang*, 44. On the 29th day of the 11th month of 1742, after moving to the Jiujiang custom house, which was about three hundred *li* away from the manufactory, Tang Ying again begged the emperor to release him from tax collection. See *Tang Ying ji*, 924–25.

61. Shih Ching-Fei, "Xiangyaqiu zuojian zhi gongyi jishu jiaoliu."

62. Quote from Bushell, *Description of Chinese Pottery and Porcelain*, 15 (modified).

63. *Tang Ying ji*, 928.

64. *Tang Ying ji*, 927, on the 20th day of the 2nd month of 1743.

65. *Tang Ying ji*, 930–31. How the accurate fine was calculated had been lost, but we could reach an approximate number by adding up the breakdown expense specified in the *Regulation and Precedents*. Moreover, I doubt that a scale which could measure to a precision of 1/100,000 of a tael existed in 1743.

66. *Tang Ying dutao wendang*, 161.

67. *Tang Ying dutao wendang*, 166.

68. *Tang Ying dutao wendang*, 67.

69. Hugh Moss points out other examples in "The Influence of Tang Ying on the Production of Imperial Porcelain Snuff Bottles," 4–16.

70. *Tang Ying dutao wendang*, 67. Tang Ying means that this *jiazi* year, which is now beginning, will be the start not only of just another sixty-year cycle but of a ten-thousand-year reign or a ten-thousand-year period of prosperity.

71. *Tang Ying ji*, 957.

72. See "Qianlong yuti shi" (Qianlong's imperial poems for inscription), in Feng Xianming, *Zhongguo gutaociwenxian jishi*, 271–88. For an insightful analysis of the Qianlong emperor's knowledge of porcelain revealed in these poems, see Hsieh Ming-Liang, "Qianlong de taoci jianshangguan."

73. *Tang Ying dutao wendang*, 4.

74. For the cost of materials and labor for each category, see "Yuanzhuo ciqi shaozao zhijia zeli" (Regulations and precedents for the manufacture of round and molded porcelain wares), in Tie Yuan and Li Guorong, *Qinggong ciqi dang'an quanji*, 3:70–83.

75. "Alms-Bowl-Shaped Urn in Ru Glaze," in Yang Jingrong, *Yanse you*, 236.

76. "Iron bone" is a literal translation. This style with (sometimes painted) dark cracks on thick translucent greenish gray glaze is often known as "iron wire" in English.

77. For the questionable early dating of some Ge wares and recent archaeological discoveries of Ge style ceramics in multiple sites, see Geng et al., *Geyao ciqi lansheng*.

78. *Tang Ying quanji*, 2:393.

79. *Tang Ying ji*, 951.

80. On the Hutian kiln site, see Liu Xinyuan, "Jingdezhen Hutianyao kaocha jiyao"; Liu, "Jingdezhen Hutianyao geqi dianxing wanlei de zaoxing tezheng jiqi chengyinkao."

81. *Tang Ying dutao wendang*, 129.

82. For d'Entrecolles's letters about porcelains, see Tichane, *Ching-te-chen*, 49–128. For the French version of the two letters, see d'Entrecolles, "Lettre du Père D'Entrecolles au Père Orry, 1 sept.1712,"; and "Lettre du Père D'Entrecolles au Père Orry, 25 janvier 1722."

83. Kerr and Wood, *Ceramic Technology*, 194.

84. "Jiangxi xunfu Lang Tingji zoujin xiyangren yinhongxu suojin wupin zhe," in Zhongguo Diyi Lishi Dang'anguan, *Kangxichao Hanwen zhupi zouzhe huibian*, 334–35.

85. Two forewords are dated to 1709 and 1710. See Lang, *Shengyin Bian*.

86. The textualization of knowledge reached far beyond any single industry such as ceramic production. The Imperial Archive and the Regulations and Precedents (*Zeli*) document all kinds of manufacturing on various scales throughout the Qing empire.

87. Wood, *Chinese Glazes*, 184.

88. *Tang Ying ji*, 951.

89. The earliest production of Jun ware is still open to debate. They might have been fired as early as the end of the Northern Song dynasty, but most of the extant early Jun wares date from the Jin and Yuan dynasties. See Lo Hui-chi, "Chuanshi Junyaoqi de shidai wenti"; Qin Dashu, "Junyao shishao niandai kao."

90. *Tang Ying dutao wendang*, 139.

91. *Tang Ying ji*, 42; *Tang Ying quanji*, 1:14.

92. Ellen Huang, in "An Art of Transformation," traces the long and convoluted history of this term and this category and excavates its deeper political significance in the Qing dynasty.

93. *Ji* actually literally means "the fresh and bright azure after a storm."

94. "Gongjin shangchuan ji oude yaobian ciqi zhe" (Memorial on the submission of the accidental porcelains in flambé glaze), in *Tang Ying ji*, 933.

95. Lan and Zheng, *Jingdezhen taolu tushuo*, 213.

96. Attributed to Zhang Jiuyue, *Notes on the Southern Kilns*, 23.

97. The attribution is based on Lang's trademark-like seals, namely *zhenlu* and *yuci chunyi tang*, imprinted on the vessels. See Lam, "Lang Tingji (1663–1715) and the Porcelain of the Late Kangxi Period"; Lu Minghua, "Langyao xiangguan wenti zaikao." "Joined color" is a modern term; this category of decoration was called "five colors" (*wucai*) in the imperial archive. This emic name might cause confusion with the *wucai* or *famille verte* popular during the Kangxi reign, but even nonspecialists would not mistake one for another category.

98. Record dated to the 20th day of the 3rd month of 1729 in *Tang Ying dutao wendang*, 132.

99. See *Tang Ying ji*, 933.

100. *Tang Ying ji*, 952.

101. Bushell, *Description of Chinese Pottery and Porcelain*, 17.

CONCLUSION

1. Tang Ying ji, 174.

2. For a study of Cai Yan's (b. 178) poetry, including the "Eighteen Songs of a Nomad Flute," see Hans Frankel, "Cai Yan and the Poems Attributed to Her." Frankel translated the title of the poem as "Song of the Barbarian Reed-Whistle in Eighteen Stanzas."

3. *Tang Ying ji*, 851.

4. *Tang Ying ji*, 853

5. *Tang Ying ji*, 851.

6. *Tang Ying ji*, 849.

7. "This is the beginning of the third song of Fengyun Hui. All use Xiao flutes and strings to provide quiet accompaniment softly." *Tang Ying ji*, 850.

8. *Tang Ying ji*, 854.

9. Tang Ying, "Zouqing laoge liuchang xiezao zhe" (Memorial on retaining Laoge to assist in the manufactory), QL10/2/25, in Tie Yuan and Li Guorong, *Qinggong ciqi dang'an quanji* , 2:357.

10. For a study of these subsequent bannermen supervisors, see Cai Hebi, "Yong Qian yuyao: Tang Ying, xiezao, dutaoguan" (The imperial kilns of the Yongzheng and Qianlong reigns: Tang Ying, manufacture assistant and ceramic supervisor), in Jiang, *Tang Ying yu tangyao guoji xueshu yantaohui lunwenji*, 7–20.

11. Lan and Zheng, *Jingdezhen taolu tushu*, book 2, in Quanguo Tushuguan Wenxian Suowei Fuzhi Zhongxin, *Zhongguo gudai taoci wenxian jilu*, 2:612–13.

12. Lai Yu-Chih. "Images, Knowledge and Empire," 7–100.

13. For Dekui's participation in jade quarrying, see Yulian Wu, "Chimes of Empire."

14. For an excellent study of the special steel chisel invented to tackle large jadestones, see Guo Fuxiang, "Qianlong gongting zhiyu xingongju 'Qinzhong gangpian' kao." For the entanglement of aesthetic quality and political significance of these jade wares, see Kleutghen, "Flowering Stone."

15. Torbert has already studied the most infamous case of bannerman Gao Pu's corruption in the jade trade. See Torbert, *The Ch'ing Imperial Household Department*, 136–71.

16. For a summary of Linking's career and his work in hydraulic junction conservancy, see "Linqing and Grand Canal Conditions in Northern Jiangsu," in Jane Leonard, *Stretching the Qing Bureaucracy in the 1826 Sea-Transport Experiment*, 19–38.

BIBLIOGRAPHY

Adamson, Glenn, Giogio Riello, and Sarah Teasley. *Global Design History*. Abingdon: Routledge, 2011.

Anderson, Christy, Anne Dunlop, and Pamela H. Smith, eds. *The Matter of Art: Materials, Practices, Cultural Logics, c. 1250–1750*. Manchester: Manchester University Press, 2015.

Andreas, Joel. *Rise of the Red Engineers: The Cultural Revolution and the Origins of China's New Class*. Stanford, CA: Stanford University Press, 2009.

Aoki Masaru 青木正ル. *Shina kinsei gikyokushi* 支那近世戲曲史 (The history of theater of modern China). Tōkyō: Kōbundō Shobō, 1955.

Ash, Eric H. "Introduction: Expertise and the Early Modern State." *Osiris* 25, no. 1 (2010): 1–24.

Bai, Qianshen. *Fu Shan's World: The Transformation of Chinese Calligraphy in the Seventeenth Century*. Cambridge, MA: Harvard University Asia Center, 2003.

Barbieri-Low, Anthony J. *Artisans in Early Imperial China*. Seattle: University of Washington Press, 2007.

Barnhart, Richard. "Figures in a Landscape." *Archives of Asian Art* 42 (1989): 62–70.

Bartlett, Beatrice. *Monarchs and Ministers: The Grand Council in Mid-Ch'ing China, 1723–1820*. Berkeley: University of California Press, 1991.

Belfrage, Esbjörn. "Chinese Watercolours from the 18th Century Illustrating Porcelain Manufacture." In *International Association of Bibliophiles XV Congress Copenhagen Transaction*, edited by Poul A. Christiansen, 124–31. Copenhagen: Danish National Library of Science and Medicine, 1992.

Bennett, Jane. *Vibrant Matter: A Political Ecology of Things*. Durham, NC: Duke University Press, 2010.

Bentley, Tamara. *The Figurative Works of Chen Hongshou (1599–1652): Authentic Voices/Expanding Markets*. Burlington, VT: Ashgate, 2012.

Berger, Patricia. *The Empire of Emptiness: Buddhist Art and Political Authority in Qing China*. Honolulu: University of Hawai'i Press, 2003.

Berliner, Nancy, et al. *The Emperor's Private Paradise: Treasures from the Forbidden City.* Salem, MA: Peabody Essex Museum; New Haven, CT: Yale University Press, 2010.

Beurdeley, Michel, and Guy Raindre. *Qing Porcelain: Famille Verte, Famille Rose, 1644–1912.* Translated by Charlotte Chesney. New York: Rizzoli, 1987.

Biot, Édouard. *Le Tcheou-li ou Rites des Tcheou.* 1851; rpt., Taipei: Chengwen, 1969.

Blair, Ann. *Too Much to Know: Managing Scholarly Information before the Modern Age.* New Haven, CT: Yale University Press, 2010.

Bol, Peter. "Seeking Common Ground: Han Literati under Jurchen Rule." *Harvard Journal of Asiatic Studies* 47, no. 2 (1987): 461–538.

———. *"This Culture of Ours": Intellectual Transitions in T'ang and Sung China.* Stanford, CA: Stanford University Press, 1992.

Bray, Francesca. *Biology and Biological Technology: Part II, Agriculture.* Cambridge: Cambridge University Press, 1984.

———. "Chinese Literati and the Transmission of Technological Knowledge: The Case of Agriculture." In *Cultures of Knowledge: Technology in Chinese History,* edited by Dagmar Schäfer, 299–325. Leiden: Brill, 2011.

———. "Towards a Critical History of Non-Western Technology." In *China and Historical Capitalism,* edited by Timothy Brook and Gregory Blue, 158–209. Cambridge: Cambridge University Press, 1999.

Bray, Francesca, Vera Dorofeeva-Lichtmann, and Georges Métailié, eds. *Graphics and Text in the Production of Technical Knowledge in China: The Warp and the Weft.* Leiden: Brill, 2007.

Brook, Timothy. "Guides for Vexed Travelers: Route Books in the Ming and Qing." *Ch'ing-shih wen-t'i* 4, no. 5 (June 1981): 32–76.

Brook, Timothy, and Gregory Blue, eds. *China and Historical Capitalism: Genealogies of Sinological Knowledge.* Cambridge: Cambridge University Press, 1999.

Brown, Claudia. *Great Qing: Painting in China, 1644–1911.* Seattle: University of Washington Press, 2014.

Brown, Claudia, and Ju-hsi Chou, eds. *Chinese Painting under the Qianlong Emperor: The Symposium Papers in Two Volumes. Phoebus* 6, no. 2. Temple: Arizona State University, 1991.

Burkus-Chasson, Anne. "Between Representations: The Historical and the Visionary in Chen Hongshou's 'Yaji.'" *Art Bulletin* 84, no. 2 (June 2002): 315–33.

———. *Through a Forest of Chancellors: Fugitive Histories in Liu Yuan's "Lingyan ge"; An Illustrated Book from Seventeenth-Century Suzhou.* Cambridge, MA: Harvard University Asia Center for the Harvard-Yenching Institute, 2010.

Bush, Susan. *The Chinese Literati on Painting: Su Shih (1037–1101) to Tung Ch'i-ch'ang (1555–1636).* Cambridge, MA: Harvard University Press, 1971.

Bushell, Stephen. *Description of Chinese Pottery and Porcelain: Being a Translation of the T'ao Shuo.* Oxford: Clarendon Press, 1910.

Bussotti, Michela, and Han Qi. "Typography for a Modern World? The Ways of Chinese Movable Types." *East Asian Science, Technology, and Medicine Journal* 40 (2014): 9–44.

Cahill, James. *Pictures for Use and Pleasure: Vernacular Painting in High Qing China.* Berkeley: University of California Press, 2010.

Cai Mei-Fen 蔡玫芬. "Guanfu yu guan Yang: Qianlun yingxiang Songdai ciqi fazhan de guanfang yinsu" 官府與官樣—淺論影響宋代瓷器發展的官方因素 (Government office and official Yang: On the official impact on the development of ceramics in Song dynasty). In *Qianxinian Songdai wenwu dazhan* 千禧年宋代文物大展 (China at the inception of the second millennium C.E.: Art and culture of the Sung dynasty, 960–1279), 321–27. Taipei: Guoli Gugong Bowuyuan, 2006.

Cao Ganyuan 曹淦源. "Qianlong huangdi, Tang Ying yu jiaopin" 乾隆皇帝、唐英與轎瓶 (Emperor Qianlong, Tang Ying, and vases for sedan chair). *Shoucangjie* 7 (2006): 61–63.

Cao Yiqiang 曹意強. "An Effort without a Response: Nian Xiyao (年希堯, ? –1739) and His Study of Scientific Perspective." *Yishushi Yanjiu* 4 (2002): 103–33.

Chang Jingzhi 常靜之. *Lun bangzi qiang* 論梆子腔 (On clapper drama). Beijing: Renmin Yinyue Chubanshe, 1991.

Chang, Kang-i Sun. *The Cambridge History of Chinese Literature.* Vol. 2. New York: Cambridge University Press, 2010.

Chang, Michael. *A Court on Horseback: Imperial Touring and the Construction of Qing Rule, 1680–1785.* Cambridge, MA: Harvard University Asia Center, Harvard University Press, 2007.

Chang Te-Chang. "The Economic Role of the Imperial Household in the Ch'ing Dynasty." *Journal of Asian Studies* 31, no. 2 (1972): 243–73.

Chen Fang-Mei 陳芳妹. "Song guqiwuxue de xingqi yu song fanggu tongqi" 宋古器物學的興起與宋仿古銅器 (The rise of Song antiquarianism and the imitation of archaic bronze). *Taida Journal of Art History* 10 (2001): 37–160.

Chen Kaijun 陳愷俊. "Yiwei jishu guanliao de ziwo xiuyang" 一位技術官僚的自我修養 (The self-cultivation of a technocrat). *Gugong wenwu yuekan* 364 (2013): 92–100.

Chen Kuo-tung 陳國棟. "Neiwufu guanyuan de waipai, wairen yu Qianlong gongting wenwu gongji zhijian de guanxi" 內務府官員的外派、外任—與乾隆宮廷文物供給之間的關係 (Imperial bondservants' provincial positions and their contribution to the acquisition of objets d'art for emperor Qianlong's court). *Taida Meishushi Yanjiu Jikan,* no. 33 (Sep. 2012): 225–69, 346.

———. "Wuyingdian zongjianzao He Shiheng: Huoyue yu 'liyi zhizheng' shijian zhong de yiwei neiwufu renwu" 武英殿總監造赫世亨- 活躍於「禮儀之爭」事件中的一位內務府人物 (He Shihen, superintendent of the Wuyindian Workshops: A "rites controversy" figure of the Department of Imperial Household). *Gugong xueshu jikan* 30, no. 1 (2012): 87–134.

Chen, Liana. "Ritual into Play: The Aesthetic Transformation of Qing Court Theater." PhD diss., Stanford University, 2009.

Chen Wen-shih 陳文石. *Ming Qing zhengzhi shehui shilun* 明清政治社會史論 (Historical investigation of the politics and society during Ming and Qing). Taipei: Taiwan Xuesheng Shuju, 1991.

Chi Jo-hsin 嵇若昕. "Cong huojidang kan yongqian liangchao de neiting qiwu yishu guwen" 從活計檔看雍乾兩朝的內廷器物藝術顧問 (The advisers for decorative art to emperor Yuan-chen and emperor Ch'ien-lung: Based on the artisans of the imperial workshops). *Soochow University Journal of History* 16 (2005): 53–105.

———. "Qianlong shiqi de Ruyiguan" 乾隆時期的如意館 (The hall of self-fulfillment in the Ch'ien-lung court). *Gugong xueshu jikan* 23, no. 3 (2006): 127–52.

———. "Qing zhonghouqi (1821–1911) Neiwufu zaobangchu nanjiang jiqi xiangguan wenti" 清中後期(1821～1911)內務府造辦處南匠及其相關問題 (Southern craftsmen in the workshops of the Imperial Household Department during the middle to late Qing period [1821–1911] and issues related to them). *Gugong xueshu jikan* 32, no. 3 (2015): 63–89.

Chiu Hui-Ying 丘慧瑩. *Tang Ying xiqu yanjiu* 唐英戲曲研究 (Study of Tang Ying's drama). Taibei Xian, Yonghe: Huamulan Wenhua Chubanshe, 2010.

Chiu, Suet-Ying. *Bannermen Tales (zidishu): Manchu Storytelling and Cultural Hybridity in the Qing Dynasty*. Cambridge, MA: Harvard University Asia Center, 2018.

Chou, Ju-hsi. "Tangdai: A Biographical Sketch." *Phoebus* 6, no. 1 (1988): 133–40.

Chou, Ju-hsi, and Claudia Brown, eds. "Chinese Painting under the Qianlong Emperor." Special issue, *Phoebus: A Journal of Art History* 6, no. 1 (1988).

Chou Wen-Hui 周文惠. "Qingchao qianqi zhizao chutan-yi Suzhou zhizao wei zhongxin" 清朝前期織造初探- 以蘇州織造為中心 (Preliminary investigation of the textile manufactory in the early Qing period: Focusing on the Suzhou textile manufactory). MA thesis, National Soochow University, 2005.

Cicero, M. Tullius. *De Officiis* (On obligations). Translated by Walter Miller. Cambridge, MA: Harvard University Press, 1913.

Clunas, Craig. *Superfluous Things: Material Culture and Social Status in Early Modern China*. Honolulu: University of Hawai'i Press, 2004.

Corsi, Elisabetta. "Nian Xiyao de shengping jiqi dui yishu he kexue de gongxian" 年希堯的生平及其對藝術和科學的貢獻 (A biography of Nian Xiayao and his contribution to science and art). *Zhongguoshi yanjiu* 3 (2000): 156.

Crossley, Pamela. *A Translucent Mirror: History and Identity in Qing Imperial Ideology*. Berkeley: University of California Press, 1999.

Crossley, Pamela, and Evelyn Rawski. "A Profile of the Manchu Language in Ch'ing History." *Harvard Journal of Asiatic Studies* 53, no. 1 (June 1993): 63–102.

Curtis, Emily. "European Contribution to the Chinese Glass of the Early Qing Period." *Journal of Glass* 35 (1993): 91–101.

———. *Glass Exchange between Europe and China, 1550–1800: Diplomatic, Mercantile and Technological Interactions*. Farnham, England: Ashgate, 2009.

———. "Qingchao de bolizhizao yu yesuhuishi zai Canchikou de zuofang" 清朝的玻璃製造與耶穌會士在蠶池口的作坊 (The manufacture of glass in the Qing dynasty and Canchikou workshop). *Gugong Bowuyuan Yuankan* 1 (2003): 62–71.

Dalian Tushuguan 大連圖書館, ed. *Dalian Tushuguan cang Qingdai Neiwufu Dang'an* 大連圖書館藏清代內務府檔案 (Qing dynasty Imperial Household Archives in Dalian Library). Beijing: Guojia Tushuguan Chubanshe, 2010.

Daston, Loraine, and H. Otto Sibum. "Introduction: Scientific Personae and Their Histories." *Science in Context* 16, nos. 1–2 (Mar. 2003): 1–8.

David, Percival. "The *T'ao shuo* and 'The Illustrations of Pottery Manufacture': A Critical Study and a Review Reviewed." *Artibus Asiae* 12, no. 3 (1949): 165–83.

Dear, Peter, ed. *The Literary Structure of Scientific Argument: Historical Studies.* Philadelphia: University of Pennsylvania Press, 1991.

———. "Mysteries of State, Mysteries of Nature: Authority, Knowledge and Expertise in the Seventeenth Century." In *States of Knowledge: The Co-production of Science and Social Order*, edited by Sheila Jasanoff, 206–24. London: Routledge, 2004.

D'Entrecolles, Père. "Lettre du Père D'Entrecolles au Père Orry, 1 sept. 1712. Sur la Manufacture de Porcelaine en Chine." In *Lettres Edifiantes et Curieuses*, 12:253–357. Paris, 1741.

———. "Lettre du Père D'Entrecolles au Père Orry, 25 janvier 1722." In *Lettres Edifiantes et Curieuses*, 16:318–67. Paris, 1724.

Despeux, Catherine, and Christine Nguyen Tri, eds. *Éducation et instruction en Chine.* Vol. 2, *Les formations spécialisées*. Leuven, Belgium: Éditions Peeters, 2003.

Di Luo. "A Grain of Sand: Yingzao Fashi and the Miniaturization of Chinese Architecture." PhD diss., University of Southern California, 2016.

Dillion, Michael. "A History of the Porcelain Industry in Jingdezhen." PhD diss., Leeds University, 1976.

Ding Haibin 丁海斌. *Qingdai "guan keji" qunti de yangcheng yu jiegou yanjiu* 清代"官科技"群體的養成與結構研究 (Studies on the formation and construction of the "official science and technology" community in the Qing dynasty). Beijing: Zhongguo Shehui Kexue Chubanshe, 2008.

Ding Ruqin 丁汝芹. *Qingdai neiting yanxi shihua* 清代內廷演戲史話 (History of court theater during the Qing dynasty). Beijing: Zijincheng Chubanshe, 1999.

Dong Han 董含. *Chunxiang zhuibi* 蓴鄉贅筆 (Superfluous jottings from Chun Village). In *Shuoling* 說鈴 (1799), compiled by Wu Zhenfang 吳震方. 1705; rpt., Taipei, Guangwen Shuju, 1980.

Du Jiaji 杜家驥. "Qingdai Baqi zhidu zhong de 'taiqi'" 清代八旗制度中的'抬旗' (The "elevation of banner" in the banner system of the Qing dynasty). *Shixue jikan* 4 (1991): 48–52.

Du Jiaji 杜家驥 and Zhang Zhenguo 張振國. "Qingdai Neiwufu guanzhi de fuzaxing jiqi tedian" 清代內務府官製的複雜性及其特點 (The complexity and character of the official system in the Imperial Household Department of the Qing dynasty). *Nankai Journal* 4 (2008): 68–73.

Du Wan 杜綰. *Stone Catalogue of Cloudy Forest* (*Yunlin shipu* 雲林石譜). Translated by Edward Schafer. Berkeley: University of California Press, 1961.

Durrant, Stephen. "Sino-Manchu Translations in the Mukden Court." *Journal of the American Oriental Society* 99 (1979): 653–61.

Edgren, Soren, ed. "Imperially Commissioned Pictures of Tilling and Weaving." *Chinese Rare Books in American Collections*. New York: China Institute, 1984.

E'ertai 鄂爾泰 et al., eds. *Baqi manzhou shizu tongpu* 八旗滿洲氏族通譜 (Complete genealogies of the Manchu clans and families of the Eight Banners). Shenyang: Liao Shen Shushe, 1989.

———. *Qinding Baqi tongzhi* 欽定八旗通志 (Comprehensive history of the Eight Banners, imperially ordained). Beijing: Beijing Airusheng Shuzihua Jishu Yanjiu Zongxin, 2009.

Elliott, Mark C. *The Manchu Way: The Eight Banners and Ethnic Identity in Late Imperial China*. Stanford, CA: Stanford University Press, 2001.

Elman, Benjamin. *Civil Examinations and Meritocracy in Late Imperial China*. Cambridge, MA: Harvard University Press, 2013.

———. *A Cultural History of Civil Examinations in Late Imperial China*. Berkeley: University of California Press, 2000.

———. *A Cultural History of Modern Science in China*. Cambridge, MA: Harvard University Press, 2006.

———. *From Philosophy to Philology: Intellectual and Social Aspects of Change in Late Imperial China*. Cambridge, MA: Council on East Asian Studies, Harvard University, 1984.

———. "The Investigation of Things (Gewu 格物), Natural Studies (Gezhixue 格致), and Evidential Studies (Kaozhengxue 考證學): Gewu in Late Imperial China, 1600–1800." In *Concepts of Nature: A Chinese-European Cross-Cultural Perspective*, edited by Hans Vogel and Günter Dux, 368–99. Leiden: Brill, 2010.

———. *On Their Own Terms: Science in China, 1550–1900*. Cambridge, MA: Harvard University Press, 2005.

Elman, Benjamin, and A. Woodside, eds. *Education and Society in Late Imperial China 1600–1900*. Berkeley: University of California Press, 1994.

Eyferth, Jacob. "Craft Knowledge at the Interface of Written and Oral Cultures." *East Asian Science, Technology and Society* 4 (2010): 185–205.

———. *Eating Rice from Bamboo Roots: The Social History of a Community of Handicraft Papermakers in Rural Sichuan, 1920–2000*. Cambridge, MA: Harvard University Asia Center, Harvard University Press, 2009.

———. "The Nature of Skill." In *Eating Rice from Bamboo Roots: The Social History of a Community of Handicraft Papermakers in Rural Sichuan, 1920–2000*, 14–18. Cambridge, MA: Harvard University Asia Center, 2009.

Fan Jinmin 范金民. "Qingdai feichu jiang ji de lishi yiyi" 清代廢除匠籍的歷史意義 (The historical significance of abolishing artisans' registration in the Qing dynasty). *Qingshi yanjiu* 96, no. 1 (1995): 108–15.

Feng Jiren. *Chinese Architecture and Metaphor: Song Culture in the Yingzao Fashi Building Manual*. Honolulu: University of Hawai'i Press, 2012.

Feng Mingzhu 馮明珠. *Emperor Ch'ien-lung's Grand Cultural Enterprise* 乾隆皇帝的文化大業. Taipei: Guoli Gugong Bowuyuan, 2002.

———. *Harmony and Integrity: The Yongzheng Emperor and His Times* 雍正：清世宗文物大展. Taibei Shi: Guoli Gugong Bowuyuan, 2009.

———. *Kangxi dadi yu taiyangwang luyi shisi tezhan: zhongfa yishu wenhua de jiaohui* 康熙大帝與太陽王路易十四特展：中法藝術文化的交會 (Emperor Kangxi and the

Sun King Louis XIV: Sino-Franco encounters in arts and culture). Taipei Shi: Guoli Gugong Bowuyuan, 2011.

Feng Xianming 馮先銘, ed. *Zhongguo gutaociwenxian jishi* 中國古陶瓷文獻集釋 (Annotated collection of historical documents on ancient Chinese ceramics). Hong Kong: Yishujia Chubanshe, 2000.

Finlay, John. "The Qianlong Emperor's Western Vistas: Linear Perspective and Trompe l'Oeil Illusion in the European Palaces of the Yuanming yuan." *Bulletin de l'École Française d'Extrême-Orient* 94 (2007): 159–93.

Finlay, Robert. *The Pilgrim Art: Cultures of Porcelain in World History*. Berkeley: University of California Press, 2010.

Fletcher, Joseph. "The Mongols: Ecological and Social Perspectives." *Harvard Journal of Asiatic Studies* 46, no. 1 (June 1986): 11–50.

Fong, Wen C., and James C. Y. Watt, eds. *Possessing the Past: Treasures from the National Palace Museum, Taipei*. New York: Metropolitan Museum of Art, 1996.

Forêt, Philippe. *Mapping Chengde: The Qing Landscape Enterprise*. Honolulu: University of Hawai'i Press, 2000.

Foucault, Michel. *The Order of Things: An Archaeology of the Human Sciences*. New York: Vintage, 1970.

———. "What Is an Author? The Author Function." Translated by Donald F. Bouchard and Sherry Simon. In *Language, Counter-Memory, Practice*, 113–38. Ithaca, NY: Cornell University Press, 1977.

Franke, Wolfgang. "Patents for Hereditary Ranks and Honorary Titles during the Ch'ing Dynasty." *Monumenta Serica* 1 (1942): 38–67.

Frankel, Hans. "Cai Yan and the Poems Attributed to Her." *Chinese Literature: Essays, Articles, Reviews* (*CLEAR*) 5, nos. 1–2 (July 1983): 133–56.

Fraser, Sarah. "The Artist's Practice in Tang Dynasty China (8th–10th Centuries)." PhD diss., University of California, Berkeley, 1996.

———. "Formulas of Creativity: Artists' Sketches and Techniques of Copying at Dunhuang." *Artibus Asiae* 59, nos. 3–4 (2000): 189–224.

———. *Performing the Visual: The Practice of Buddhist Wall Painting in China and Central Asia, 618–960*. Stanford, CA: Stanford University Press, 2004.

Fu Yiling 傅衣凌. *Mingqing shidai shangren ji shangye ziben: Mingdai jiangnan shimin jingji shitan* 明清時代商人及商業資本：明代江南市民經濟試探 (Merchants and commercial capital in the Ming and Qing period: Preliminary investigation of Burgher economy in Jiangnan during the Ming dynasty). Beijing: Zhonghua Shuju, 2007.

Fu Yuhong 傅育紅. "Shaozao ciqi zhangcheng zhiding hou yuyao jingfei de hexiao" 燒造瓷器章程制定後禦窯燒造經費的核銷 (The fiscal verification of imperial porcelain manufacture cost after the establishment of the regulation system for porcelain manufacture). *Gugong Bowuyuan Yuankan*, no. 11 (2006): 73–80.

Fu Zhenlun 傅振倫 and Zhen Li 甄勵. "Tang Ying ciwu nianpu changbian" 唐英瓷務年譜長編 (Chronology of Tang Ying's ceramic work). *Jingdezhen taoci* 2 (1982): 18–66.

Gao Bin 高斌. *Guzai caotang shiji* 固哉草堂詩集 (Poetry from Guzai thatched hut). In

Qingdai shiwen ji huibian 清代詩文集彙編 (Compilation of poetry and prose of Qing dynasty). Vol. 273. Shanghai: Shanghai Guji Chubanshe, 2010.

Gao Xiaoran 高曉然. "Falangcai shaozao guocheng zhong de jijian wuzheng" 琺瑯彩燒造過程中的幾件物證 (Some material evidence of the productive process of *falang* enameled wares). *Gugong Bowuyuan Yuankan* 2 (2010): 102–12.

———. "Guifu shenggong shenglai zhibi: Jianlun qianlong shiqi taoci zhong de qiqiao zhizuo" 鬼斧神工神來之筆—簡論乾隆時期陶瓷中的奇巧之作 (Marvelous achievement: Brief discussion of the ingenious works of ceramics during the Qianlong period). *Nanfang Wenwu* 4 (2006): 109–13.

Ge Zhaoguang 葛兆光. *An Intellectual History of China.* Vol. 1, *Knowledge, Thought, and Belief before the Seventh Century CE* (*Zhongguo sixiang shi, juan 1* 中國思想史 卷一). Translated by Michael Duke and Josephine Chiu-Duke. Leiden: Brill, 2014.

Gell, Alfred. "The Technology of Enchantment and the Enchantment of Technology." In *Anthropology, Art and Aesthetics*, edited by J. Coote and A. Shelton, 40–66. Oxford: Clarendon, 1992.

Geng Baochang 耿寶昌 et al. "Geyao ciqi lansheng" 哥窯瓷器攬勝 (Exploration of porcelain from the Ge kilns). Special issue, *Zijincheng*, no. 275 (2017).

———. "Jiang Qi and Tang Ying" 蔣祈與唐英. *Gugong Bowuyuan Yuankan* 1 (1999): 49–51.

———. "Mantan Tang Ying yu tangyao ciqi" 漫談唐英與唐窯瓷器 (Tang Ying and the porcelains of Tang kiln). In *Dutaoguan wenhua yu Jingdezhen* 督陶官文化與景德鎮 (The culture of ceramic supervisor and Jingdezhen), edited by Zhao Caiquan et al., 1–17. Nanchang: Jiangxi Meishu Chubanshe, 2011.

———. *Mingqing ciqi jianding* 明清瓷器鑒定 (Authentication of the porcelain of the Ming and Qing dynasties). Beijing: Zijincheng Chubanshe, 1993.

Gerritsen, Anne. *The City of Blue and White: Chinese Porcelain and the Early Modern World.* Cambridge: Cambridge University Press, 2020.

———. "Global Design in Jingdezhen: Local Production and Global Connections." In *Global Design History*, edited by Glenn Adamson, Giogio Riello, and Sarah Teasley, 25–33. Abingdon, England: Routledge, 2011.

———. "Porcelain and the Material Culture of the Yuan Court (1279–1368)." *Journal of Early Modern History* 16 (2012): 241–73.

Gerritsen, Anne, and Stephen McDowall. "Material Culture and the Other: European Encounters with Chinese Porcelain, ca. 1650–1800." *Journal of World History* 23, no. 1 (March 2012): 87–113.

Giès, Jacques. "'Perspectiva' ou 'Science de la vision' de Nian Xiyao (?–1739): Le paradoxe recurrent de la rencontre Chine-Occident." In *Les très riches heures de la cour de Chine: Chefs-d'oeuvre de la peinture impériale des Qing 1662–1796*, edited by Marie-Catherine Rey, 13–43. Paris: Musée Guimet des Arts Asiatiques, 2006.

Gillette, Maris Boyd. *China's Porcelain Capital: The Rise, Fall, and Reinvention of Ceramics in Jingdezhen.* London: Bloomsbury, 2016.

Ginzburg, Carlo. *The Cheese and the Worms: The Cosmos of a Sixteenth-Century Miller.* Baltimore, MD: Johns Hopkins University Press, 1980.

Goepper, Keh. "Tang-tai, Ein Hofmaler der Ch'ing-Zeit." PhD diss., Ludwig-Maximilians-Universitat, Munich, 1956.

Golas, Peter. *Picturing Technology in China: From Earliest Times to the Nineteenth Century*. Hong Kong: Hong Kong University Press, 2015.

———. "Technical Representation in China: Tools and Techniques of the Trade." *East Asian Science, Technology, and Medicine* 20 (2003): 11–44.

Goldman, Andrea. *Opera and the City: The Politics of Culture in Beijing, 1770–1900*. Palo Alto, CA: Stanford University Press, 2012.

Grafton, Antony. *Leon Battista Alberti: Master Builder of the Italian Renaissance*. Cambridge, MA: Harvard University Press, 2002.

Gu Pingdan 顧平旦. "Cao Yin 'Taiping leshi' zaju chutan" 曹寅《太平樂事》雜劇初探 (Preliminary study of Cao Yin's *Festivity in a Peaceful Era*). *Hongloumeng xuekan* 4 (1986): 294–99.

Gu Yingtai 谷應泰. *Mingshi jishi benmo* 明史紀事本末 (Reporting origin and result of events in the history of the Ming dynasty). Taipei: Taiwan Shangwu Yinshuguan, 1983.

Guan Zengjian and Konrad Herrman, trans. *Kao Gong Ji: The World's Oldest Encyclopedia of Technology*. Leiden: Brill, 2014.

Gugong Bowuyuan. *Qinggong Neiwufu zaobanchu dang'an zonghui* 清宮內務府造辦處檔案總匯 (Archive of the Imperial Workshops in the Imperial Household Department of Qing dynasty). Beijing: Renmin Chubanshe, 2005.

Gugong Bowuyuan Ming-Qing Dang'an Bu 故宮博物院明清檔案部, ed. *Li Xu zouzhe* 李煦奏摺 (Memorial by Li Xu). Beijing: Zhonghua Shuju, 1976.

Guo Daiheng and He Yan 郭黛姮 賀豔. *Shenzang jiyi yichan zhong de Yuanmingyuan: Yangshifang tudang yanjiu, 1* (Yuanmingyuan-heritage in deep memory: Studies of archive in the bureau of design). Shanghai: Shanghai Yuandong Chubanshe, 2016.

Guo Fuxiang 郭福祥. "Qianlong gongting zhiyu xingongju 'Qinzhong gangpian' kao: Jianlun zuozan jishu yu qinggong daxing yuqi zhizuo de guanxi" 乾隆宮廷制玉新工具"秦中鋼片"考—兼論鑿鏨技術與清宮大型玉器制作的關系 (An examination of "a steel disc made in qinzhong": A concurrent discussion about the techniques and large-size jade carving of the imperial Qing court). *Gugong Bowuyuan Yuankan*, no. 1 (2017): 79–98.

Guo Moruo 郭沫若. "Bangui de zaifaxian" 班簋的再發現 (Rediscovery of the Bangui vessel). *Wenwu* 9 (1972): 2–13.

Guojia Tushuguan, ed. *Qingdai Yangshilei jianzhu tudang zhan* 清代樣式雷建築圖檔展: 華夏建築義江的傳世絕響 (Exhibition of Yangshi Lei architectural archives of the Qing dynasty: Masterpieces of architectural conceptions of ancient China). Beijing: Guojia Tushuguan, 2004.

Hammers, Roslyn Lee. "Perspectives in Early Qing-Dynasty Pictures of Tilling and Weaving and Pictures of Cotton." *Historia Scientiarum* 21, no. 1 (2011): 3–19.

———. *Pictures of Tilling and Weaving: Art, Labor and Technology in Song and Yuan China*. Hong Kong: Hong Kong University Press, 2011.

Han Wei 韓魏. "Songdai fanggu zhizuo de yangban wenti" 宋代仿古製作的樣本問題 (The "model" in the replication of antiques during the Song dynasty). In *Songyun:*

Sichuan jiaocang wenwu jingcui 宋韵—四川窖藏文物精粹 (Charm of Song dynasty: Selection from the archaeological discovery of a hoard in Sichuan), 288–96. Beijing: Zhongguo Shehui Kexue Chubanshe, 2006.

Hanan, Patrick. *The Chinese Vernacular Story*. Cambridge, MA: Harvard University Press, 1981.

Hay, Jonathan. "The Kangxi Emperor's Brush-Traces: Calligraphy, Writing, and the Art of Imperial Authority." In *Body and Face in Chinese Visual Culture*, edited by Wu Hung and Katherine Tsiang Mino, 311–34. Cambridge, MA: Harvard University Press, 2004.

———. *Sensuous Surfaces: The Decorative Object in Early Modern China*. Honolulu: University of Hawai'i Press, 2010.

———. *Shitao: Painting and Modernity in Early Qing China*. Cambridge: Cambridge University Press, 2001.

He Beijie 何蓓潔. "Yangshi lei shijia yanjiu" 樣式雷世家研究 (Study of the lineage of designer Lei). MA thesis, Tianjin University, 2007.

Hearn, Maxwell. "Document and Portrait: The Southern Tour Paintings of Kangxi and Qianlong." *Phoebus* 6, no. 1 (1988): 91–131.

Ho Ping-Ti. *Studies on the Population of China, 1368–1953*. Cambridge, MA: Harvard University Press, 1959.

Hong Wei 宏偉. "Qingdai Wanqi Baqi Menggu wenren En-hua jiqi 'Baqi wenyi bianmu" 清代晚期八旗蒙古文人恩華及其《八旗藝文編目》 (The Mongolian literati En-Hua of Eight Banners in the late Qing dynasty and her *Catalogue of Eight Banners' Art and Literature*). *Mongguxue Jikan*, no. 1 (2016): 1–10.

Hong Zhou et al., eds. *Baqi Manzhou shizu tongpu* 八旗滿族氏族通譜 (Comprehensive genealogy of the Eight Banner Manchu clans). Shenyang: Liaohai Chubanshe, 2007.

Hongxi Meishuguan. *Chinese Art: Chinese Art from the Ching Wan Society Collection*. Taipei: Chang Foundation, 1998.

Hostetler, Laura. *Qing Colonial Enterprise: Ethnography and Cartography in Early Modern China*. Chicago: University of Chicago Press, 2001.

Hou Hao-chih 侯皓之. "Keshen qingjin: Cong dang'an lun Haiwang qirenqishi yu zai zaobanchu de zuoyong" 恪慎勤謹— 從檔案論海望其人其事與在造辦處的作用 (Prudential and talented: Study of Haiwang's contribution to the Imperial Workshops). *Gugong Xueshu Jikan* 30, no. 3 (2013): 237–80.

Hsieh Ming-Liang 謝明良. "Qianlong de taoci jianshangguan" 乾隆的陶瓷鑑賞觀 (Qianlong's connoisseurship on ceramics). *Gugong xueshu jikan* 21 (2003): 1–38, 299.

Hsieh Yu-chen 謝玉珍. "Mingchu guanfang yongqi renwuwen de yihan" 明初官方用器人物紋的意涵 (The meanings of early Ming official wares decorated with human figures). *Gugong xueshu jikan* 25 (2007): 127–32.

Huang Bian 黃汴. *Tianxia shuilucheng* 天下水陸程 (Routes of transportation over rivers and lands). Taiyuan: Shanxi Renmin Chubanshe, 1992.

Huang Chao 黃超 and Paul A. Van Dyke. "Hoppo Tang Ying 唐英 (1750–1751) and the Development of the Guangdong Maritime Customs." *Journal of Asian History* 51, no. 2 (2017): 223–56.

Huang, Ellen. "An Art of Transformation: Reproducing Yaobian Glazes in Qing-Dynasty Porcelain." *Archives of Asian Art* 68, no. 2 (Oct. 2018): 133–56.

———. "China's China: Jingdezhen Porcelain and the Production of Art in the Nineteenth Century." PhD diss., University of California, San Diego, 2008.

———. "From the Imperial Court to the International Art Market: Jingdezhen Porcelain Production as Global Visual Culture." *Journal of World History* 23, no. 1 (Mar. 2012): 115–45.

Huang Li-Chun 黃麗君. "Baqizhidu yu zuqun rentong: Qing qianqi Zhongchao guanxishi zhong de Neiwufu gaoli zuoling Jinshi jiazu" 八旗制度與族群認同：清前期中朝關系史中的內務府高麗佐領金氏家族 (The banner system and ethnic identity: The Jin family and its ethnic identity from the perspective of Sino-Joseon studies). *Qingshi yanjiu*, no. 2 (May 2019): 64–77.

———. "Hesu jiqi yizuo qibentou yanjiu" 和素及其譯作七本頭 研究 (A study of Hesu and his collection of translation Ci Ben Deo). *Taiwan daxue lishi xuebao* 58 (2017): 91–150.

———. "Huangdi jiqi baoyi nucai: Lun Qingdai huangquan yu Neiwufu guanliao tizhi" 皇帝及其包衣奴才：論清代皇權與內務府官僚體制 (The emperors and their bondservants: Interaction between imperial wills and bureaucratic institutions of the Imperial Household Department in the Qing dynasty). PhD diss., National Taiwan University, 2014.

Huang Qinghua 黃清華. "Beiyiwang de Tangyao jiaqi" 被遺忘的唐窯佳器 (The forgotten fine wares from the Tang kiln). *Gugong wenwu yuekan* 363 (2013): 110–19.

———. "Lang yao yu Kangxi Guanyao guanxi kaoshi" 郎窯與康熙官窯關係考釋. In *Yanxun xiuse: Kangxi ciqi yu gongting yishu zhenpin tezhan* 延薰秀色：康熙瓷器與宮廷藝術珍品特展 (Beauty's lasting fragrance: Special exhibition of porcelain from the Kangxi reign and court art), 18–29. Beijing: Poly Art Museum, 2011.

Huang Wei 黃薇 and Huang Qinghua 黃清華. "Yuan qinghua ciqi zaoqi leixing de xin faxian: Cong shizheng jiaodu lun yuanqinghua ciqi de qiyuan" 元青花瓷器早期類型的新發現—從實證角度論元青花瓷器的起源 (New discovery of an early style of Yuan blue-and-white porcelain: Empirical discussion of the origin of Yuan blue-and-white porcelain). *Wenwu* 11 (2012): 79–88.

Huang Yi-nong 黃一農. "Hongyi dapao yu Huang Taiji chuangli de Baqi Hanjun" 紅夷大砲與皇太極創立的八旗漢軍 (Red Barbarian Cannon and the Hanjun Banner founded by Hong Taiji). *Lishi yanjiu*, no. 4 (2004): 74–105.

Hummel, Arthur. *Eminent Chinese of the Ch'ing Period (1644–1912)*. Washington, DC: Library of Congress, 1944.

Huo Hua 霍華. "Qing guanyao jiqingyou fencai qianlong xingweitu zhuanxuanpin yanjiu" 清官窯霽青釉粉彩乾隆行圍圖轉鏇瓶研究 (Study of the revolving vase decorated with the painting of Qianlong's hunting over sky-blue *fencai* glaze). *Dongnan wenhua* 2 (1997): 132–40.

Idema, Wilt. *Two Centuries of Manchu Women Poets: An Anthology*. Seattle: University of Washington Press, 2017.

Idema, Wilt, Wai-yee Li, and Ellen Widmer, eds. *Trauma and Transcendence in Chinese Literature*. Cambridge, MA: Harvard University Asia Center, Harvard University Press, 2006.

Ingold, Tim. *The Perception of the Environment: Essays on Livelihood, Dwelling and Skill*. London: Routledge, 2000.

Jami, Catherine. "Western Learning and Imperial Scholarship: The Kangxi Emperor's Study." *East Asian Science, Technology and Medicine* 27 (2007): 144–70.

Jasanoff, Sheila, ed. *States of Knowledge: The Co-production of Science and Social Order*. London: Routledge, 2004.

Ji Cheng 計成. *Yuanye* 園冶. Translated as *The Craft of Gardens* by Alison Hardie. New York: Better Link Press, 2012.

Jiang Jianxin 江建新. "Tang ying 'Taocheng jishi beiji' jiqi chutu canbei yiwen jiaoshi" 唐英《陶成紀事碑記》及其出土殘碑遺文校釋 (Annotated broken stela inscription: Tang Ying's *Report on the Accomplishment of Porcelains*). In *Dutaoguan wenhua yu Jingdezhen* 督陶官文化與景德鎮, edited by Zhao Caiquan 趙彩泉 et al., 304–12. Nanchang: Jiangxi Meishu Chubanshe, 2011.

———. *Tang Ying yu Tangyao guoji xueshu yantaohui lunwenji* 唐英與唐窯國際學術研討會論文集 (Proceedings of the international conference on Tang Ying and the Tang kiln). Beijing: Hualing Chubanshe, 2016.

———. "Yuanqinghua yu Fuliang Ciju jiqi yaochang" 元青花與浮梁磁局及其窯場 (Yuan dynasty blue-and-white, Fuliang Porcelain Bureau and its kilns). *Zhongguo guojia bowuguan guankan* 119 (2013): 76–115.

Jiang Qi 蔣祁. *Taoji jiaozhu* 陶記校注. Annotated by Bai Kun白焜. *Jingdezhen taoci* no. 4 (1981): 36–52.

Jin Jian 金簡. *Wuying dian juzhenban chengshi* 武英殿聚珍版程式. Translated by Richard Rudolph as *A Chinese Printing Manual*. Los Angeles: Ward Ritchie Press, 1954.

Johnson, David, et al. *Popular Culture in Late Imperial China*. Berkeley: University of California Press, 1985.

Johnson, Tara M. *Acculturation: Implications for Individuals, Families and Societies*. New York: Nova Science, 2011.

Ju Qingyuan 鞠清遠. "Yuandai xiguanjianghu yanju" 元代係官匠戶研究 (Study of the institutionalized artisanal households of the Yuan dynasty). *Shi huo* 1 (1935): 11–45.

Keliher, Macabe. *The Board of Rites and the Making of Qing China*. Oakland: University of California Press, 2019.

———. "The Manchu Transformation of Li: Ritual, Politics, and Law in the Making of Qing China, 1631–1690." PhD diss., Harvard University, 2015.

Kern, Martin. *Statecraft and Classical Learning: The Rituals of Zhou in East Asian History*. Leiden: Brill. 2009.

Kerr, Rose, and Nigel Wood. *Ceramic Technology*. Science and Civilisation in China, vol. 5, part 12. Cambridge: Cambridge University Press, 2004.

Kessler, Lawrence. "Chinese Scholars and the Early Manchu State." *Harvard Journal of Asiatic Studies* 31 (1971): 179–200.

Klein, Ursula, and E. C. Spary, eds. *Materials and Expertise in Early Modern Europe: Between Market and Laboratory*. Chicago: University of Chicago Press, 2009.

Kleutghen, Kristina. "Flowering Stone: The Aesthetics and Politics of Islamic Jade at the Qing Court." In *Eighteenth-Century Art Worlds: Global and Local Geographies of Art*, edited by Michael Yonan and Stacey Sloboda, 19–33. London: Bloomsbury Visual Arts, 2019,

———. *Imperial Illusions: Crossing Pictorial Boundaries in the Qing Palaces*. Seattle: University of Washington Press, 2015.

Ko, Dorothy. *Cinderella's Sisters: A Revisionist History of Footbinding*. Berkeley: University of California Press, 2005.

———. *Every Step a Lotus: Shoes for Bound Feet*. Berkeley: University of California Press, 2001.

———. *The Social Life of Inkstones: Artisans and Scholars in Early Qing China*. Seattle: University of Washington Press, 2017.

Kong Shangren 孔尚任. *Kong Shangren quanji jijiao zhuping* 孔尚任全集輯校注評 (Complete annotated and commented works of Kong Shangren). Edited and annotated by Xu Zhengui. Jinan: Qilu Shushe, 2004.

Krahl, Regina. "The Yongzheng Emperor and the Qing Court Collection." *Transactions of the Oriental Ceramic Society* 80 (2015–16): 121–37.

Kuhn, Philip. *Soulstealers: The Chinese Sorcery Scare of 1768*. Cambridge, MA: Harvard University Press, 1990.

Lai Hui-Min. *Qianlong huangdi de hebao* 乾隆皇帝的荷包 (Emperor Qianlong's privy purse). Taipei: Academia Sinica Institute of Modern History, 2014.

Lai Yu-Chih. "Images, Knowledge and Empire: Depicting Cassowaries in the Qing Court." *Transcultural Studies* 1 (2013): 7–100.

Lam, Peter Y. K. 林業強. "Cangu yunxin: Liuyuan sheji ciyang kao" 參古運新：劉源設計瓷樣考 (Cangu Yunxin: Investigation of Liu Yuan's design). In *Gugong bowuyuan bashi huadan gutaoci guoji xueshu yantaohui lunwenji* 故宮博物院八十華誕古陶瓷國際學術研討會論文集 (Proceedings of the international conference on ancient ceramics in honor of the eightieth anniversary of the Palace Museum), 11–24. Beijing: Zijincheng Chubanshe, 2007.

———. *Jixia qingshang: Huaihaitang cang qingdai yuyao cipin* 機暇清賞：懷 海堂藏清代御窰瓷缾 (Ethereal elegance: Porcelain vases of the imperial Qing—the Huaihaitang collection). Hong Kong: University of Hong Kong Press, 2007.

———. "Lang Tingji (1663–1715) and the Porcelain of the Late Kangxi Period." *Transactions of the Oriental Ceramic Society* 68 (2003–4): 27–49.

———. "Porcelain Manufacture Illustrations of the Qing Dynasty" 廣州藝術博物院院刊. *Journal of Guangzhou Museum of Art: Special Edition on Exhibition of Souvenir from Canton*, no. 1 (2004): 21–49.

———. "Tang Ying (1682–1756): The Imperial Factory Superintendent at Jingdezhen." *Transactions of the Oriental Ceramics Society* 1, no. 63 (1998–99): 65–82.

———. "Toward a Dating Framework for Qianlong Imperial Porcelain." *Transactions of the Oriental Ceramic Society* 74 (2009–10): 1–34.

Lan Pu 藍浦 and Zheng Tinggui 鄭廷桂. *Jingdezhen taolu tushuo* 景德鎮陶錄圖說 (Illustrated and annotated Jingdezhen *taolu*). Edited by Mian Lian 冕連. 1815; Jinan: Shandong Huabao, 2004.

Lang Tingji 郎廷極. *Ji Tang yao fa* 集唐要法 (Principal methods for writing a poem by assembling selections of Tang poetry). In *Congshu jicheng chubian* 叢書集成初編, edited by Wang Yunwu, vol. 2614. Shanghai: Shangwu Yinshuguan, 1935–40.

———. *Shengyin bian* 勝飲編 (Wonderful beverage). In *Congshu jicheng, chubian* 叢書集成初編, vol. 1685. Beijing: Zhonghua Shuju, 1985.

Latour, Bruno. "Gabriel Tarde and the End of the Social." In *The Social in Question: New Bearings in History and the Social Sciences*, edited by Patrick Joyce, 117–32. London: Routledge, 2002.

Lau, D. C. *Mencius*. Rev. ed. New York: Penguin, 2004.

Lawton, Thomas. "An Eighteenth Century Chinese Catalogue of Calligraphy and Painting: An Annotated Translation of Sections Three and Four." PhD diss., Harvard University, 1970.

Lazarist Mission Press 北京遣使會編. *Beitang Tushuguan cang xiwen shanben mulu* 北堂圖書館藏西文善本目錄 (Catalog of the Pei-T'ang Library). Beijing: Guojia Tushuguan Chubanshe, 2009.

Ledderoser, Lothar. *Ten Thousand Things: Module and Mass Production in Chinese Art*. Princeton, NJ: Princeton University Press, 2000.

Lee, George J. "Numbered Chun Ware." *Transactions of the Oriental Ceramic Society* 21 (1945–46): 53–64.

Lei Binyan 雷炳炎. *Qingdai shehui baqi guizu shijia shili yanjiu* 清代社會八旗貴族世家勢力研究 (Study of the bannermen aristocratic clans in the Qing society). Beijing: Zhongguo Shehui Kexue Chubanshe, 2016.

Lenoir, Timothy, ed. *Inscribing Science: Scientific Texts and the Materiality of Communication*. Stanford, CA: Stanford University Press, 1998.

Leonard, Jane. *Stretching the Qing Bureaucracy in the 1826 Sea-Transport Experiment*. Leiden: Brill, 2019.

Leroi-Gourhan, André. *Gesture and Speech*. Translated by Anna Bostock Berger. Cambridge, MA: MIT Press, 1993.

Li Baoping. "Numbered Jun Wares: Controversies and New Kiln Site Discoveries." *Transactions of the Oriental Ceramic Society* 71 (2006–7): 65–77.

Li Bozhong 李伯重. *Jiangnan de zaoqi gongyehua* 江南的早期工業化：1550–1850 年 (Early industrialization in Jiangnan, 1550–1850). Beijing: Shehui Kexue Wenxian Chubanshe, 2000.

Li, Cheng. "The Rise of Technocracy: Elite Transformation and Ideological Change in Post-Mao China." PhD diss., Princeton University, 1992.

Li, Chu-Tsing. *A Thousand Peaks and Myriad Ravines: Chinese Paintings in the Charles A. Drenowatz Collection*. Artibus Asiae Supplementum 30. Anscona: Artibus Asiae, 1974.

Li Dan. "Mingmo Qingchu Chaoxian yimin Jinshi Xindali jiazu yanjiu" 明末清初朝鮮

移民金氏新達理家族研究 (The study of Choson immigrants of the Kim's Xindali clan in the late Ming dynasty and early Qing dynasty). *Zhongzhou xuekan*, no. 5 (May 2018): 134–38.

Li Dou 李斗. *Yangzhou huafang lu zhu* 揚州畫舫錄註 (Annotated chronicle of the painted barques of Yangzhou). Annotated by Zhou Chundong. Jinan: Shandong Youyi Chubanshe, 2001.

Li Jiazhi 李家治 et al. *Zhongguo gudai taoci kexue jishu chengjiu* 中國古代陶瓷科學技術成就 (The scientific and technological achievements of premodern Chinese ceramics). Shanghai: Shanghai Keji Chubanshe, 1985.

Li Jinlu 李僅錄 and Wang Guangyao 王光堯. "Beijing xinchutu Tang Ying qie Keji ci guihuiguan" 北京新出土唐英妾可姬瓷骨灰罐 (The porcelain ash urn of Tang Ying's concubine, Keji, recently excavated from Beijing). In *Dongfang bowu*, vol. 14. Hangzhou: Zhejiang Daxue Chubanshe, 2005.

Li Qijiang 李其江 等 et al. "Mingqing shiji jiangji zhidu de biange dui Jingdezhen jishu fazhan de yingxiong" 明清時期匠籍制度的變革對景德鎮製瓷技術發展的影響 (Effect of craftsman register reform on development of porcelain-making technique in Jingdezhen during Ming and Qing dynasties). *China Ceramic Industry* 19, no. 5 (2012): 26–28.

Li Qingquan 李清泉. "Fenben: Cong Xuanhua Liaomu bihua kan gudai huagong de gongzuo moshi" 粉本—從宣化遼墓壁畫看古代畫工的工作模式 (Copybook: Studying the working models of ancient painters through the frescoes in the Liao tombs in Xuanhua). *Nanjing yishu xueyuan xuebao* 1 (2004): 36–39.

Li Wai-yee. "The Representation of History in the Peach Blossom Fan." *Journal of the American Oriental Society* 115, no. 3 (Jul.–Sep. 1995): 421–33.

Li Yu 李漁. *A Tower for the Summer Heat* (Xiayi lou 夏宜樓). Translated by Patrick Hanan. New York: Columbia University Press, 1998.

Li Zijun 李子軍. "Qionglai shi faxian jinian mingwen yinmo" 邛崍市發現紀年銘文印模 (Dated and inscribed mold discovered in Qionglai). *Chengdu wenwu* 1 (1996): 10.

Liao Baoxiu 廖寶秀. *Huali caici: Qianlong yangcai* 華麗彩瓷：乾隆洋彩 (Stunning decorative porcelains from the Ch'ien-lung reign). Taipei: Guoli Gugong Bowuyuan, 2008.

Liao Beng 廖奔. *Zhongguo xiqu shenqiang yuanliu shi* 中國戲曲聲腔源流史 (The origin and transformation of Chinese theatrical singing styles). Taipei: Guanya Wenhua Shiye Youxiangongsi, 1992.

Lin Boting 林柏亭, ed. *Daguan: Beisong tuyao tezhan* 大觀：北宋汝窯特展 (Grand view: Special exhibition of ju ware from the northern Sung dynasty). Taipei: National Palace Museum, 2006.

Lin, Li-chiang 林麗江. "The Creation and Transformation of Ancient Rulership in the Ming Dynasty (1368–1644): A Look at the *Dijian tushuo* (Illustrated Arguments in the Mirror of the Emperors)." In *Perceptions of Antiquity in Chinese Civilization*, edited by Dieter Kuhn and Helga Stahl, 321–59. Heidelberg: Edition Forum, 2008.

———. "The Proliferation of Images: The Ink-stick Designs and the Printing of the *Fang-shih mo-p'u* and the *Ch'eng-shih mo-yuan*." PhD diss., Princeton University, 1998.

Little, Stephen. *Chinese Ceramics of the Transitional Period, 1620–1683*. New York: China House Gallery, China Institute in America, 1983.

Liu Chaohui 劉朝暉. *Mingqing yilai Jingdezhen de ciye yu shehui kongzhi* 明清以來景德鎮的瓷業與社會控制 (The porcelain industry and social control in Jingdezhen since the Ming and Qing periods). Shanghai: Shanghai Shudian Chubanshe, 2010.

Liu Fengyun 劉鳳雲. "Shiba shiji de jishu guanliao" 十八世紀的技術官僚 (Technocrats in the eighteenth century). *Qingshi yanjiu* 2 (2010): 17–20.

Liu, Lydia He. *Translingual Practice: Literature, National Culture, and Translated Modernity—China, 1900–1937*. Stanford, CA: Stanford University Press, 1995.

Liu Wenfeng 劉文峰. *Shan shaan shangren yu bangzi xi kaolun* 山陝商人與梆子戲考論 (The study of merchants of Shanxi and Shaanxi and clapper theater). Beijing: Wenhua Yishu Chubanshe, 2011.

Liu Xiaomeng 劉小萌. "Guanyu Qingdai Neiwufu shijia" 關於清代內務府世家 (On the clans in the Imperial Household Department of the Qing dynasty). In *Mingqing shi luncong* 明清史論叢—孫文良教授誕辰七十周年紀念文集 (A symposium on Ming Qing history: Festschrift for Professor Sun Wenliang's seventieth anniversary), 138–58. Shengyang: Liaoning Daxue Chubanshe, 2004.

———. *Manzu cong buluo dao guojia* 滿族從部落到國家 (From tribe to state: An early history of the Manchus). Beijing: Zhongguo Shehui Kexue Chubanshe, 2007.

Liu Xinyuan 劉新園. "Jiang Qi Taoji zhuzuo shidai kaobian" 蔣祈陶記著作時代考辨 (Research on the period of the "Tao Ji": A discussion of differences in the porcelain manufacture technology, market, and taxes, etc., between the Southern Song and Yuan Dynasty in Jingdezhen). *Jingdezhen taoci* (1981): 5–35.

———. "Jingdezhen Hutianyao geqi dianxing wanlei de zaoxing tezheng jiqi chengyinkao" 景德鎮湖田窯各期典型碗類的造型特徵及其成因考 (The features of the principal types of Hutian kiln bowls of various periods and their origin). *Wenwu* 11 (1980): 50–60.

———. "Jingdezhen Hutianyao kaocha jiyao" 景德鎮湖田窯考察紀要 (Reconnaissance of ancient kiln sites at Hutian in Jingdezhen). *Wenwu* 11 (1980): 39–49.

———. "Yuanqinghua teyi wenshi he Jiangzuoyuan suoshu Fuliang Ciju yu Huaju" 元青花特異紋飾和將作院所屬浮梁磁局與畫局 (Research on Yuan blue-and-white wares with unique pattern decoration, Fuliang Porcelain Bureau and Huaju Bureau). *Jingdezhen taoci xueyuan yuanbao* 3, no. 1 (1982): 9–20.

Liu Xu 劉昫. *Jiu tang shu* 舊唐書 (Old history of the Tang dynasty). Taipei: Taiwan Shangwu Yinshuguan, 1983.

Lo Hui-chi 羅慧琪. "Chuanshi Junyaoqi de shidai wenti" 傳世鈞窯器的時代問題 (The numbered Chun wares and their manufacturing dates). *Taida Meishushi Yanjiu Jikan* 4 (1997): 109–83.

Loehr, George. "Missionary-Artist at the Manchu Court." *Transactions of the Oriental Ceramic Society* 34 (1962–63): 51–67.

———. "The Sinicization of Missionary Artists and Their Works at the Manchu Court during the Eighteenth Century." *Cahiers d'Histoire Mondiale* 8 (1963): 795–803.

Long, Pamela. *Artisan/Practitioners and the Rise of the New Sciences, 1400–1600*. Corvallis: Oregon State University Press, 2011.

Louis, Francois. *Design by the Book*. New York City: Bard Graduate Center, 2017.
Lü Chenglong 吕成龍. "Kangxi chao Langyao ciqi pinzhong chutan" 康熙朝郎窯瓷器品種初探 (Preliminary exploration of the categories of porcelains from Lang's kilns during the Kangxi reign). In *Dutaoguan wenhua yu Jingdezhen* 督陶官文化與景德鎮 (The culture of ceramic supervisor and Jingdezhen), edited by Zhao Caiquan and Jiang Hua, 74–91. Nanchang: Jiangxi Meishu Chubanshe, 2011.
Lü Jian 吕堅. "Kangxikuan huafalang suoyi" 康熙款畫琺瑯瑣議 (Discussion of the painted enameled wares with Kangxi's mark). *Gugong Bowuyuan yuankan* 3 (1981): 93–94.
Lu Minghua 陸明華. "Langyao jiqi zuopin yanjiu: Xincailiao de faxian yu qishi" 郎窯及其作品研究—新資料的發現與啟示 (Study of the Lang kiln wares: Discovery of new materials and its indication). *Shanghai Bowuguan guankan* 7 (1996): 92–110.
———. "Langyao xiangguan wenti zaikao" 郎窯相關問題再考 (Reexamining issues related to the Lang kiln wares). *Shanghai Bowuguan guankan* 12 (2012): 303–20.
———. "Qingchu Jingdezhen yuyaochang chengyin kao" 清初景德鎮御窯廠成因考 (Investigation of the establishment of the Imperial Manufactory of Porcelain in Jingdezhen during the early Qing period). *Shanghai Bowuguan guankan* 6 (1992): 306–22.
Luhmann, Nicklas. *Art as a Social System*. Translated by Eva M. Knodt. Stanford, CA: Stanford University Press, 2000.
Luo Yinghui 羅映輝. *Bangziqiang changqiang jiegou yanjiu* 梆子腔唱腔結構研究 (The study of the structure of the singing style of clapper drama). Beijing: Renmin Yinyue Chubanshe, 1994.
Ma Wenkuan. "Ping Jiangqi Taoji zhuzuo shidai kaobian: Yu Liu Xinyuan xiansheng shangque" 評《蔣祈〈陶記〉著作時代考辨》—與劉新園先生商榷 (A review of the thesis "Inquiry into the date of writing of the Taoji by Jiang Qi": Discussion with Mr. Liu Xinyuan). *Kaogu xuebao* 3 (2008): 395–414.
Ma Ya-chen 馬雅貞. *Kehua zhanxun: Qingchao diguo wugong de wenhua jiangou* 刻畫戰勳：清朝帝國武功的文化建構 (Marking the military medals: The cultural construction of military achievement of the Qing empire). Beijing: Shehui Kexue Chubanshe, 2016.
Mackerras, Colin. *Chinese Theater from Its Origins to the Present Day*. Honolulu: University of Hawaiʻi Press, 1983.
———. "The Growth of the Chinese Regional Drama in the Ming and Ch'ing." *Journal of Oriental Studies* 9, no. 1 (1971): 58–91.
Mao Ruifang 毛瑞芳. "Beitang shumu: jilu xixuedongjian de zhongyao wenxian" 《北堂書目》：記 錄西學東漸的重要歷史文獻 (The catalogue of the Pei-T'ang Library: An important record of the introduction of Western learning to China). *Journal of Historiography* 4 (2007): 112–18.
Mao Wen-Fang 毛文芳. *Wan Ming xianshang meixue* 晚明閑賞美學 (Aesthetics of leisurely appreciation in late Ming). Taipei: Taiwan Xuesheng Shuju, 2000.
McCausland, Shane. "The Emperor's Old Toys: Rethinking the Yongzheng (1723–35)

'Scroll of Antiquities' in the Percival David Foundation." *Transactions of the Oriental Ceramic Society* 66 (2012): 65–75.

McKendrick, Neil, and John Brewer. *The Birth of a Consumer Society: The Commercialization of Eighteenth-Century England*. London: Europa, 1982.

McMahon, Daniel. "Dynastic Decline, Heshen, and the Ideology of the Jiaqing Reforms." In *Rethinking the Decline of China's Qing Dynasty*, 42–58. New York: Routledge, 2015.

Menegon, Eugenio. "Interlopers at the Fringes of Empire: The Procurators of the Propaganda Fide Papal Congregation in Canton and Macao, 1700–1823." *Cross-Currents: East Asian History and Culture Review* 7, no. 1 (May 2018): 30–69.

Meng Fanshu 孟繁樹. "Lun qianjia shiqi changjiang liuyu de bangziqiang" 論乾嘉時期長江流域的梆子腔 (A study of the *bangzi qiang* in the regions along the Yangzi River during the reigns of Qianlong and Jiaqing). In *Zhonghua xiqu* 中華戲曲 (Chinese theater), vol. 9, 147–63. Taiyuan: Shanxi Shifan Daxue Xiqu Wenwu Yanjiusuo, 1990.

Mitchell, Timothy. *Rule of Experts: Egypt, Techno-Politics, Modernity*. Berkeley: University of California Press, 2002.

Mitchell, W. J. T., and Mark B. N. Hansen. *Critical Terms for Media Studies*. Chicago: University of Chicago Press, 2010.

Moll-Murata, Christine, Jianze Song, and Hans Ulrich Vogel. *Chinese Handicraft Regulations of Qing Dynasty: Theory and Application*. Munich: Iudicium, 2005.

Mosca, Matthew. "Empire and the Circulation of Frontier Intelligence: Qing Conceptions of the Ottomans." *Harvard Journal of Asiatic Studies* 70, no. 1 (2010): 147–207.

Moser, Jeffrey. "Recasting Antiquity: Ancient Bronzes and Ritual Hermeneutics in the Song Dynasty." PhD diss., Harvard University, 2010.

Moss, Hugh. *By Imperial Command: An Introduction to Ch'ing Imperial Painted Enamels*. Hong Kong: Hibya, 1976.

———. "The Influence of Tang Ying on the Production of Imperial Porcelain Snuff Bottles." *Journal of the International Chinese Snuff Bottle Society* (Spring 2009): 4–16.

Mukerji, Chandra. *Territorial Ambitions and the Gardens of Versailles*. Cambridge: Cambridge University Press, 1997.

Mullaney, Thomas. "The Moveable Typewriter: How Chinese Typists Developed Predictive Text during the Height of Maoism." *Technology and Culture* 53, no. 4 (Oct. 2012): 777–814.

Murck, Christian F., ed. *Artists and Traditions: Uses of the Past in Chinese Culture*. Princeton, NJ: Princeton University Art Museum, 1976.

Murray, Julia. "From Textbook to Testimonial: The Emperor's Mirror, an Illustrated Discussion (*Dijian tushuo/Teikan zusetsu*) in China and Japan." *Ars Orientalis* 31 (2001): 65–101.

Nappi, Carla. *The Monkey and the Inkpot: Natural History and Its Transformations in Early Modern China*. Cambridge, MA: Harvard University Press, 2009.

Naquin, Susan, and Evelyn Rawski. *Chinese Society in the Eighteenth Century*. New Haven, CT: Yale University Press, 1987.

Needham, Joseph, et al. *Science and Civilisation in China*. Vol. 5, *Chemistry and Chemical Technology*, part 7, *Military Technology*. Cambridge: Cambridge University Press, 1986.

Nie Chongzheng 聶崇正. "Tan Qingdai chen zikuan huihua" 談清代臣'字'款繪畫 (Study of paintings signed with "your subject" from the Qing dynasty). *Wenwu*, no. 4 (1984): 77–78.
Nienhauser, William H., Jr., et al., eds. *The Indiana Companion to Chinese Literature*. Bloomington: Indiana University Press, 1986–98.
Niiniluoto, Ilkka, Matti Sintonen, and Jan Woleński. *Handbook of Epistemology*. Dordrecht: Springer Netherlands, 2004.
Ning Chia. "The Li-Fan Yuan in the Early Ch'ing Dynasty." PhD diss., Johns Hopkins University, 1992.
Owen, Stephen. *Traditional Chinese Poetry and Poetics: Omen of the World*. Madison: University of Wisconsin Press, 1985.
Ozaki Nobumori 尾崎洵盛. *Shinchō no Kan'yō* 清朝の官窯 (Imperial porcelain manufactory of the Qing dynasty). Tōkyō: Heibonsha, 1960.
Pagani, Catherine. *Eastern Magnificence and European Ingenuity: Clocks of Late Imperial China*. Ann Arbor: University of Michigan Press, 2001.
Park, J. P. *Art by the Book: Painting Manuals and the Leisure Life in Late Ming China*. Seattle: University of Washington Press, 2012.
Park, Katharine, and Loraine Daston, eds. *Cambridge History of Science*. Vol. 3, *Early Modern Science*. Cambridge: Cambridge University Press, 2006.
Peng Tao 彭濤. "Mingdai huanguan zhengzhi yu Jingdezhen de taozheng" 明代宦官政治與景德鎮的陶政 (The eunuch politics of the Ming Dynasty and ceramic administration in Jingdezhen). *Nanfang wenwu*, no. 2 (2006): 111–20.
Perdue, Peter. *China Marches West*. Cambridge, MA: Harvard University Press, 2005.
Peterson, Willard. *Bitter Gourd: Fang I-chih and the Impetus for Intellectual Change*. New Haven, CT: Yale University Press, 1979.
———, ed. *The Cambridge History of China*. Vol. 9. Cambridge: Cambridge University Press, 2002.
Pietz, William. "The Problem of the Fetish I." *RES: Anthropology and Aesthetics* 9 (Spring 1985): 5–17.
Porter, David. *The Chinese Taste in Eighteenth-Century England*. Cambridge: Cambridge University Press, 2010.
Qi Meiqin 祁美琴. "Neiwufu Gaoshi jiazu kao" 內務府高氏家族考 (Investigation of the Gao clan of the Imperial Household Department). *Studies in Qing History* 2 (2000): 108–14.
———. *Qingdai baoyi qiren yanjiu* 清代包衣旗人研究 (Study of *booi* bannermen in the Qing dynasty). Beijing: Renmin Chubanshe, 2019.
———. *Qingdai Neiwufu* 清代內務府 (The Imperial Household Department in the Qing dynasty). Shenyang: Liaoning Minzu Chubanshe, 2009.
———. "Qingdai Neiwufu Baoyi dui Qingdai Wenhua de Gongxian" 清代內務府包衣對清代文化的貢獻內蒙古社會科學 (The contribution to the culture of the Qing dynasty from *booi* of the Imperial Household Department). *Inner Mongolia Social Science* 3 (1997): 55–58.

Qian Decang 錢德蒼, ed. *Zhui Bai Qiu* 綴白裘 (The collected treasure, or stitching together white fur). Annotated by Wang Xieru 汪協如. Beijing: Zhonghua Shuju, 1941.

Qin Dashu 秦大樹. "Jingdezhen Yuyaochang yizhi 2014 nian fajue shouhuo yu xiangguan wenti yanjiu" 景德鎮禦窯廠遺址2014年發掘收獲與相關問題研究 (Discovery from the excavation of the Imperial Porcelain Manufactory site in Jingdezhen in 2014). *Wenwu*, no. 8 (2017): 69–88.

———. "Junyao shishao niandai kao" 鈞窯始燒年代考 (On the starting date of the production of Jun ware). *Huaxia Kaogu* 2 (2004): 75–94.

Qingshi Guan 清史館. *Qingshi gao* 清史稿 (History of the Qing dynasty). Beijing: Zhonghua Shuju, 1976–77.

Quanguo Tushuguan Wenxian Suowei Fuzhi Zhongxin 全國圖書館文獻縮微複製中心, ed. *Zhongguo gudai taoci wenxian jilu* 中國古代陶瓷文獻輯錄. Beijing: Guojia Tushuguan, 2003.

Rabier, Christelle, ed. *Fields of Expertise: A Comparative History of Expert Procedures in Paris and London, 1600 to present.* Newcastle, England: Cambridge Scholars, 2007.

Rawski, Evelyn. *The Last Emperors: A Social History of Qing Imperial Institutions.* Berkeley: University of California Press, 1998.

Rawski, Evelyn, and Jessica Rawson. *China: The Three Emperors, 1662–1795.* London: Royal Academy of Arts, 2005.

Rawson, Jessica. "Central Asian Silver and Its Influence on Chinese Ceramics." *Bulletin of the Asia Institute*, n.s., 5 (1991): 139–51.

Reitz, S. C. Bosch. "On the Numbers in the Base of Chün Ware." *Metropolitan Museum of Art Bulletin* 11, no. 8 (Aug. 1916): 173–75.

Roberts, Lissa L., Simon Schaffer, and Peter Dear, eds. *Mindful Hands: Inquiry and Invention from the Late Renaissance to Early Industrialisation.* Amsterdam: University Presses, 2007.

Robinson, David M., ed. *Culture, Courtiers, and Competition: The Ming Court* (1368–1644). Cambridge, MA: Harvard University Asia Center, Harvard University Press, 2008.

Rowe, William. *Saving the World: Chen Hongmou and Elite Consciousness in Eighteenth-Century China.* Stanford, CA: Stanford University Press, 2001.

Ruitenbeek, Klaas. *Carpentry and Building in Late Imperial China: A Study of the Fifteenth-Century Carpenter's Manual Lu Ban Jing.* Leiden: E. J. Brill, 1990.

Saeki Yūichi 佐伯有一 and Tanaka Issei 田仲一成, eds. *Niida Noboru Hakushi shū Pekin kōshō girudo shiryōshū* 仁井田陞博士輯北京工商ギルド資料集 (Guild sources of merchants' and artisans' guilds in Beijing, compiled by Dr. Niida Nororu). Tōkyō: Tōkyō Daigaku Tōyō Bunka Kenkyūjo Fuzoku Tōyōgaku Bunken Sentā, 1975–83.

Saitō Kikutarō 斎藤菊太郎. "Gen jidai sometsuke sagasu I & II: Jūyon seiki chūyō no gen no sometsuke to gen kyoku" 元代染付考(上下)—十四世紀中葉の元青花と元曲 (Yuan blue-and-white and Yuan drama in the middle of the fourteenth century). *Kobijutsu* 古美術 18–19 (1967): 5–41, 49–74.

Sato, Sarah 佐藤サアラ. "Ming jidai Kanyō ni okeru seika tōsai no ichi" 明代官窯における成化闘彩の位置 (The position of *doucai* [joint colors] in the Ming official kilns). *Tōyō tōji* 東洋陶磁 1, no. 35 (2005–6): 56–59.

Sawyer, Keith. *Explaining Creativity: The Science of Human Innovation*. New York: Oxford University Press, 2012.
Schäfer, Dagmar. *The Crafting of the Ten Thousand Things: Knowledge and Technology in Seventeenth-Century China*. Chicago: University of Chicago Press, 2011.
———, ed. *Cultures of Knowledge: Technology in Chinese History*. Leiden: Boston: Brill, 2012.
———, ed. *Gongting yu difang: Shiqi zhi shiba shiji de jishu jiaoliu* 宮廷與地方：十七至十八世紀的技術交流 (The court and the local: Technological exchange during the seventeenth and the eighteenth centuries). Beijing: Zijincheng Chubanshe, 2010.
———. "Inscribing the Artifact and Inspiring Trust: The Changing Role of Markings in the Ming Era." *East Asian Science, Technology and Society* 5, no. 2 (2011): 239–65.
———. "Knowledge by Design." In *The Structures of Practical Knowledge*, edited by Matteo Valleriani, 280–81. Cham, Switzerland: Springer, 2017.
Scheier-Dolberg, Joseph. "Yu Zhiding (ca. 1646–ca. 1716) and the Envisioning of the Early Qing World." PhD diss., Columbia University, 2018.
Schlesinger, Jonathan. *A World Trimmed with Fur: Wild Things, Pristine Places, and the Natural Fringes of Qing*. Stanford, CA: Stanford University Press, 2017.
Schorkowitz, Dittmar, and Ning Chia, eds. *Managing Frontiers in Qing China: The Lifanyuan and Libu Revisited*. Leiden: Brill, 2017.
Sena, Yunchiahn Chen. *Bronze and Stone: The Cult of Antiquity in Song Dynasty China*. Seattle : University of Washington Press, 2019.
Shan Guoqiang. "Style of the Painting of Beauties at the Qing Court." *Zijincheng* 3 (1995): 16–22.
Shang Gang 尚剛. "Yuandai taoshi liangti" 元代陶事兩題 (Two topics on porcelain manufacture in the Yuan dynasty). *Wenwu* 9 (2017): 48–53.
Shang Wei. "The Literati Era and Its Demise (1723–1840)." In *The Cambridge History of Chinese Literature*, vol. 2, edited by Kang-i Sun Chang and Stephen Owen, 245–342. Cambridge: Cambridge University Press, 2010.
———. "Truth Becomes Fiction When Fiction Is True: The Story of the Stone and the Visual Culture of the Manchu Court." *Journal of Chinese Literature and Culture* 2, no. 1 (April 2015): 207–48.
Shao Yiping 邵毅平. "Doupeng xianhua: Zhongguo gudian xiaoshuo zhong de guangjia jiegou" 豆棚閒話：中 國古典小說中的框架結構 (Idle talk under the bean arbor: The framework of Chinese classical short stories). In *Zhonghua wenshi luncong* 中華文史論叢 (Investigation of Chinese literature and history), vol. 66, 140–77. Shanghai: Shanghai Guji Chubanshe, 2001.
Shapin, Steven. "Here and Everywhere." *Annual Review of Sociology* 21 (1995): 289–321.
Shen Chien-tung. "The 'Method' and 'Mode' of Traditional Craftsmanship: A Case Study of Workshop Techniques in the Sung Dynasty." *Gugong Xueshu Jikan* 22, no. 4 (2005): 31–59.
Shen, Grant Guangren. *Elite Theatre in Ming China, 1368–1644*. London: Routledge, 2005.
Shi Zhihong. *Central Government Silver Treasury: Revenue, Expenditure and Inventory Statistics, ca. 1667–1899*. Leiden: Brill, 2016.

Shih Ching-Fei 施靜菲. "Mengyuan gongting zhong ciqi shiyong chutan" 蒙元宮廷中瓷器使用初探 (Imperial use of porcelain under the Mongols). *Guoli Taiwan Daxue Meishushi Yanjiu Jikan* 15 (2003): 169, 203–99.

———. *Riyue guanghua: Qinggong huafalang* 日月光華：清宮畫琺瑯 (Radiant luminance: The painted enamelware of the Qing imperial court). Taipei: National Palace Museum, 2012.

———. "Xiangyaqiu zuojian zhi gongyi jishu jiaoliu: Guangdong, Qinggong yu Shensheng Luoma Diguo" 象牙球所見之工藝技術交流: 廣東、清宮與神聖羅馬帝國 (Concentric ivory spheres and the exchange of craft techniques: Canton, the Ch'ing court and the Holy Roman Empire)." *Gugong xueshu jikan* 25, no. 2 (2007): 87–138.

Shih Ching-Fei and Peng Ying-Chen. "Cong wenhua mailuo tantao qingdai youshangcai mingci: Falang cai, yangcai, yu fencai" 從文化脈絡探討清代釉上彩名詞—琺瑯彩; 洋彩與粉彩 (On the origin and development of three terms for Qing dynasty overglazed enamels: *Falangcai, yangcai,* and *fencai*). *Gugong Xueshu Jikan* 29, no. 4 (2012): 1–74.

Sigaut, François. "Technology." In *Companion Encyclopedia of Anthropology*, edited by Tim Ingold, 420–59. London: Taylor and Francis, 2002.

Simon, Herbert A. *Administrative Behavior: A Study of Decision-Making Processes in Administrative Organizations*. New York: Free Press, 1997.

Smith, Pamela. *The Business of Alchemy*. Princeton, NJ: Princeton University Press, 1994.

Smith, Pamela, Amy R. W. Meyers, and Harold J. Cook, eds. *Ways of Making and Knowing: The Material Culture of Empirical Knowledge*. Ann Arbor: University of Michigan Press, 2014.

Smith, Pamela, and Benjamin Schmidt, eds. *Making Knowledge in Early Modern Europe: Practices, Objects, and Texts, 1400–1800*. Chicago: University of Chicago Press, 2007.

Song Yingxing. *T'ien-Kung K'ai-Wu: Chinese Technology in the Seventeenth Century*. Translated by E-tu Zen Sun and Shiou-chuan Sun. University Park: Pennsylvania State University, 1966.

Spence, Jonathan D. *Ts'ao Yin and the K'ang-hsi Emperor: Bondservant and Master*. New Haven, CT: Yale University Press, 1966.

Stary, Giovanni. "Fundamental Principles of Manchu Poetry." In *The International Conference on Chinese Border Area Studies*, edited by the Editorial Committee for Academic Papers on the International Conference on China Border Area Studies, 187–221. Taipei: National Chengchi University, 1970.

Stuart, Jan, and Evelyn Rawski. *Worshiping the Ancestors: Chinese Commemorative Portraits*. Washington, DC: Freer Gallery of Art, Arthur M. Sackler Gallery, Smithsonian Institution; Stanford, CA: Stanford University Press, 2001.

Su Jincheng 蘇金成. "Zhongguo chuantong zongjiao huihua zhong fenben de yingyong" 中國傳統宗教繪畫中粉本的應用 (The use of *fenben* in traditional Chinese religious painting). *Meishu* 3 (2017): 121–25.

Sun Yue 孫悅. "Cuitao Tang Ying yu Qingdai guanyao" 榷陶唐英與清代官窯 (Ceramics supervisor Tang Ying and the Qing dynasty official kiln). MA thesis, Institute of Fine Arts of China, 2010.

———. "Laoge shiji luekao" 老格事蹟考 (A brief investigation of Laoge's activities). *Shenyang Gugong Bowuyuan yuankan*, no. 2 (2015): 57–64.

Tan, Tian Yuan. "Traditions and Transitions in Eighteenth-Century Qu Poetry: The Case of Jiang Shiquan (1725–1785)." In *Linking Ancient and Contemporary: Continuities and Discontinuities in Chinese Literature*, edited by Tiziana Lippiello, Chen Yuehong 陳躍紅, and Maddalena Barenghi, 229–45. Venice: Edizioni Ca' Foscari, 2016.

Tang Quan 唐權. "Woyu zhixi: Cao Yin 'Riben dengci' yanjiu" 倭語之戲：曹寅日本燈詞研究 (Playing with Japanese words: Studies of Cao Yin's *The Joyous Japanese Songs*). *Journal of Tsinghua University (Philosophy and Social Sciences)* 28, no. 2 (2013): 52–65.

Tang Ying 唐英. *Gubaitang xiquji* 古柏堂戲曲集 (Collection of drama from the Old Cypress Mansion). Edited by Zhou Yude 周育德. Shanghai: Shanghai Guji Chubanshe, 1987.

———. *Jike Pipa Ting shi* 輯刻琵琶亭詩 (Poetry anthology on Pipa Pavillion). Woodblock edition, housed in Shanghai library. Jiujiang: Gubai Tang, 1746.

———. *Tang Ying dutao wendang* 唐英督陶文檔 (Archival records of Tang Ying's supervision of porcelain production). Edited by Zhang Faying. Beijing: Xueyuan Chubanshe, 2012.

———. *Tang Ying ji* 唐英集 (Selection of Tang Ying's works). Edited by Zhang Faying. Shenyang: Liaoshen Shushe, 1991.

———. *Tang Ying quanji* 唐英全集 (Complete works of Tang Ying). Edited by Zhang Faying. Beijing: Xueyuan Chubanshe, 2008.

Tichane, Robert. *Ching-te-chen: Views of a Porcelain City*. New York: New York State Institute for Glaze Research, Painted Post, 1983.

Tie Bao, ed. *Weiqing zhai quanji* 惟清齋全集 (Oeuvre from the Weiqing study). In *Xuxiu siku quanshu* (Supplement to the complete library of the Four Treasuries), vol. 1476. Shanghai: Shanghai Guji Chubanshe, 1995–2002.

———. *Xichao yasong ji* 熙朝雅頌集 (Imperial anthology of dynastic hymns and odes of the bright reign). Shengyang: Liaoning University Press, 1990.

Tie Yuan 鐵源 and Li Guorong 李國榮, eds. *Qinggong ciqi dang'an quanji* 清宮瓷器檔案全集 (Comprehensive archive of porcelain at the Qing court). Beijing: Zhongguo Huabao Chubanshe, 2008.

Tong Yihua. *Ming dai Chenghua ciqi tezhan* 明代成化瓷器特展. Taipei: Guoli Gugong Bowuyuan, 1984.

Torbert, Preston. *The Ch'ing Imperial Household Department: A Study of Its Organization and Principal Functions, 1662–1796*. Cambridge, MA: Harvard University Press, 1977.

Toulmin, Stephen, and Allan Janik. *Wittgenstein's Vienna*. New York: Simon and Schuster, 1973.

Tsai, Henry. *The Eunuchs in the Ming Dynasty*. New York: State University of New York Press, 1996.

Ts'ai Ho-pi 蔡和璧. "Qingchao Tang Ying shiqi de Junyao shaozao" 清朝唐英時期的鈞窯燒造." *Yishujia* 130 (1986): 226–31.

Wang Ayling 王瑷玲. "Gai kundiao hesizhu tiandao renxin: Lun tang ying zhi xiju jiaohuaguan yuqi jingdianxing siwei zhi goujian" 改崑調合絲竹天道人心(- 論

唐英之戲劇教化觀與其"經典性,"思維之建構 (On Qing dramatist Tang Ying's didacticism and canonicity of his drama). *Zhongguo wenzhe yanjiu jikan* 32 (2008): 73–108.

Wang Cheng-hua. "Material Culture and Emperorship: The Shaping of Imperial Roles at the Court of Xuanzong 1426–35." PhD diss., Yale University, 1998.

Wang Ching-Ling 王靜靈. *Praying for Myriad Virtues: On Ding Guanpeng's the Buddha Preaching in the Berlin Collection*. Dortmund, Germany: Verlag Kettler, 2017.

Wang, Chu-P'ing 王竹平. "Cong kexuefenxi wenxian huigu kan falangcai, yangcai yu fencai de fenlei yu mingming" 從科學分析文獻回顧看琺瑯彩; 洋彩與粉彩的分類與命名 (Nomenclature for painted enamel on porcelain in the Qing dynasty: A scientific viewpoint). *Gugong xueshu jikan* 29, no. 3 (2012): 115–66.

———. "Cong tiehongcai tan Kangyong shiji Jingdezhen yangcaici de shaozao" 從鐵紅彩談康雍時期景德鎮洋彩瓷的燒造 (Investigation of the *yangcai* enameled porcelain in Jingdezhen during the Kangxi and Yongzheng reigns through the iron red pigment). *Gugong Wenwu Yuekan* 358 (2013): 46–57.

Wang Guangyao 王光堯. "Cong Gugongcang Qingdai zhici guanyang kan Zhongguo gudai guanyang zhidu—Qingdai yuyaochang yanjiu zhier" 從故宮藏清代製瓷官樣看中國古代官樣制度—清代御窯廠研究之二 (Ancient Chinese official sample wares from the perspective of Qing dynasty ceramic samples in the collection of the Palace Museum: Studies in Qing dynasty official kilns 2). *Gugong Bowuyuan yuankan* 6 (2006): 1–28.

———. *Mingdai gongting taoci shi* 明代宮廷陶瓷史 (History of court ceramics of the Ming dynasty). Beijing: Zijincheng Chubanshe, 2000.

———. "Qianlong cibangui 乾隆瓷班簋 (Porcelain Ban gui vessel of the Emperor Qianlong). *Gugong Bowuyuan yuankan* 4 (1999): 57–64.

———. *Zhongguo gudai guanyao zhidu* 中國古代官窯制度 (The system of premodern Chinese official kilns). Beijing: Zijincheng Chubanshe, 2004.

———. *Zhongguo gudai guanyao zhidu II* 中國古代官窯制度 二 (The system of premodern Chinese official kilns II). Beijing: Gugong Chubanshe, 2017.

Wang Guangyao 王光堯 and Guo Xingkuan 郭興寬, eds. *Guanyang yuci: Gugong Bowuyuan cang qingdai zhici guanyang yu yuyao ciqi* 官樣御瓷：故宫博物院藏清代制瓷官样与御窑瓷器 (Official design and imperial porcelain: Models for production and porcelain from imperial manufacture in the collection of the Palace Museum). Beijing: Zijincheng Chubanshe, 2007–8.

Wang Hongxu 王鴻緒. *Ming shigao* 明史稿 (Manuscript of the history of the Ming dynasty). Taipei Xian: Wenhai Chubanshe, 1962.

Wang Qiheng 王其亨 and He Beijie 何蓓潔. "Zhu Qiqian 'Yangshi Lei Kao' jiaozhu (Annotations on Zhu Qiqian's textual research on the Yangshi Lei family). *Jianzhu xuebao* 1 (2007): 84–87.

Wang, Shen. "Wang Yuanqi and the Orthodoxy of Self-Reflection in Early Qing Landscape Painting." PhD diss., University of Pennsylvania, 2010.

Wang Yao-ting 王耀庭. "Yuci huazhuangyuan Tang Dai" 御賜畫狀元唐岱 (Imperial champion painter Tang Dai). *Gugong wenwu yuekan* 392 (Nov. 2015): 18–29.

———. *Zhuanyi moxie* 傳移摹寫 (The tradition of representing art: Originality and reproduction in Chinese painting and calligraphy). Taipei: Guoli Gugong Bowuyuan, 2007.

Wang Yifeng 王屹峰. *Zhongguo Nanfang yuanshici yaoye yajiu* 中國南方原始瓷窯業研究 (A study of green proto-porcelain production in South China). Beijing: Zhongguo Shudian, 2010.

Wang Yiping 王怡蘋. *Yuanmingqing guanyao fanlianhua wenshi zhi yanjiu* 元明清官窯蕃蓮花紋飾之研究 (Indian lotus design on imperial kiln porcelain of the Yuan, Ming and Qing dynasties). Beijing: Shehuikexue Wenxian Chubanshe, 2017.

Wang Zhengyao 王政堯. "Manzu ruguan yu Qingqianqi xiju wenhua" 滿族入關與清前期戲劇文化 (The theatrical culture of Manchu before conquest and during early Qing). *Qingshi yanjiu*, no. 2 (1994): 37–46.

———. *Qingdai xiju wenhua kaobian* 清代戲劇文化考辨 (Investigation of the theatrical culture of the Qing dynasty). Beijing: Yanshan Wenhua Chubanshe, 2014.

Wang Zhizhang 王芷章. *Qing Shengpingshu zhilue* 清昇平署志略 (A short history of the Shengpingshu). Beijing: Guoli Beiping Yanjiuyuan Shixue Yanjiuhui, 1937.

Wang Zhonghan 王鍾翰. *Neiwufu shijia kao* 內務府世家考 (Research on the clans in the Imperial Household Department). In *Qingshi xukao*, 524–41. Taipei: Huashi Chubanshe, 1993.

Wang Zongmu 王宗沐 et al., eds. *Jiangxisheng dazhi* 江西省大志 (The great gazetteer of Jiangxi province). Beijing: Zhonghua Shuju, 2018.

Wei Litong 魏荔彤. *Huaifang shi bieji* 懷舫詩別集 (Individual poetry anthology of Huaifang). Jinan: Qilu Shushe, 2001.

Wei Qingyuan 韋慶遠. *Mingqing shi xuxi* 明清史續析 (Further investigation of Ming and Qing history). Guangzhou: Guangdong Renmin Chubanshe, 2006.

Wenren, Jun 聞人軍, trans. *Ancient Chinese Encyclopedia of Technology: Translation and Annotation of Kaogong ji* 考工記 (*The Artificers' Record*). New York: Routledge, Taylor and Francis, 2013.

Whiteman, Stephen. "Creating the Kangxi Landscape: Bishu Shanzhuang and the Mediation of Qing Imperial Identity." PhD diss., Stanford University, 2011.

———. "Kangxi's Auspicious Empire: Rhetorics of Geographic Integration in the Early Qing." In *Chinese History in Geographical Perspective*, edited by Jeffrey Kyong-McClain and Du Yongtao, 33–54. Lanham, MD: Lexington Books, 2015.

———. *Where Dragon Veins Meet: The Kangxi Emperor and His Estate at Rehe*. Seattle: University of Washington Press, 2020.

Wilhelm, Hellmut. "The Po-hsueh Hung-ju Examination of 1679." *Journal of the American Oriental Society* 71 (1951): 60–66.

Will, Pierre-Etienne. "L'apprentissage du métier de fonctionnaire à la fin de la période impériale." In *Éducation et instruction en Chine*. Vol. 2, *Les formations spécialisées*, edited by Catherine Despeux and Christine Nguyen Tri, 7–47. Leuven, Belgium: Éditions Peeters, 2003.

Wölfflin, Heinrich. *Principles of Art History: The Problem of the Development of Style in Later Art*. Translated by M. D. Hottinger. 1932; New York: Dover, 1950.

Wong Yu-wen 翁宇雯. "Zhenzhu de zhuisuizhe: Mingwu zong jiqi guanyao Huihui wen qimin" 真主的追隨者：明武宗及其官窯回回文器皿 (The follower of Allah: Ming Wu-tsung and the ceramics with Huihui characters of the Cheng-te Official Kiln). *Gugong wenyu yuekan* 29, no. 2 (2011): 147–208.
Wood, Nigel. *Chinese Glazes: Their Origins, Chemistry, and Recreation*. Philadelphia: University of Pennsylvania Press, 1999.
Wu Gan 吳敢. "Zhui bai qiu 'xukao shang'" 綴白裘敘考上 (Introduction and investigation of *The Collected Treasure*). *Xuzhou Shifan Jiaoyu Xueyuan xuebao* (Journal of Xuzhou Normal University) 16, no. 1 (2001): 1–6.
Wu Hung. "Emperors' Masquerade: Costume Portraits of Yongzheng and Qianlong." *Orientations* 26, no. 7 (1995): 25–41.
Wu Shizhou 吳十洲. *Qianlong yi ri* 乾隆一日 (One day of Qianlong's life). Jinan: Shandong Huabao Chubanshe, 2006.
Wu, Silas H. L. 吳秀良. *Communication and Imperial Control in China: Evolution of the Palace Memorial System, 1693–1735*. Cambridge, MA: Harvard University Press, 1970.
———. "Nanshufang zhi jianzhi jiqi qianqi de fazhan" 南書房之建置及其前期的發展 (The establishment and the early development of the Southern Study). *Si yu yan* 5 (1968): 6–12.
Wu, Yulian. "Chimes of Empire: The Construction of Jade Instruments and Territory in Eighteenth-Century China." *Late Imperial China* 40, no. 1 (June 2019): 55–71.
Wu Zhaoqing 吳兆清. "Qingdai Zaobanchu de jigou he jiangyi" 清代造辦處的機構和匠役 (The institution and personnel of the Imperial Workshops of the Qing dynasty). *Historical Archive* 4 (1991): 79–89.
Wu Zhuo 吳卓. "Jesuit Missionaries in China and the Imperial Workshops in the Imperial Household Department of the Qing Court." *Jiuzhou Xuelin* 2, no. 2 (2004): 67–73.
Xiang Xiaoying 項曉瑛. "Tang Ying jiqi xiqu chuangzuo" 唐英及其戲曲創作 (Tang Ying and his drama). MA thesis, Eastern Normal University. 2008.
Xu Biao 徐飈. *Liangsong wuzhi wenhua* 兩宋物質文化 (Material culture of two Song dynasties). Nanjing: Jiangsu Meishu Chubanshe, 2007.
Xu Kai 徐凱. "Lun Jin Jian" 論金簡 (On Jin Jian). In *Hanguo xue lunwen ji* 韓國學論文集 (Studies of Korea), edited by Beijing Daxue Hanguoxue Yanjiu Zhongxin, book 10, 168–78. Shenyang: Liaoning Minzu Chubanshe, 2003.
Xu Song 徐松, ed. *Song huiyao jigao* 宋會要輯稿. Beijing: Zhonghua Shuju, 1957.
Yang Boda 楊伯達. "Kangxi kuan hua falang chutan" 康熙款畫琺瑯初探 (Preliminary investigation of the painted enameled wares with Kangxi's reign mark). *Gugong Bowuyuan yuankan* 4 (1980): 42–48.
Yang Huiling 楊惠玲. *Xiqu banshe yanjiu: Ming Qing jiaban* 戲曲班社研究：明清家班 (A study of a family opera troupe during the Ming and Qing dynasties). Xiamen: Xiamen Daxue Chubanshe, 2006.
Yang Jingrong 楊靜榮, ed. *Yanse you* 顏色釉 (Monochrome glaze). Shanghai: Shanghai Kexue Jishu Chubanshe, 1999.
Yang Zhengtai 楊正泰, ed. *Tianxia shuilu lucheng* 天下水陸路程 (Routes of

transportation over rivers and lands under heaven). Taiyuan: Shanxi Renmin Chubanshe, 1992.
Yao Yijun 姚藝君. "Xiansuo shengqiang ciyuan kao" 弦索聲腔辭源考 (The etymology of Xiansuo singing style). *Zhongguo yinyue* 4 (2016): 87–92.
Ye Peilan 葉佩蘭. *Gugong Bowuyuan cang wenwu zhenpin quanji: Falangcai fencai* 故宮博物院藏文物珍品全集 琺瑯彩粉彩 (*Falang* enamel and *fencai* enamel). Shanghai: Shanghai Kexue Jishu Chubanshe, 1999.
Ye Xiaoqing. *Ascendant Peace in the Four Seas: Drama and the Qing Imperial Court.* Hong Kong: Chinese University Press, 2012.
———. "Ascendant Peace in the Four Seas: Tributary Drama and the Macartney Mission of 1793." *Late Imperial China* 26, no. 2 (Dec. 2005): 89–113.
Yeh, Wen-hsin, ed. *Becoming Chinese: Passages to Modernity and Beyond.* Berkeley: University of California Press, 2000.
Yi Qing 易晴 and Cui Yong 崔勇, eds. *Qingdai jianzhu shijia yangshi Lei zupu jiaoshi* 清代建築世家樣式雷族譜校釋 (Annotation to the architect Lei's family genealogy from the Qing dynasty). Beijing: Zhongguo Jianzhu Gongye Chubans, 2015.
Yin Falu 陰法魯. "Mantan bili" 漫談觱篥 (On Bili). *Zhongguo Dianji yu Wenhua*, no. 2 (1993): 102–3.
Yu Hui 余輝. "Shiba shiji fuwu yu jingcheng wangfu huandi de renwu huajia" 十八世紀服務於京城王府宦邸的人物畫家 (Figural portrait painters in the princely mansions of Beijing in the eighteenth century). *Gugong Bowuyuan yuankan* 6 (2002): 63–70.
Yu Pei-Chin 余佩瑾. *Dejiaqu: Qianlong huangdi de taoci pinwei* 得佳趣：乾隆皇帝的陶瓷品味 (Obtaining refined enjoyment: The Qianlong emperor's taste in ceramics). Taipei: Guoli Gugong Bowuyuan, 2012.
———, ed. *Jincheng xuying: Qing Yongzheng falang caici* 金成旭映：清雍正琺瑯彩瓷 (Porcelain with painted enamels of the Qing Yongzheng period [1723–1735]). Taibei Shi: Guoli Gugong Bowuyuan, 2013.
———. "Lang Shining (1688–1766) yu ciqi" 郎世寧與瓷器 (Giuseppe Castiglione [1688–1766] and porcelain). *Gugong xueshu jikan* 32, no. 2 (Dec. 2014): 1–37.
———. "Pinjian zhi qu: Shiba shiji de taoci puce jiqi xiangguan de wenti" 品鑑之趣—十八世紀的陶瓷譜冊及其相關的問題 (The appeal of connoisseurship: Eighteenth-century ceramic manuals and related questions). *Gugong xueshu jikan* 22, no. 2 (2004): 133–66.
———. "Qianlong guanyao yanjiu: Zuowei shengwang de lixiang yixiang" 乾隆官窯研究：作為聖王的理想意象 (A study of Qianlong official wares and the ideal of a sagacious ruler). PhD diss., National Taiwan University, 2011.
———. "Shanzhi liuguang ce de huizhi ji xiangguan wenti" 埏埴流光冊的繪製及相關問題 (The making of the "Shanzhi liuguang" album and related problems). *Gugong wenwu yuekan* 404, no. 11 (2016): 46–60.
———. "Tang Ying jianzao zhuanxinpin jiqi xiangguan wenti" 唐英監造轉心瓶及其相關問題 (Tang Ying's supervision of the making of revolving vases and related issues). *Gugong xueshu jikan* 31, no. 4 (2014): 205–49.

———. "Taoye tuce suojian Qianlong Huangdi de lixiang guanyao" 陶冶圖冊所見乾隆皇帝的理想官窯 (The Qianlong emperor's ideal imperial kiln, as seen in the illustrated album of ceramics making). *Gugong xueshu jikan* 30, no. 3 (2013): 185–220.

Yu Tongyuan 余同元. *Chuantong gongjiang xiandai zhuanxing yanjiu* 傳統工匠現代轉型研究 (Modern transformation of traditional craftsmen). Tianjin: Tianjin Guji Chubanshe, 2012.

Yuan Mei 袁枚. *Suiyuan shihua buyi* 隨園詩話補遺 (Poetry criticism from the garden of harmony, supplement). Xianggang: Xianggang Yimei Tushu Gongsi, 1960.

Yun Lu 允祿 et al. *Huangchao liqi tushi* 皇朝禮器圖式 (Illustrated regulations for ceremonial paraphernalia of the Qing dynasty). 18 vols. Beijing: Wuyin Dian print, 1759 and 1795.

Zeng Gong 曾鞏 (attr.). *Longping ji* 隆平集 (The collection of magnificent pacification). Siku quanshu edition (Chinese Text Project), accessed on March 15, 2017.

Zeng Yongyi 曾永義. "Bangziqiang xi xintan" 梆子腔系新探 (A new look at the *bangzi qiang*). *Zhongguo Wenzhesuo yanjiu jikan* 30 (2007): 143–78.

———. "Lunshuo xiqu yasu zhi tuiyi" 論說戲曲雅俗之推移 (On the evolution of the criteria between elegant and vulgar drama). *Xiju tanjiu* 3 (2009): 249–96.

———. "Yuan zaju tizhi guilu de yuanyuan yu xingcheng" 元雜劇體製規律的淵源與形成 (The origin and development of the formal rules of northern drama of the Yuan dynasty). *Journal of Chinese Literature in National Taiwan University* 3 (1990): 203–52.

Zhang Daoyi 張道一, trans. *Kao Gong Ji zhuyi* 考工記註譯 (Annotation and translation of *Artificers' Record*). Xi'an: Shanxi Renmin Meishu Chubanshe, 2004.

Zhang Fukang 張富康. *Zhongguo gutaoci de kexue* 中國古陶瓷的科學 (The science of ancient Chinese ceramics). Shanghai: Shanghai Renmin Meishu Chubanshe, 2000.

Zhang Jiasheng 張佳生. *Qingdai Manzu zhici shilun* 清代滿族詩詞十論 (Ten studies of Manchu *shi* and *ci* poetry during the Qing dynasty). Shenyang: Liaoning Minzu Chubanshe, 1993.

Zhang Jiuyue 張九鉞 (attr.). *Notes on the Southern Kilns* (*Nanyao biji*). Edited by Wang Jing. Guilin: Guangxi Normal University Press, 2012.

Zhang Juling 張菊玲. *Qingdai Manzu zuojia wenxue gailun* 清代滿族作家文學概論 (Survey of bannermen literary authors from the Qing dynasty). Beijing: Zhongyang Minzu Xueyuan Chubanshe, 1990.

Zhang Rong 張榮, ed. *Guangning qiushui: Qinggong zaobanchu boliqi* 光凝秋水： 清宮造辦處玻璃器 (Luster of autumn water: Glassware of the Imperial Workshops of the Qing court). Beijing: Zijin Cheng Chuban She, 2005.

Zhang Yajin 張雅晶. "Qingdai Wanyan shi Hesu shiji kao" 清代完顏氏和素事蹟考 (Examination of Hesu of the Wanggiyan clan from the Qing dynasty). In *Manxue luncong*, vol. 1, 254–65. Shenyang: Liaoning Minzu Chubanshe, 2011.

Zhang Yingying 張映瑩. *Zhongguo gudai yingzao lei gongguan* 中國古代營造類工官 (The artisan officials of building in premodern China). Beijing: Wenwu Chubanshe, 2011.

Zhang Zhao et al., eds. *Shiqu baoji* 石渠寶笈 (Treasure cabinet of the stone canal). Shanghai: Shanghai Guji Chubanshe: Xinhua Shudian Shanghai Faxingsuo Faxing, 1991.

Zhang Zhaoping 張兆平. "Kangxi chao zhuming manwen fanyijia Hesu" 康熙朝著名滿文翻譯家和素 (He Su, a renowned Manchu translator of the Kangxi reign). *Gugong Bowuyuan yuankan* 168, no. 4 (2013): 143–50.

Zhao Bing. "Administration, savoir techniques et impériale: Tang Ying 唐英 (1682–1756)." *Revue de Synthèse* 131, no. 3 (2010): 307–41.

———. "Erudition, expertise, technique et politique: Autour de la querelle de la datation du Taoji." *Arts Asiatiques* 61 (2006): 143–64.

———. "Traduction annotée du Taoji." In *La splendeur du feu: Chefs-d'œuvre de la porcelaine chinoise de Jingdezhen du XIIe au XVIIIe siècle*, edited by Gilles Cabrero, 182–99. Paris: Centre Culturel de Chine, 2004.

Zhao Binwen 趙炳文. "Shilunshu Qingdai fanyi shijia Hesu" 試論述清代繙譯世家和素 (Preliminary discussion of Hesu from an eminent lineage of translators of the Qing dynasty). In *Qingdai dang'an yu qinggong wenhua: Dijiujie qinggongshi yantaohui lunwenji* 清代檔案與清宮文化—第九屆清宮史研討會論文集 (Proceedings of the Ninth Conference of the Qing Court History: Archive and culture), 489–99. Beijing: Zhongguo Dang'An Chubanshe, 2010.

Zhao Ziqiang 趙自強. "Lun Qingdai de Nei Fanshu Fang" 論清代的內翻書房 (On the Inner Court Bureau of Translation in the Qing). *Qingshi yanjiu* 2 (1992): 22–28, 38.

Zhejiang Sheng Wenwu Kaogu Yanjiusuo. *Zhejiang kaogu jinghua* 浙江考古精華 (Selection from the archaeological discoveries in Zhejiang province). Beijing: Wenwu Chubanshe, 1999.

Zheng Naizhang 鄭乃章 and Zhang Qingyu. "Jingdezhen yao yizu zhaozi de xingzhi yu gongneng yanjiu" 景德鎮窯一組照子的形式與功能研究 (Studies of the forms and functions of some fire testers in Jingdezhen kilns). *Zhongguo taoci* 49 (2013): 67–79.

Zheng Xinmiao 鄭欣淼 et al., eds. *Douse zhengyan: Gugong cang Qingdai yuyao jingpin ji* 鬥色争妍：故宮藏清代御窯瓷器精品集 (Fire and color: Imperial kiln porcelain from the Palace Museum collection). Amoi: Museu de Arte de Macau, 2011.

Zhongguo Diyi Lishi Dang'anguan 中國第一歷史檔案館. *Kangxichao Hanwen zhupi zouzhe huibian* 康熙朝漢文硃批奏摺匯編 (The collected Chinese-language secret palace memorials of the Kangxi reign). Beijing: Dang'an Chubanshe, 1984.

———. *Qinggong Yuegang'ao shangmao dang'an quanji* 清宮粵港澳商貿檔案全集 (Archive of the trade between the Qing court and Guangdong, Hong Kong, and Macau). Beijing: Zhongguo Shudian, 2002.

Zhongguo Diyi Lishi Dang'anguan 中國第一歷史檔案館, Xianggang Zhongwen Daxue Wenwu Guan 香港中文大學文物館. *Qinggong Neiwufu Zaobanchu dang'an zonghui* 清宮內務府造辦處檔案總匯 (Archive of the Imperial Workshops in the Imperial Household Department of the Qing dynasty). Beijing: Renmin Chubanshe, 2005.

Zhongguo Guojia Tushuguan 中國國家圖書館. *Qingdai yangshilei jianzhu tudang zhan: Huaxia jianzhu yijiang de chuanshi juexiang* 清代樣式雷建築圖檔展：華夏建築藝匠的傳世絕響 (Exhibition of Yangshi Lei architectural archives of the Qing Dynasty: Masterpieces of architectural conceptions of ancient China). Beijing: National Library of China, 2007.

———. *Zhongguo Guojia Tushuguan cang qinggong shengpingshu dang'an jicheng* 中國家

圖書館藏清宮升平署檔案集成 (Archive of the Bureau of Ascending Peace collected in the National Library). Beijing: Zhonghua Shuju, 2011.

Zhongyang Yanjiuyuan 中央研究院, ed. *Mingshilu* 明實錄 (Veritable record of the Ming dynasty). Nan'gang: Zhongyang Yanjiuyuan Lishi Yuyan Yanjiusuo, 1961–66.

Zhu Jiajin 朱家溍. "Qingdai hua falang qi zhizao kao" 清代畫珐瑯器製造考 (Investigation of the production of painted enamel wares in the Qing dynasty). *Gugong Bowuyuan yuankan* 3 (1982): 67–76.

———. *Qingdai neiting yanju shimokao* 清代內廷演劇始末考 (Investigation of the beginning and end of court theater in the Qing dynasty). Beijing: Zhongguo Shudian Chubanshe, 2007.

Zhu Jinfu 朱金甫. "Lun Kangxi shiqi de nanshufang" 論康熙時期的南書房 (On the Southern Study during the Kangxi period). *Gugong Bowuyuan Yuankan* 2 (1990): 27–38.

Zito, Angela. *Of Body and Brush: Grand Sacrifice as Text/Performance in Eighteenth-Century China*. Chicago: University of Chicago Press, 1997.

Zong Tinghu 宗廷虎 and Li Jinling 李金苓. *Zhongguo jiju shi* 中國集句史 (The history of assembling verses in China). Jinan: Shandong Wenyi Chubanshe, 2009.

Zuo Ya. "The Production of Written Knowledge under the Rubric of Jiyi." *East Asian Science, Technology and Society: An International Journal* 4 (2010): 255–73.

INDEX

Page numbers in italics refer to illustrations. Plates follow p. 104.